# Eight Symphonic Masterworks
of the Nineteenth Century

# Eight Symphonic Masterworks of the Nineteenth Century

*A Study Guide for Conductors*

Leonard Slatkin

ROWMAN & LITTLEFIELD
Lanham • Boulder • New York • London

Published by Rowman & Littlefield
An imprint of The Rowman & Littlefield Publishing Group, Inc.
4501 Forbes Boulevard, Suite 200, Lanham, Maryland 20706
www.rowman.com

86-90 Paul Street, London EC2A 4NE

Copyright © 2024 by The Rowman & Littlefield Publishing Group, Inc.

*All rights reserved.* No part of this book may be reproduced in any form or by any electronic or mechanical means, including information storage and retrieval systems, without written permission from the publisher, except by a reviewer who may quote passages in a review.

British Library Cataloguing in Publication Information Available

**Library of Congress Cataloging-in-Publication Data**

Names: Slatkin, Leonard, author.
Title: Eight symphonic masterworks of the nineteenth century : a study guide for conductors / Leonard Slatkin.
Description: Lanham : Rowman & Littlefield Publishers, 2024. | Series: Scores to settle ; volume II | Includes bibliographical references and index. | Summary: "Leonard Slatkin delves into eight of the most beloved orchestral pieces of the nineteenth century and tackles problems conductors face before stepping onto the podium, providing tips that will help bring these works to life on the stage. He covers works by Mussorgsky, Berlioz, Brahms, Dvořák, Sibelius, Beethoven, Rimsky-Korsakov, and Tchaikovsky"— Provided by publisher.600
Identifiers: LCCN 2024027131 | ISBN 9781538187180 (cloth) | ISBN 9781538187203 (ebook) | ISBN 9781538187197 (paper)
Subjects: LCSH: Beethoven, Ludwig van, 1770-1827. Symphonies, no. 3, op. 55, E♭ major. | Mussorgsky, Modest Petrovich, 1839-1881. Kartinki s vystavki. | Berlioz, Hector, 1803-1869. Symphonie fantastique. | Brahms, Johannes, 1833-1897. Symphonies, no. 1, op. 68, C minor. | Dvořák, Antonín, 1841-1904. Symphonies, no. 9, op. 95, E minor. | Sibelius, Jean, 1865-1957. Symphonies, no. 2, op. 43, D major. | Rimsky-Korsakov, Nikolay, 1844-1908. Shekherazada. | Tchaikovsky, Peter Ilich, 1840-1893. Symphonies, no. 6, op. 74, B minor | Orchestral music—19th century—Analysis, appreciation. | Conducting.
Classification: LCC MT125 .S56 2024 | DDC 784.2/09034—dc23/eng/20240617
LC record available at https://lccn.loc.gov/2024027131

∞™ The paper used in this publication meets the minimum requirements of American National Standard for Information Sciences—Permanence of Paper for Printed Library Materials, ANSI/NISO Z39.48-1992.

To all those who strive to make their dreams a reality

"The unexamined life is not worth living."

—Socrates

"The thing is that I'm naturally curious about a lot of different disciplines in music, and I enjoy doing them. And as long as people are nice enough to let me, I'll keep on trying."

—André Previn

"There is nothing greater than the joy of composing something oneself and then listening to it."

—Clara Schumann

"We are what we pretend to be, so we must be careful about what we pretend to be."

—Kurt Vonnegut, *Mother Night*

"What's another word for Thesaurus?"

—Steven Wright

# Contents

| | |
|---|---|
| Introduction to Volume II | 1 |
| Ludwig van Beethoven: Symphony No. 3, "Eroica" | 3 |
| Modest Mussorgsky, orch. Maurice Ravel: *Pictures at an Exhibition* | 27 |
| Hector Berlioz: *Symphonie fantastique* | 55 |
| Johannes Brahms: Symphony No. 1 | 87 |
| Antonín Dvořák: Symphony No. 9, "From the New World" | 111 |
| Jean Sibelius: Symphony No. 2 | 139 |
| Nikolai Rimsky-Korsakov: *Scheherazade* | 169 |
| Pyotr Ilyich Tchaikovsky: Symphony No. 6, "Pathétique" | 191 |
| Bibliography | 221 |
| About the Author | 223 |

# Introduction to Volume II

When it comes to pinning down a timeframe for any artistic movement, music always seems to lag behind its counterparts, and Romanticism is no exception. Although isolated works of Romantic literature and visual art can be traced back to the eighteenth century, not until Beethoven revolutionized the musical world in the early part of the nineteenth century did we assign a name to the new kind of music that was starting to appear.

The newfound freedom of expression extended to not only the works themselves but also the performance practice. The straightforward Baroque and Classical periods gave way to a more spontaneous style of presentation, which in turn led to the need for a conductor. Usually considered not much more than time-beaters, these orchestra leaders developed a series of rules to show ensembles how they should play the music. The earliest podium-minders included Lully, Spohr, von Weber, and Mendelssohn. Indeed, almost all the conductors were composers, right through Berlioz and Wagner.

Upon the emergence of conductors such as Hans Richter and Felix Mottl, we began to separate the creator from the leader. These conductors added a new depth of expression, creating a more individualized style in terms of keeping time as well as developing independence between their two arms. Much of what they did still applies today.

In this edition, we will examine eight of the most famous works that emanated from the Romantic era. Stylistically, the pieces contain marked differences and thus need to be approached individually. All eight pieces under consideration go well beyond the world of keeping time. Even the earliest of the compositions, Beethoven's Third Symphony, still confounds many conductors. Sometimes the composers featured in this book provide a few clues as to how to lead their work, including Berlioz in the *Symphonie fantastique*. In other cases, such as the Second Symphony of Sibelius, the difficulties need to be sorted out by the conductor.

As I examine each piece, I try to provide a roadmap for not only the technical difficulties but the musical ones as well. Often, a given problem has more than one viable solution; therefore, I offer various options, leaving you to decide which suits your interpretation.

The most practical way to utilize the information in this volume is to have the score or book in hand, with the other on a monitor or tablet, although it is certainly possible to work with hard copies of both. These scores are available on the International Music Score Library Project (IMSLP.org). In addition, the digitized scores in the New York Philharmonic's Archives can serve as a helpful resource, although they are not downloadable.

The works discussed in the following pages are all unrivaled masterpieces and therefore subject to numerous opinions on how to conduct them. My suggestions are based on almost sixty years of leading each of these pieces many times, with many orchestras. Yet, each time I do so, I always learn something new. One of the great pleasures of the conductor's art is the joy of discovery.

I would like to thank Joshua Gersen, Takao Kanayama, David Loebel, and Yaniv Segal for their help with editing the musical matters of each piece, and Leslie Karr for copyediting.

Let's begin our exploration.

# Ludwig van Beethoven: Symphony No. 3, "Eroica"

"Music is the one incorporeal entrance into the higher world of knowledge which comprehends mankind, but which mankind cannot comprehend."

—Ludwig van Beethoven

Joseph Willibrord Mähler, Public domain, via Wikimedia Commons

# 4  Ludwig van Beethoven: Symphony No. 3, "Eroica"

If one work ever redefined music, this is it. Monumental in scale and scope, it is a mountain that every conductor must climb, understanding that they may never reach its peak. Such are the mysteries and subtleties contained within this symphony.

Revolutions do not happen overnight. Although the "Eroica" is arguably one of the most innovative musical creations in history, Beethoven had been preparing himself for years, waiting for the right moment to launch this daunting work. By the end of 1805, he had already written his first two symphonies, six string quartets, nine violin sonatas, and twenty-two piano sonatas. He had flexed his muscles and was ready to move to the next level.

The work was not an immediate success, with several critics finding it too long and noting that the Finale did not live up to the expectations presented by the previous movements. In fact, the other work on the program at the premiere—another symphony in E♭, this one by Anton Eberl—was received more enthusiastically than Beethoven's Opus 55.

With the backstory of Napoleon lurking, rarely do I think about the politician when performing this symphony. That the composer scratched out the dedication to Napoleon—upon learning that Bonaparte had declared himself Emperor—does not carry musical weight in terms of how I perform the piece. Rather, I look at it as the symphony that changed musical thought.

I chose this symphony over Beethoven's other eight in the form because it presents the greatest structural challenge for the conductor, even more than the Fifth or Ninth. At worst, it can seem like an eternity before the symphony concludes, and at best, we can feel ourselves inching forward in our understanding of the work's complexities.

Several editions of "Eroica" are available for performance and study. At one point, I had six different sets of the nine symphonies, plus the supplemental material (sometimes illuminating, other times frustrating) that came with the scores. Musicians of my generation did not have to deal with these newer discoveries when we were first learning and performing Beethoven's symphonies. As material was unearthed, we had to decide whether to incorporate it into our interpretations.

Most of the changes were minor—a dynamic here, a rest there, etc. There were other emendations that could make a difference, but these seemed more scholarly than musical. Traditions were passed along from generation to generation. Not until Toscanini presented the nine Beethoven symphonies did interpretations start to take on more distinct personalities.

The great Italian maestro's predecessors and contemporaries, including Furtwängler, engaged in a more liberal interpretation of the music, making alterations to the scores for various reasons. Toscanini tried to restore a degree of objectivity to the canon, but he was not blameless when it came to tailoring the works to suit his needs.

The premiere of the Third took place in the relatively small Theater an der Wien in 1805. In contrast, by the start of the twentieth century, orchestras were playing in much larger venues, and the size of the ensemble had increased twofold. The instruments themselves had also undergone changes, in particular the brass, which could now be played chromatically. This freed up conductors—who assumed that Beethoven was limited in the notes he could utilize due to the restrictions of the horns and trumpets of his time—to alter the text and allow for the newly available pitches.

The above issues might sometimes dominate the conductor's conception of the piece. When this occurs, the architectural design of the symphony can disappear in favor of a missing-the-forest-for-the-trees approach. Even though we will look at some of the possibilities, it is usually for the sake of clarity and the goal of getting from beginning to end.

It is fascinating to read other books and articles that have been written about how to conduct this as well as the other Beethoven symphonies. Among the sources I consulted is a remarkable essay from 1907 by conductor Felix Weingartner who, just as Gustav Mahler did during this time, made alterations to the printed material.[1] Almost a century later, in 1992, the distinguished conductor and pedagogue Norman del Mar published his take on performance practice of the symphonies.[2] By then, a lot of information had been gleaned regarding historically informed methods of presentation, and at certain points, del Mar clearly takes on Weingartner. It makes for a very interesting comparison. And to further muddy the waters, Norman's son, Jonathan, took the lead on editing new editions of the symphonies, which were published by Bärenreiter between 1996 and 2000.[3]

The search for the truth never ends, but at some point we do have to ask ourselves, "How literal must we be, and is the composer always right?" Sometimes, assuming we have the background and knowledge, just using common sense can work best.

In 2000, I presented a two-week festival in Washington, D.C., at the height of the historically informed performance craze. I had a concert idea that was quite the opposite. With the assistance of various scholars, we presented four Beethoven symphonies in editions prepared by Mahler. A lot of Mahler's alterations seem nonsensical today—four oboes playing the famous cadenza in the first movement of the Fifth, for example. Not only did we employ all the forces required by Mahler, but we also followed the indications in his scores to get a rough idea of how he interpreted the works.

For this score study, we will use the Breitkopf & Härtel edition from 1999 (publisher plates 5233).[4] It includes not only rehearsal letters but bar numbers as well. (Be aware of potential discrepancies with measure numbers in the various editions.) To convey the essential information a conductor needs to lead the "Eroica," I will mostly stick to what is in the Breitkopf edition. However, I will occasionally reference what past researchers and performers concluded, and perhaps you might find a nugget or two that strikes an interesting chord.

With one important difference, the instrumentation of "Eroica" is the same as Beethoven's first two symphonies. The woodwinds are in pairs, but now there are three horns instead of two. A couple of trumpets and a set of timpani, along with the usual complement of strings, round out the list of players. The horns and trumpets mostly play in E♭, but in the slow movement, some of them switch to instruments in C to help cover the notes that were not available on the valveless instruments.

## First Movement: Allegro con brio

The opening tempo is marked *Allegro con brio*, and it carries with it a metronome marking of ♩. = 60. *Con brio* almost always applies to an Allegro, and for our purposes, simply means "with life." Few topics are more hotly debated than how quickly or slowly Beethoven wanted his music to be played. Some interpreters stick to the letter of the text, and others argue that the metronomes of the time were potentially inaccurate and that Beethoven was not familiar enough with them.

I have a somewhat different spin. The metronome was not invented until 1817. The first seven of Beethoven's symphonies had already appeared without the metronome markings. He wrote the second movement of his Eighth in honor of the new contraption. He was almost entirely deaf by this time, but more importantly, he was putting in the speeds many years after the pieces were written.

Time changes everything, and as evident in recordings by well-respected composer/conductors, they do change their minds about the tempos of their own works. Even if the metronome Beethoven used was precise, more than likely his sense of proportion had changed. The most we can truly understand are the relative tempos between the movements. As the great man himself said, "One must feel the tempos."

Also high on the discussion list is the length of the opening two notes. In his first two symphonies, we have introductions before the main material of the movement begins. Here he includes just two bars with one emphatic note on each downbeat. Bernstein referred to these as "Thor's hammer blows." With just two notes, Beethoven shatters the musical ethic of the time, and this is what must be conveyed to the orchestra.

Even though it is possible to conduct the opening with one beat to the bar, this approach can take away from the power of not only the chords but also the stunning effect of the two rests. Do not even attempt to start conducting until you have the sound and speed firmly entrenched in your mind.

Upon listening to recordings of twenty conductors leading this opening, I discovered numerous different opinions on the length of the chord. Some play it very short; others give it a bit of heft. You can find what I think is a very good solution by looking at the last two bars of this movement. Although the disposition of the notes is different, the effect is almost the same as the start: two firm E♭ chords.

The violins have a three- and four-note indication. If these are to be played short and crisp, then divisi must be employed. In the first violins, one half of the section can play the top two notes, leaving the lower notes to the other half of the section. Since two of those notes are replicated in the second violins, I would suggest that half of that section just play the upper E♭ and the remaining second violins play the bottom two notes.

Along with a few of my fellow conductors, I opt to take these two bars slightly slower than the tempo that commences in the third bar. This is what I do in those final measures as well, hoping that some symmetry has been achieved. I don't actually conduct in one or three. The upbeat is preceded by an almost invisible gesture, as if I were giving two/three, but after the downbeat, I don't move until the upbeat to the second bar. In my younger days, I followed the patterns I learned from the older generation of conductors and stayed in three, perhaps around ♩ = 132. Now, I move along a bit and take a quicker approach starting in the third bar.

To coordinate the opening, I advise starting the first rehearsal at the third measure so that the orchestra learns your tempo for the body of the movement. Then, go back and add the first two measures. Once the musicians understand the principle, you can conduct in one beat, regardless of the metronome mark you choose to take.

The first few pages present numerous decisions to make, and many of the problems will recur several times in the movement. For example, the tune can be bowed as the phrasings indicate, or you can ask the cellos to take another stroke in the second bar. I prefer separate bows for the first and second measures, a down bow for the third and fourth bars, and an up bow for the crescendo.

In almost every composer's output, we are confronted with the *sforzando* marking. What does it mean, and how do we apply it? From my perspective, the marking must be considered in the context of the passage in which it occurs. The first of these is in **m. 9**, and we have no dynamic to guide us. This decision, as with so many others, is a matter of personal preference. I choose not to exaggerate it to avoid interrupting the line of the theme.

Similarly, when a crescendo or diminuendo is marked but no dynamic indicates how loud or soft it should be, we must use our best instincts. In the case of the two bars commencing at **m. 13**, we should get loud enough to ensure that the *subito piano* is clear at **m. 15**. Therefore, this crescendo can go almost to *forte*.

A common dilemma for musicians is how to distinguish between *sforzando* and *forte/piano*. To make decisions, it is crucial to look carefully at what is on the page before moving forward with what can loosely be called an interpretation. The section between **m. 23** and **m. 34** presents several possibilities regarding dynamics and phrasing. I believe that the operative dynamic during these eleven bars is *piano*. If we interpret *sforzando* to indicate not a dynamic but simply an expression mark, as there are no indications of *forte* to be found, those should be played as accents rather than as a continual storm of loud notes.

Conductors of earlier generations always took a breath to separate the slurs in this section, as if there were an eighth-note or even quarter-note rest before each *sforzando*. Mahler went so far as to write in down bows for each of these. Having performed this work for many years and now taking somewhat brisker tempos than I used to, I opt to connect each phrase, with no break until **m. 33**. At that point, Beethoven adds dots to the isolated quarter notes but does not change the basic dynamic of *piano*. He then writes a two-bar crescendo to finally get us to the first *fortissimo* of the movement.

As the size of the string section increased at the end of the nineteenth century, so did the habit of doubling the woodwinds and brass. Both Weingartner and Mahler indicate that this moment (**m. 37**) is the first in which these extra instruments should be utilized. Mahler takes it one step further by introducing an E♭ clarinet into the mix. I don't think anyone performs it with this instrumentation these days, but it was certainly interesting to hear once.

It was not the convention of the period to phrase the brass melodies in the same way as the woodwinds or strings. Hence, the horns and trumpets do not have the same slurs as the other instruments. However, you can aim for consistent phrasing if you do so discreetly. Eight bars before **reh. A** (**m. 37**) is an excellent example of where you must decide whether the various instruments should all match or not.

Some conductors like to make a slight diminuendo in the bar before **reh. A**. I think this depends on what tempo you choose. If the speed is on the brisk side and the hall is somewhat reverberant, a diminuendo makes sense to be able to hear the notes right after the downbeat. If the opposite is true, then the *subito piano* can certainly stand on its own. You might need to rehearse it both ways to see which solution works best.

The ensuing dialogue between the woodwinds and first violins needs careful balancing as well as agreement on the length of the last note. The cellos and basses can play the quarters short, but the last one does not have a dot and serves as a gentle landing rather than a lighthearted moment. Again, keep in mind that the *sforzando* marks in **mm. 53–54** are within the context of the *piano* dynamic.

The sudden *fortissimo* phrase beginning on the second beat of **m. 55**, played marcato, can be ever-so-slightly held back, just to increase the tension. The next four bars should be beautiful, almost out of place with much of the movement, only to be interrupted by the crescendo four bars before **reh. B**. If needed, you can move ahead in the bar before **reh. B**, but be careful not to get so fast that the next passage is a blur. I usually have the brass and timpani hold to *mezzo forte* starting at **m. 65**. I normally go into three, primarily as an aid to the eighth-note pickups that are in the instruments other than the violins.

This intense activity is under the influence of a single *forte* dynamic. While I understand the temptation to play this music quite loudly, that takes away from the climax of this section at **m. 81**. This effect is best achieved by having all the winds play *mezzo forte* at **m. 71**.

Now we come to the second theme, a gentle moment with some delicious harmonic surprises. The downbeat of **reh. C** cannot be played too long, lest the note on the second beat be covered up by the reverberation. There is always some confusion when notes have both a slur and a dot at the same time. You must decide what the proper length of these should be. No matter your conclusion, the strings and winds must agree to achieve consistent phrasing. This whole section is sometimes performed a bit more rubato, with slight hesitations every so often. Turn your attention to the double basses at **m. 86**. Here Beethoven has written a line for them independent from the cellos, and it makes sense to bring out passages such as these.

There are two ways to accomplish the transition to **reh. D**. You can hold back **m. 99**, but only by a little, and then accelerate back to the main tempo, perhaps starting three bars before **reh. D** itself. Otherwise, you can suddenly be in the tempo immediately at **reh. D**. In either case, you must achieve a true *pianissimo* in **m. 99**. The strings should not bounce the bow too much going into **reh. D**. Depending on your comfort level and that of the orchestra, you can either conduct in three or in one. Balance is difficult in the fifth bar after **reh. D**, so normally I decrease the volume of the strings, as well as the horns, trumpets, and timpani, to *mezzo forte* here, with a crescendo to *fortissimo* in **m. 116**.

Four measures before **reh. E**, the strings have six down-bow strokes that must be played equally. Unless the hall is very dry, wait just a brief moment for the reverberation of the last chord to die away before commencing the *subito piano*. Another option is to start the cellos and basses a bit stronger and make a diminuendo. Balance between the strings is necessary from the fourth measure after **reh. E** to hear the eighth notes equally.

The dramatic three bars that begin at **m. 144** have the strange indication of single *forte*. I have never heard anyone observe this, and it does not make musical sense to drop down here. However, it is important to give comparable weight to all three beats in the second violins and violas. Some conductors back away from the last notes of these bars, but I think they must sound strong and conclusive. The three even-more-declamatory chords that follow are usually held back slightly.

To repeat or not to repeat? When I began my career, no one ever took the first ending. It added five minutes to what is already a long movement. Then, starting in the 1960s, conductors began to not only take faster tempos but also observe the repeat. I recorded it this way but very rarely take the repeat in concert.

Somehow, the second ending always ends up feeling a bit slower than the main tempo. We have to get back to tempo, and the place to do it is **m. 166**, preceded by a slight ritard. Beethoven includes lots of felicitous details to bring out, such as the various *sforzandos*, which give distinction to the different registers in which they are played, and bowings that need to be accomplished elegantly. The first violins can play all the eighth notes up bow in **m. 168**, as well as the succeeding times this occurs. Note that **m. 178** is a *subito pianissimo*, and the crescendo that follows goes up one dynamic to *piano*. Do not drop back down here.

The passage at **reh. F** presents major balance issues. To bring out the theme in the lower strings, I ask them to change bows every measure rather than every two measures as Beethoven indicates. This spot benefits from the split violin section, with the second violins located on the conductor's right, but the winds and brass must adjust their dynamic down to about *mezzo forte*, no matter where the seconds are placed. The same applies to the alternating passages in the violins, with the quicker passage played loudly and the syncopations brought down.

At **m. 194**, the low strings and woodwinds should play notes of equal length. It can be useful to rehearse them separately to help the musicians understand the dialogue aspect here. The crescendo that begins at **m. 208** can increase to *mezzo forte* before dropping back down to *piano*. Six bars before **reh. G**, the seconds have to cut through the slightly noisy surroundings, but remember, this passage is only single *forte*. This gives us the opportunity to really make something of the *subito fortissimo* two bars before **reh. G**.

In the old days, orchestras used to play **m. 236** somewhat loudly. I prefer to keep the *sforzandos* at *mezzo forte*. At **m. 244**, you have to make a decision about which line is the most important to bring out. In my mind, it is the lower strings; therefore, I think the crescendo in the other instruments should only increase to *forte* at the most.

Another big decision presents itself at **reh. H**. How you perform this whole passage depends entirely on how you phrased at **m. 29**. I enjoy connecting the slurs rather than separating them, but this is purely a matter of taste. The notes in the lower strings that have a dot must be played emphatically.

The famous dissonance four bars before **reh. I** should be as strong as possible. I think that Beethoven put in the single *forte* just to remind us that we are still quite loud. The key here is to make sure the musicians who play the E♮ are forceful enough to shock even today's listeners. I usually take just a bit of time before playing the first note at **reh. I** and then start this slightly heavier, making a slight accelerando to get back to tempo by **m. 284**. One way to accomplish this is to have the strings play all down bows to start and then switch to up/down on the second beat of the third bar.

The unique interjection of a new theme should have a different feel to it than anything that has occurred previously—more expressive, I think, with little crescendos and diminuendos in the tune. I ask for just a slight crescendo at **m. 291** and then *subito piano* in the next bar.

The trumpets can get in the way at **m. 304**, so I usually take them down to *mezzo forte*, but they can make a crescendo through the quarter notes and then drop back after the *sforzando*. Two bars before **reh. K** is a sudden *fortissimo*. The canon at **m. 338** is clear, but you will always have to ask the second flute to play louder than the first when those instruments enter. Keep in mind that the crescendo does not commence until eight bars before **reh. L**.

The fifth measure after **reh. L** can be performed a bit nasal in tone and aggressively. This gives an effective contrast to the upcoming *subito piano*. Here is a suggestion to get from the pizzicato to the arco in **mm. 381–82** and subsequent bars: Ask the violins and violas to pluck with the left hand, giving them ample opportunity to get the bows ready to play at the tip. All four notes should be plucked in the same manner to achieve a similar sound for each.

The notes in **mm. 394–95** have often puzzled musicians and scholars. Wagner even went so far as to change the second violin note to a G♮. This delicious anticipation of the recapitulation requires what might seem like a set of wrong notes, especially if you are able to get the triple *pianissimo* in the strings and the horn playing very softly as well. Then, Beethoven indicates a *subito* single *forte*, followed immediately by another *subito* dynamic increase to *fortissimo*.

What a fantastic surprise Beethoven has for us here. Audiences must have expected a straightforward reprise of the opening section, especially if the repeat was observed. But no, the composer changes direction from the fifth bar and gets us to F major! The horn solo can be tricky, as the horn often gets behind the strings.

Another unexpected dissonance occurs at **m. 438**, where the E♭ seems incongruous but makes perfect sense at the same time. The remainder of this recapitulation follows pretty much the same idea as was presented the first time around. I prefer to have the timpanist play most of the louder notes with a hard mallet, bringing out the sixteenth notes at **m. 520**.

The Coda begins at **reh. S**, and in some ways, we can think that the composer could have stayed in E♭ and written a fitting conclusion to the movement soon after. But when Beethoven introduces that third theme in the development, the traditional rules go out the window. What we have is an extended Coda (140 bars long!) that incorporates all the elements that came before.

The conductor must be very clear with the preparation and beat starting at **m. 567**. It can be done in either one or three, but in both instances, a precise downbeat is needed to bring in the first violins together. I introduce a slight hairpin at **m. 581** for both violin sections. As it was with the violins, so it must be with the third horn at **m. 589**. You can also ask them to play up a little so that everyone else can adjust to their rhythm.

An infamous passage starts at **m. 595**. The idea of an independent double bass part, separate from cellos and bassoons, was still novel, and it occurs several times in this symphony. However, this spot is almost always difficult for the ensemble. Firstly, unless the orchestra is very experienced, the basses will play too softly to be heard. Secondly, they will also be uniformly late with the pickup note. You must tell them to anticipate this just a bit earlier than usual but not rush into the downbeat.

Eight bars before **reh. U**, aim for equal length with the quarter note alterations, which also must fit with the series of two-beat phrases in the violas and cellos. At **reh. U** we arrive at the Coda proper. Try to stay in one, and keep the tempo moving. The violins should think of this in a lighthearted way and should not overemphasize the *sforzandos*. I ask them to play the second note of the third bar of the phrase on the short side. Balance the canon between the first violins and the horns so that one does not overwhelm the other.

At **reh. V**, we should hear the woodwind and lower string lines equally—this means making sure that the other instruments are not too loud at the start. The final iteration of the theme allows us the opportunity to take advantage of notes Beethoven did not have during his time. For example, look at the trumpets starting in **m. 655**. For four bars, they play the tune, but then they play repeated B♭s for the next four bars. Most conductors ask them to double the melodic line for the complete eight bars.

Before concluding the movement, we have more decisions to make. The first is at **m. 681**, where it is possible to either separate or sustain the chords depending on whether you ask the strings to take all down bows or use a regular up/down motion. In any event, most conductors agree that the upbeat to **m. 685** should be short. Then, the brass and timpani can drop down after the first beat just a little and make a crescendo five bars before the end.

The final two notes depend on what you did at the start of the movement. If you conducted it in tempo, then do so again here. And if you held it back, then it is appropriate to do so here as well.

## Second Movement: Marcia funebre; Adagio assai

Few musical figures are more hotly debated than that which opens the monumental slow movement of the "Eroica." The questions are simple enough: Should the double basses play the grace notes before or on the beat? At what speed? Beethoven does not help matters, as he is inconsistent with these notes later in the movement. How do we decide?

Let's see what is written before those notes are sounded. First of all, the movement is marked *Marcia funebre*. That should give us a clue. The tempo indication is *Adagio assai*, ♪ = 80, a bit fast for a funeral march. The meter is 2/4, but given that we are told about the eighth notes, clearly this movement must be conducted in four. I conduct it on the back side of 60. The *sotto voce* indication reinforces the *pianissimo* dynamic, implying that the sound is not only soft but distant as well.

These notes evoke a military drum, and if they were played on that instrument, they would sound before the beat. The composer does not indicate that the grace notes are triplets, as he does in the sixth bar. However, that does not mean that they should come on the bar line. Logic sometimes overtakes what we see on the page. From my point of view, these little notes come before the downbeat and are played in a manner similar to the triplets.

Since this is a march, albeit a slow one, I give three small, silent beats to start. The basses are usually quite far away from the first violins and cannot always hear the opening two notes clearly. Once you show the fiddles the first note, immediately grab the attention of the basses. In the fourth measure, be sure to sustain the basses' G, as this gives the second violins' F♯ more bite.

From my perspective, the oboe should imitate the first violins at the opening. If the oboe entrance is too free, the architecture of the movement has already been taken apart by the time the violins get the same figure again. The rhythmic accompaniment should be played on the string with the eighth note at full value. The conductor should decide how loud and soft the crescendos and diminuendos are based on what the oboist plays.

**Rehearsal A** brings us to the first fully *espressivo* moment in the warm relative key of E♭ major. Although marked *piano*, this part of the tune needs a slightly fuller tone than what has occurred before, with the crescendo going to perhaps *mezzo forte*. Hold the quarter note for its full length at **m. 20** and use the downbeat of the next bar as the cutoff. This gesture should be quite abrupt and followed by very little motion until the lead-in to the third beat. In **m. 24**, I find it helpful for the first violins to take a breath before reiterating the G.

Start **m. 27** loudly enough to make a truly big diminuendo. Three bars later, we get to break our rule of the *sforzando* reflecting the previous dynamic. Clearly, this is meant to be a shock and should be played quite strongly. What follows is in keeping with the similar passage earlier, but now the instrumental groups have traded places. The second violin line contains a possible error in **m. 58**, where Beethoven places the *sforzando* on the second eighth note and ties that G over to the next one. In my experience, this does not really work, so I prefer to have everyone play the *sforzando* on the third eighth note.

The chord at **m. 60** presents an unusual balance problem. All the notes are doubled by at least one other instrument except for the F in the second bassoon. If you have the luxury of doubled winds, two of them can play this note. If not, just ask the second bassoonist to play out a bit more than his or her colleagues.

Many conductors move the *Maggiore* section forward a bit. Alterations to tempo are often dictated by a change from major to minor and vice-versa, and considering the length of this movement, the contrast might be needed. No matter what, the lead-in to the *Maggiore* should not sound like it is the end of the movement, so do not slow down. In fact, if you wish to have a faster tempo at the *Maggiore*, I suggest starting to move forward in the previous bar so that the melodic lines in the lower strings are equal in tempo before and after the key change. Regarding the two-bar crescendo before **m. 76**, I advise starting it in **m. 75** to avoid covering up the woodwinds.

In the bar before **reh. C**, both violin sections wind up on the top note only; they do not sustain the lower notes. Do not let the strings overwhelm the oboe's presentation of the moving notes. Similarly, make sure that the balance of the dialogue between the violins and woodwinds is equal from **m. 86**.

Just as we delayed the crescendo before **m. 76**, I suggest doing the same starting at **m. 92**, but this time I advise waiting for three measures before increasing the volume. Four measures before the double bar, we have a *forte/piano* that should sound scary. Just when we are led to believe that the cadence will have some sort of conclusive gesture, we get a jolt. The most effective way to achieve this is to ask the strings to start right at the frog and pull very quickly to somewhere near the tip. To avoid running out of bow, they should change to an up bow in the next measure.

The following section appears to be a recapitulation of the opening, with some slight alterations here and there. However, the music takes an extreme turn starting in **m. 114**, where we have a double fugue, with two elements vying for dominance. Many conductors move the tempo forward a bit for this section, probably concerned that the half notes cannot be sustained at a slow tempo. I disagree with that assessment. This section contains so much tension that it can never seem slow enough for me, as long as that suspense is maintained. To compensate for the held-back pace, I ask the strings who have the half notes to take two bows per note. This works very well to create the intensity needed. If you have doubled woodwinds, or if someone is acting as an assistant, they should join in for the long notes.

All the sixteenth notes should be played on the string with a very heavy marcato. You may need to adjust bowings in this section if they work against what is on the printed page. Although Beethoven did write low open Cs for the double basses, he did not utilize them very often. Neither should we. Keep this sound reserved for very special places.

For example, four bars before **reh. D**, I have often heard this phrase, as well as the one at **m. 139**, dropped down an octave in the basses. To my ears, the effect is diminished if we give away the color too early, so I stick to what is written for the first C. Note that Beethoven could easily have asked the timpani to play a C at this point but chose the G instead. We should honor that.

Scholarly opinions differ on the horn passage at **m. 135**. In the following examples, both might be correct. Weingartner writes, "[T]he first and second horns should play in unison with the third, as this latter is too weak alone."[5] In contrast, Del Mar states, "[T]he celebrated 3rd horn solo of bars 135–9 . . .

should on no account be doubled, other than by the clarinets with which Beethoven supported it."[6] To each his own.

I think **m. 139** is the place to allow the double basses to go to the lower C. With the timpani playing the G, it comes across as a kind of dissonance, or at least an anomaly. The next few measures also benefit from bow changes on the long, sustained notes. Getting back to the basses, they have a trill on an E♭ in **m. 144**. It is always a bit underwhelming, and there is nothing you can do about it. Perhaps adhering to the printed octave is best for **m. 143** before asking them to drop back down for the low D.

Several important *sforzandos* occur from **mm. 145–48**, and to make them truly effective, start each measure on an up bow to allow for a down bow in the middle of the bar. A weighty crescendo reinforces the cadence one bar before **reh. E**. Then, wait just a moment before giving the note in the middle of that measure. Ask for all down bows on the eighth notes, certainly.

The climax of this section is open to debate. Normally, we continue to sustain the *fortissimo* until the downbeat of the third bar, as written, but Mahler interestingly makes a diminuendo over the course of the three notes, completely altering the meaning of the phrase. I find that choice unconvincing because the point of climax seems wrong. We should gradually allow the music to relax during the decrescendo bar to create a smooth transition for the return of the tune.

Just when it appears that we might be headed for a gentle Coda, Beethoven once again surprises the listener with the softest possible A♭ in the first violins, played on the A string. The cellos and basses should take two bows for the explosive A♭ that follows, adding a slight lift before the next bar. When the other strings come in, they should do the same, and your fourth beat should establish both a release point for the chord and the tempo for the next section.

At **m. 160**, it is certainly permissible to move ahead slightly, especially if you have taken a relaxed tempo for the *fugato*. Be diligent about the brass dynamics; they should not overwhelm the lower strings. The diminished arpeggio that occurs from **m. 164** is an interesting detail to bring out. Adjust the dynamics in all the instruments so that this line is heard distinctly but do so in a way that does not seem exaggerated. This is best accomplished with the strings playing on the string rather than off. Sadly, you cannot do much about the flutes being the only instruments to finish the phrase. I suppose you could ask both (assuming you only have two) to play the first three notes as strongly as possible and then ask the second flute to stay in the upper octave for the second group.

**Measure 168** has tremendous power if the basses and cellos play a heavy and long eighth note. The listener should feel a little uncomfortable with the clash of the G♮ against those who are playing the A♭. Bring out, but take care not to exaggerate, the accents in the upcoming measures.

To keep symmetry with what has come before, the first violins' third beat in **m. 180** requires a comma after it so that the B♭ that follows conveys the same upbeat meaning as earlier. This is a place where many conductors perform the section a little louder than the first time. With the depth of sound that today's string sections can produce, I rather enjoy the richer sonority here. The tempo can be held back, but only slightly, as the most active part of the movement begins at **m. 191**. My preference is for the violins to play on the string with a well-articulated bow stroke.

Often, what sounds like a mistake can be attributed to the performers backing away from an offending note or two. For example, at **m. 199**, the tonic and dominant come together, and it seems like one of them is wrong. However, if you ask the woodwinds, who move together on the C and B♮, not to make the diminuendo until the last beat, it helps illuminate Beethoven's intention.

This was probably unintentional, but two bars before **reh. H**, the third horn has a four-note motive that is strikingly similar to the opening of the Fifth Symphony. I usually ask the musician to bring this out and play the sixteenth notes at least *mezzo forte*, keeping that dynamic for the downbeat of the next bar.

The Coda starts at **reh. H** with a figure reminiscent of the second movement of Haydn's "Clock" Symphony (No. 101). Because of the slower tempo, this figure should be played on the string. Note that when the first violins enter, they are marked at *piano* but have no diminuendo. Clearly the *pianissimo* is *subito*, but the problem has to do with the final note of the previous bar. Since this breaks the repeated note pattern by jumping up an octave, do we consider it an upbeat to the next measure or the ending of the phrase we have been playing? I choose the latter by waiting ever so slightly before commencing the fifth bar.

I had never really noticed it until a musician in the National Symphony Orchestra told me that a guest conductor brought out the F♯ in **m. 222**. If it is played just a bit longer, the effect of this leading tone to the dominant on the strong beat of the bar is quite disconcerting. We do not expect the dissonance of the F♯ in the cellos to be as potent against the G as it sounds.

*Subito piano* marks and hairpins abound as we head into the last few bars. This final passage can certainly be played more slowly than any tempo previously chosen. At this point, we have lost the feeling of the funeral march and come to a place that is almost devoid of a sustained tempo.

On one occasion, I heard a conductor change the flute notes in **m. 236** to correspond with the first violins. This is a clear choice that Beethoven made and should not be altered. When we arrive at the last iteration of the tune, pay attention to the balance between the timpani and the strings' pizzicatos. You can deal with the first violins with your left hand and concentrate on the low strings for the sake of ensemble. Observe the length of the last notes on each of the wind chords.

Three measures before the end of the movement, I begin to subdivide my beat. The next bar is in eight, and unless the orchestra really knows the piece, someone will likely come in early. Try to capture everyone's attention before this measure starts and be as clear as possible. Then, turn your focus to the lower strings so that they know exactly where to place the first note of the triplets. Even though the slur seems to indicate otherwise, I usually connect the last two bars with no separation or breath. Finally, hold on to the last note as long as possible and give a very discreet cutoff to prevent either premature applause or coughing.

### Third Movement: Allegro vivace

After what should be a lengthy pause, the Scherzo comes as a complete rejection of the seriousness of the funeral march. We need some time to recover from what should be a harrowing experience. The very nature of the form dictates that this is the most straightforward movement in the symphony. But Beethoven being Beethoven, he nevertheless distinguishes his vision of a Scherzo from that of any of his compositional predecessors.

We start out with the usual 3/4 meter and the instruction *Allegro vivace* with a metronome marking of ♩. = 116. For a change, this speed works perfectly and can be utilized for the Trio as well. It gives enough forward momentum to feel a sense of anticipation at nearly every phrase point. Establish the tempo with the orchestra by giving a whole bar of preparation prior to the initial entry, plus the one that serves as the downbeat of the movement. Internally, the conductor must feel the pulse well before commencing. If you decide to keep the Trio in the same tempo, think about that section as well as the one you are about to start. We will address this issue in a moment.

The opening of the movement is a six-bar introduction to the oboe tune. This must have caught both the musicians and the audience off guard when the symphony was first performed. Make sure that the tempo you choose allows for the eighth-note figure in **m. 9** to be heard and articulated clearly.

We must wait ninety-two bars before any change of dynamic takes place. Keeping these measures *pianissimo* is no easy task. Almost every orchestra needs to be reminded of this dynamic, especially at **m. 53**, where musicians tend to overplay the accents and to allow the texture to incite them to play louder. Even the entrance of the oboe can create the illusion that the dynamic level has increased. For the conductor, a clear, small beat is the only solution. The larger the gesture, the louder the music will get.

The explosive crescendo one bar before **reh. A** is difficult to achieve. Sometimes it sounds like a *subito forte*. We are going from the softest *pianissimo* to the strongest *fortissimo* in just one measure. I suppose it is possible, although not practical, to assign a different dynamic to each of the notes here. Since the brass and timpani do not enter until **reh. A**, perhaps the intended effect is closer to a *subito fortissimo*. In any event, try to make the crescendo as incremental as possible.

The third bar after **reh. A** presents a balance issue, as the imitation figure in the lower strings can be completely obscured by the other instruments. Certainly, the musicians playing the quarter-note rhythmic element should drop down immediately. If this is not enough to allow the canon to get through, then some of the woodwinds also need to lessen their volume level.

On occasion, the upbeat to **reh. B** can come just a bit too soon. Listen carefully here and ask the musicians to feel the second-beat rest. At **m. 129**, if the strings do not already have it marked in their parts, you can ask them to play each note up bow. This provides an even lighter sound and balances nicely with the woodwinds. Observe the repeat, as is integral for Scherzo form. When you come to the second ending, emphasize the last two bars to maintain strength after most of the instruments have stopped playing.

On to the dilemma of the Trio: The first decision has to do with the tempo. If you stay with the basic speed of the Scherzo, this section is not so problematic—except at the upbeat and landing of the horns, where you may wish to delay the downbeat very slightly.

What is the dynamic? This passage represents something akin to a hunting call, which might lead us to think that the whole passage is meant to be played loudly. However, the only dynamic indicated before the crescendo is *piano* in the strings. The horns have just a single *sforzando* in each of their phrases, and we know that this is not a dynamic in and of itself but is relative to the overall volume of the whole passage. Conductors are divided on whether this section is loud or soft. I take the latter approach, because the crescendo, from my perspective, means that what comes before it is more restrained. In either case, the horns can insert a slight lift between the pickup and downbeat of the Trio (**m. 167**).

As to the tempo, similar to the eighth-note passage in the oboe near the start of the movement, the second horn must have enough time to fit in the eighth notes. Here is something interesting: The recapitulation of the opening horn motif again does not have a dynamic indication, but the last phrase ended *forte*. Does that mean that this second statement should be performed differently than the first time? This is certainly a possible interpretation and could create quite a dramatic effect.

If the tempo has slowed down, you can regain it at the pickup to **m. 198**. The same dynamic decisions must hold for the horns' restatement of the hunting motif. Usually, I allow for some relaxation in the horns at **m. 238**. Another nice touch is to observe the *subito pianissimo* at **m. 248**, changing the color of the Trio.

The phrasing in both the first and second endings is almost always confusing to those who have rests. The first ending sounds like, and is, a four-bar phrase. But the lead-in to the second ending is just three bars. Musicians will have heard it the first time and may assume it is the same on the repeat. You will probably have to clarify this at rehearsal.

Everything is as it was for the return of the Scherzo proper, save for those unusual four bars in cut time (*Alla breve*, **mm. 381–84**). Although there are dots on the half notes, most conductors add a great deal of weight here and ask for more of a marcato articulation rather than staccato.

The brief Coda begins with the timpani, hopefully using hard sticks for rhythmic and pitch clarity. The harmonic changes in the strings are also important. The crescendo beginning in **m. 431** is a continual increase in dynamic that culminates in the final three *fortissimo* chords. I ask the instruments entering at **m. 435** to start at *piano* because the increase in numbers already makes the dynamic seem louder, and then they continue the crescendo to *fortissimo*.

Beethoven puts a fermata in the silence of the last bar. That should be a message to all of us that he does not want an *attacca* transition into the Finale.

## Fourth Movement: Allegro molto

As with the majority of the symphony, the Finale is unlike anything written before it in terms of the extraordinary way it combines variations, fugues, and other musical devices.

It is instructive, but not necessary, to be familiar with the three pieces through which Beethoven develops the theme of this movement. The germ of the theme first appears as a dance tune, the seventh in a series of twelve dances written in 1801 (Contredanses WoO 14). Beethoven developed the tune in a highly original piano work (Variations and Fugue in E♭ Major for

Piano, Op. 35, 1802), as well as in the last section of his only full ballet, *The Creatures of Prometheus* (Op. 43), written in 1801. This all took place almost three years before the completion of the last movement of the Third Symphony. These compositions give us a glimpse into how Beethoven thought and worked on his music.

We start out at an almost outrageously fast metronome mark for the opening *Allegro molto*. At ♩ = 76, not only are the sixteenth notes almost unplayable, but they can also only sound like a blur at best. On top of the tempo, you have to deal with the two slurred grace notes in the first violins. When played before the beat, they can sound to the listener like a mistake. I suppose the argument for placing them on the beat makes sense if you also accept that the same logic applies at the start of the second movement. I just ask for them to be played as close to the downbeat as possible, and I conduct this introduction in two.

Conductors are divided on whether to add a ritard before the fermata in **m. 11**. This is a truly personal decision and works either way. The greater problem is how long to wait before starting the strings' pizzicatos to allow the musicians to move their bows away from the string but not put them down completely. Perhaps the start of this section should have an "I wonder what comes next?" feeling to it.

Mahler likens the pizzicatos to a baby's first steps, to be taken tentatively, and he exaggerates the dynamics so that the third and fourth bars are *pianissimo*. He even goes so far as to make a slight accelerando through the four eighth notes in the seventh bar of the phrase. He then follows the same phrasing in the measures where the woodwinds are playing. I do not recommend attempting this. However, I do think this entire section can be taken just a bit slower than the introduction.

The fermatas in **m. 31** and **m. 39** can be tricky in terms of when to release the note and commence the continuation of the theme. If you do exactly what is written, more than likely the upbeat in the strings will be covered up by the resonance of the winds and timpani. My solution is to hold the fermata and then imagine that this whole bar starts again. Thus, you give both the first and the second beats, cutting off the winds just after the second. It is up to you to decide which hand does what. This gives the strings a better chance of being heard clearly while still playing softly. Naturally, you want the strings and woodwinds to be equal in balance for the conversation they are having.

Next, we move on to the variations at **m. 44**. One item that often gets overlooked, or perhaps misinterpreted, is the indication *dolce* in both the theme and the more active line underneath. Most of the time, conductors will opt for either a gentle accent on the long notes or even a slight separation. I take the composer literally here and play the notes legato and connected. The moving lines are done with a gentler stroke but still separated. The long half notes are a consistent feature throughout the movement unless Beethoven specifies otherwise.

In the B-section of the first variation, the second violin interjections (**m. 53**) should be on the aggressive side, but I do not recommend playing all three notes down bow. Everyone seems to agree that in the editions that show two fermatas for the first violins in **m. 55**, the first is clearly a mistake. As opposed to the earlier fermatas, the winds or brass are not playing; thus we do not need a space after the sustained note.

The pickup to **m. 60** is best played quickly to ensure that the two sixteenth notes do not sound like two of the ensuing triplet eighths. Continue to play the main tune sustained and very legato for four bars. At **m. 71**, be mindful that the eighth note at the end of the bar is within the duple rhythm and not the triplet.

A few conductors slightly expand the pickup to **m. 76**. The scoring is a bit thick here, so be sure that the first violins are heard equally with the woodwinds. Since the tune at **m. 84** is usually preceded by a pickup note, I insert a crescendo on the last two eighth notes of **m. 83** to lead into the *forte* rather than conduct a *subito forte* on the downbeat.

One of the most difficult spots, in terms of ensemble, starts in the end of **m. 91** and ends at the fermata. Although the first desks of strings can usually hear the oboe clearly, the others cannot. Invariably, the first violins are rarely together with their colleague in the wind section. You usually have to rehearse these two lines separately and carefully gauge the brief ritard before the fermata. The remaining instruments must play softly enough so that these two groups can hear each other.

The final fermata (four bars before **reh. A**) should be a bit longer than the previous ones, and it is possible to expand the next note a little for dramatic effect. But the real decision has to do with the tempo. You have most likely played this whole variation section at a slightly slower speed than the opening few bars. Here is an opportunity to get back to the initial tempo if you wish, either at **m. 104** or directly at **reh. A**.

As Norman Del Mar points out, the section starting at **m. 117** should be thought of in phrase groups. This is achieved by thinking of each entry of the fugal subject as the start of a new period. I continue to play the half-note theme long and sustained but switch to the lighter, shorter style in the fifth bar of each phrase. The contrast between long and short can really enhance this remarkable passage. For a change, the *sforzandos* can be taken out of context and really brought out when they occur.

We have not yet discussed what Beethoven means when he writes *più forte*, as in **m. 167**. More interpreters think this is another way of indicating a crescendo (or shorthand for *più e più forte*), but some believe that it is more like a sudden increase in dynamic. Your choice.

Getting into **reh. B** can be a tad tricky. A *subito piano* coming after a *fortissimo* often means that the first note of the *piano* bar gets lost in the acoustic. But it doesn't really make sense to insert a slight break, so the only solution is to find a dynamic that works to make the new passage clearly audible while creating a contrasting sonic profile.

Finding optimal balance at **m. 183** is just a matter of getting the flutes and oboes as soft as possible in these somewhat higher registers. When we get to **m. 191**, it can be difficult to hear the flute solo, so we can help Beethoven out here. I reduce the number of strings to three stands of first and second violins, two stands of violas and cellos, and one stand of basses. The *tutti* returns on the second note of **m. 198**. Conductors usually place a crescendo in this bar, but you are certainly free to try it as written. In my experience, it sounds awkward without a crescendo.

Leading us into the rustic G-minor section is another powerful crescendo at **m. 206**, best accomplished by playing the repeated notes on the string. At **reh. C**, I usually get a very robust sound by having the cellos and basses play the four-note motif long and sustained before observing the *molto marcato* indication that Beethoven marks four bars later. This entire passage is heavy and thickly scored, making the scale played by the flute in **m. 213** very difficult to hear. Mahler's solution is to have his added E♭ clarinet double the flute. If you do not have four flutes, ask the second to play this run as well. Even though you lose the upper octave of the tune, it is already covered by the oboe. Usually, this is enough to allow the passage to be heard. At **m. 227**, once again I have the four-note motif played in a sustained manner. However, in the subsequent phrase (**mm. 233–34**), note that the violas, cellos, and basses stop tracking the expected melody. Instead, Beethoven presents us with two aggressive, dissonant notes, which I bring out with a sustained *sforzando* as indicated.

At **reh. D**, the repeated G♮s should be on the heavy side, as if the piece were ending. This includes the eighth note in the third bar, which is marked *subito piano* and must be much gentler. A bit of relaxation is in order for the C-major section that precedes the next fugal statement.

While **m. 277** presents an inversion of the tune, it should be played in the same way as it was previously. As in the earlier fugato, it is helpful to be keenly aware of the phrase structure each time this motif occurs. If you have kept the first violins at *pianissimo*, you should have no problem hearing the flutes in **mm. 292–96**. Pay attention to the *sforzando* indications in the flutes and horns.

The dramatic statement on the upbeat at **reh. E** certainly should allow for the trumpets to go up to *fortissimo*. After four notes, however, they should go back down to *mezzo forte*, along with the other brass and timpani. The cellos and second bassoon have an interesting but often unheard line at **m. 334**, and it is important to allow the chromatic scale to be audible. At **mm. 342–43**, I alter the phrasing to emphasize the pungent C♭. The first note is separate, and then I slur every two notes, giving the passage a slightly off-balance feel. Most conductors add a ritenuto three bars before the *Poco andante*. Two bows on the fermata help to extend the length of this bar to conclude this section.

Although not the Coda proper, some argue that the *Poco andante* is the beginning of the final buildup that concludes the symphony. Most certainly it presents a relief from all the motion that has occurred, but nevertheless, it is structurally just a highly modified variation. The metronome indication is a bit fast, and most conductors take a more relaxed tempo for this section.

I recommend waiting, without moving, before beginning the tender oboe solo. It is not necessary to beat the preceding three eighths, as if the movement started all over again. The easing of tension must come suddenly, as if no one is expecting it. At **m. 354**, it is possible to ask the winds to take a breath before the last eighth note, and if you do, remember to ask them to take another breath in **m. 362**.

The three-against-four that begins in **m. 365** should be obvious to the listener, and perhaps it is advisable to move the tempo forward ever so slightly. I also like to bring out the bassoons and horns starting at **m. 373**, but not so much as to cover up the other instruments.

Although virtually all conductors make a crescendo in the bar before **reh. F**, this is not indicated by Beethoven. I once tried it as a *subito fortissimo*, as marked, but found it very unsettling. At **reh. F**, most conductors double the first horn with at least two, and sometimes more, horns. However, Beethoven has already doubled the line with clarinets and bassoons, and they must balance with the lower strings instead of sounding like a concerto for the brass.

Some adjustments in dynamics are necessary to hear everything that is going on between **reh. F** and **reh. G**. I advise that this section be played on the string, very marcato. This enables you to control the volume level and lends more weight to the passage.

Be careful not to rush at **m. 404**. A more deliberate tempo, just one click or so slower on the metronome, can be useful. The crescendo that commences in **m. 408** needs to be judged very carefully. It is supposed to last ten bars but often reaches its climax too soon. To mitigate this tendency, ask the first violins to start the crescendo on the second half of the half note instead of the quarters. You can write in whatever dynamic you believe will work for each of these long notes to help the musicians gauge how loud to be at each point. Again, be cognizant that Beethoven often uses *più forte* when indicating a crescendo.

You might find it interesting to learn that Mahler not only made a rather large crescendo in **m. 419** but also added an equally lugubrious rallentando.

The final portion of this section relies on a very steady pulse from the cellos. They should play slightly off the string but close enough to allow for any tempo fluctuation that might occur in the other instruments. The double-bass G♯s are quite wonderful if played long and loud enough within the given dynamic.

The final major difficulty has to do with getting into the Presto. The metronome mark of $\quarternote = 116$ seems too fast to allow for clear articulation of the thirty-second notes. This is a matter to consider very seriously, as it determines the tempo for this explosive Coda, but how you start it is even more important.

First of all, there is the problem of reconciling the three-against-two in the bars leading up to the Presto, with the cellos seemingly at odds with the other instruments in the orchestra. Do we make a ritard prior to the Presto or just barrel right in, *subito*? How do the strings know what tempo you will choose?

The last one of these difficulties is simple to resolve. Just play it one time starting at the Presto itself. The orchestra will remember the tempo after that. I think that just a split second of silence helps set up this ending, and I also make a slight ritard and a diminuendo, as if the work were about to fade away. Technically, what you have to do is pause when you give the fourth beat and let the musicians finish the phrase. Then, you give the new tempo just as they are finishing the old one.

The timpanist always has a good time with the four bars that start at **m. 457**. The timpani should not overwhelm the scale passages, though. Everyone seems to have their own idea about how long the notes should be played starting at **m. 461**. Here I believe we can trust Beethoven by playing long quarters and short eighths, including in the last three bars. Notably, it is important to hear the woodwind scales clearly five measures before the end. The final note is certainly not a fermata but should be sustained long enough to feel like the conclusion of an epic, but satisfying, struggle.

## Conductor's Etiquette

When you return to the stage after the initial bow, it is customary to acknowledge the three horns, followed by the oboe and flute. After that, if you wish, you can simply indicate for the rest of each section to rise.

\*\*\*

"Music is a higher revelation than all wisdom and philosophy."

—Ludwig van Beethoven

## Notes

1. Felix Weingartner and Jessie Crosland, *On the Performance of Beethoven's Symphonies* (London: Breitkopf & Härtel, 1907).

2. Norman Del Mar, *Conducting Beethoven* (Oxford: Clarendon Press, 1992).

3. Ludwig van Beethoven, *Symphonies 1–9*, ed. Jonathan Del Mar (Kassel: Bärenreiter Urtext, 1996–2000).

4. Ludwig van Beethoven, *Symphony No. 3 in E-flat Major, "Eroica," op. 55*, ed. Peter Hauschild (Wiesbaden, Germany: Breitkopf & Härtel Urtext, 1999).

5. Weingartner and Crosland, *On the Performance of Beethoven's Symphonies*, 43.

6. Del Mar, *Conducting Beethoven*, 38.

# Modest Mussorgsky, orch. Maurice Ravel: *Pictures at an Exhibition*

"My music must be an artistic reproduction of human speech in all its finest shades. That is, the sounds of human speech, as the external manifestations of thought and feeling must, without exaggeration or violence, become true, accurate music."

—Modest Mussorgsky

Рузана Ширинян, Public domain, via Wikimedia Commons

## 28  Modest Mussorgsky, orch. Maurice Ravel: *Pictures at an Exhibition*

One of the first pieces many young listeners are exposed to, *Pictures at an Exhibition* has been orchestrated more than forty times. It exists in versions for steel drum and accordion, and in genres ranging from electronic to rock. In short, this work is included in almost every top-ten list of popular classical compositions. Therefore, every conductor must learn how to lead it.

Despite the work's ubiquity, the conductor still has many decisions to make, especially these days. The work's history is somewhat complicated. Written in 1874, it is a suite of ten pieces, some preceded by a promenade. The pictures that are represented are based on drawings by Viktor Hartmann, who was not only an artist but also an architect and designer. Mussorgsky and Hartmann were friends, and Hartmann's premature death in 1873 caused the composer to sink into a deep depression.

A year later, inspired by a retrospective exhibit of the artist's collection, Mussorgsky wrote his piano suite, completing it in only three weeks. The Russian musical world was somewhat shaken by this piece, as music of the time was mostly patriotic in nature, and the suite was considered a form of "musical radicalism" in terms of its rhythms and harmonies.

The print edition of the piano suite, which was edited by Nikolai Rimsky-Korsakov, was not published until 1886, five years after Mussorgsky's death from alcoholism. Rimsky-Korsakov altered several passages, and many errors began to creep into the solo part. Almost from the first performance, pianists began to tinker with Mussorgsky's original, adjusting awkward chords and adding notes in places that they felt needed to be filled out. Much depended on which edition the soloist was using, with several in circulation from the start of the twentieth century. The first scholarly version did not arrive until 1931.[1]

The nature of the Hartmann pictures themselves added to the confusion. By the time the critical edition was published, only a few of the originals had survived. When we study and perform the piece, as with other descriptive works, we can only use the titles to help us interpret the musical meaning.

The orchestral version we perform most often is the one arranged by Maurice Ravel in 1922 at the invitation of Serge Koussevitzky. For many years, it was thought to be the first transcription. However, at least three previous attempts preceded it, the first in 1886 by Mikhail Tushmalov, a student of Rimsky-Korsakov. Of course, this led to speculation that the latter had a hand in it as well. This version only includes seven of the ten pictures and omits most of the promenades.

Sir Henry Wood's colorful rendition, featuring camel bells and other exotic instruments as well as numerous alterations to the piano text, appeared in 1915 and was subsequently withdrawn once the Ravel arrangement became available in 1922.

Simultaneously, Leo Funtek, a Slovenian living in Finland, orchestrated the whole work in the very same year as Ravel. His version is much closer to the original than the noted Frenchman's. However, Ravel's came with restrictions—Koussevitzky published the work himself and held on to the rights for several years, preventing other conductors from performing it and prompting several competing arrangements.

Among the more interesting transcriptions are those by Leonidas Leonardi, Leopold Stokowski, Lucien Cailliet, Vladimir Ashkenazy, Alexander Gorchakov, and Douglas Gamely, an Australian composer whose very unusual version of "The Great Gate of Kiev" includes a chorus and organ.

Back in the 1980s, I put together various orchestrations of the different movements and created three separate "Pictures" suites. I often preceded live performances with a comparison play-and-talk to demonstrate how they were different from the Ravel orchestration. Later, I decided to go back to the so-called authentic piano version to see how much of it I could incorporate into the existing Ravel. I readjusted dynamics, reinstated the bars that Ravel omitted, and corrected notes to keep as much of the original intact as possible.

Our discussion will focus primarily on how to conduct the Ravel arrangement in the score published by Boosey & Hawkes.[2] Rehearsal numbers are indicated, and they occur often enough that you can easily start at one rather than in the middle of a phrase.

Several versions of the piano version are available, and at one time, Boosey published an edition of the Ravel orchestration with the piano version printed at the bottom. Occasionally, I will point out where alterations might be helpful, but my main goal is to communicate how to conduct the piece. One caveat: The Ravel orchestration is still under copyright in the United States but not in other countries.

The orchestration is as follows: three flutes (third doubling piccolo), three oboes (third doubling English horn), two clarinets in B$^\flat$ and A, one bass clarinet in B$^\flat$ and A, two bassoons, one contrabassoon, one alto saxophone in E$^\flat$, four horns in F, three trumpets in C, three trombones, one tuba, timpani, percussion (side-drum, bass drum, rattle, whip, cymbals, triangle, tam-tam, glockenspiel, bell—referring to a note on the typical orchestral chime set, xylophone), celesta, two harps, and strings. Performance time is approximately thirty-two to thirty-five minutes.

## Promenade I

The lack of metronome marks probably accounts for the wide variance in conductors' speeds, not only for the different movements but also for the work as a whole. Part of the complication has to do with the opening instruction from Mussorgsky: *Allegro giusto, nel modo russico; senza allegrezza, ma poco sostenuto*. Let's see: Properly fast, in the Russian way; without mirth, but slightly sustained. Hmm.

What does the music and history tell us? We know that the composer was somewhat heavy in girth, and scholars have inferred that the eleven beats of walking music represent him waddling through the museum. In any event, the main question that immediately confronts the conductor is whether to lead the first two bars. We encounter this same situation in works such as *The Rite of Spring* and *Prelude to the Afternoon of a Faun*. You can either start off by discreetly conducting to show the trumpeter what tempo you would like, or you can just nod to that player and see what they choose. If it is too slow, you can pick up the tempo in the third bar or vice versa.

For me, the real problem is what happens between the last note of the second bar and the start of the next. For all the notes to be truly equal, they have to be played at the same length. However, the soloist must take a breath just before the third bar, which usually results in shortening the last note of the second bar. If you are fortunate enough to have four trumpets in your orchestra, the extra musician can play the *tutti* to resolve the difficulty. If not, then you should tell the trumpet player to play each note equally and the other instruments to start slightly later to allow for a breath.

The same applies to the next passage at **reh. 1** as well. The dynamic is single *forte*, so it should sound noble rather than aggressive. As with so many composers, we are confronted with a discrepancy when it comes to the differentiation between bars marked 3/2 and those marked 6/4. At **reh. 2**, the bar is clearly divided into two groups of three beats. But in the next measure, even though the stems show one thing, the phrase structure is really three sets of two beats—in other words, a 3/2. However, it is certainly feasible to split this up in whatever way feels natural to you.

This incongruity, at least here, does not matter much to the orchestra, and it usually sounds just fine. But it becomes a problem as the promenade moves along because your beat pattern may not look like what the players are expecting from the time signature. Showing how the music flows is important not only for the musicians but also for the audience. These meter groupings also have physical implications for you in terms of where you place the beats and how you communicate your concept of the work as a whole.

The second bar of **reh. 3** is certainly correct in this respect, as there are lines on each of the three beats. But another of our usual troubles crops up in the fourth bar, where we are not told the ending dynamic of this diminuendo or the one where the strings imitate the woodwinds. In both cases, I think that starting *mezzo forte* and going down to *piano* makes sense and works well. Make sure that the third oboe and first horn are heard clearly in this bar.

It follows that a *subito mezzo forte* must be played on the downbeat one measure before **reh. 4**, and the crescendo leads us to the single *forte*. The horns are the only instruments to play the fanfare sixteenth notes, so they usually need to be encouraged to play them a bit louder. Observe the accents as you proceed to the end of the movement. They do not always occur when you expect them.

In the third bar of **reh. 4**, I separate the three groups of two notes with a little lift following the second note. The same applies to the two-note groups in the bar before **reh. 5**. My guess is that about 50 percent of conductors make a slight ritard over the last couple of beats, and the others play it straightforward. In any event, the final note should not be shorter than the others.

## 1. Gnomus (The Gnome)

This is probably the most complicated of the pictures in terms of its technical requirements for the conductor. Whether you choose to pause before starting or opt to begin the movement *attacca*, having the desired tempo firmly in your head at the end of the promenade is very important.

I like to think that the composer is casually strolling through the gallery and is suddenly shocked to see a grotesque image, so I pause only momentarily before violently launching into this piece. Even though the movement is marked *Vivo* and conducted in one, if the tempo is too fast, the notes can become a blur, taking away from the barbaric quality of the melody that comes through in the piano version.

This is the first major change I make to the Ravel orchestration. To convey more violence, I have half of the strings in each section play the notes separated and near the frog each time this pattern occurs; later, I ask all the musicians to do this. A tempo of ♩. = 92 seems fast enough. I conduct the bar before the *Meno vivo* in three, setting up the next few bars at the indicated slower tempo and accounting for the fermata in the piano edition.

Three measures before **reh. 7**, I have the violas and cellos add the low C to the two eighth notes to better correspond with the solo piano version. Obviously, they cannot do this in the next bar. It is up to you whether you wish to observe Mussorgsky's fermata in the second bar of **reh. 7**; I do not.

The same octave situation in the violas and cellos comes up again four bars before **reh. 8**.

Aligning the pizzicatos at **reh. 8** is the most difficult part of the next section. When you give your preparation beat, make sure that you are feeling three quarter notes and, if needed, ask the strings to do the same. Ravel gets quite fancy at **reh. 9**, completely changing Mussorgsky's intentions. If you play it as printed, keep in mind that the glissandos in the strings are continuous and should not linger on the first note of any given bar. To me, the harp always feels a bit weak two measures before **reh. 10**, so I recommend doubling this.

However, at **reh. 9**, Ravel completely ignores the piano version, in which Mussorgsky repeats the music of **reh. 8**, played in the same way. Lately, I have preferred to eliminate Ravel's alternate section between **reh. 9** and **reh. 10**, instead asking the musicians to play the passage between **reh. 8** and **reh. 9** twice before moving on.

At the second bar of **reh. 10**, even though you are in one, you can conduct the third beat with your left hand. (This is also a possibility two bars before **reh. 8**.) Try to bring out the grace note in the woodwinds and harp. In the piano version, this note is slightly sustained, whereas Ravel shortens it. While the score gives no indication to slow down three measures before **reh. 11**, many of us hold back this bar and conduct it in three. For some reason, Ravel does not include a diminuendo in the third trombone and tuba. Of course, the piano automatically makes one, and it is even printed in the part, so you certainly can do it as well. The final note is short and abrupt.

The *Poco meno mosso, pesante*, although written in four, is usually conducted in two. Again, doubling the harps makes sense. Everything is sustained and heavy, but the *mezzo forte* dynamic should not be overplayed to ensure that the interjections of the *Vivo* make an impact. Almost all the notes here are legato, but we have a decision to make in the bar before the *Vivo*. We can see that the last note is short, but what about the one before it? I make this brief, as well, adding a diminuendo before violently attacking the 3/4 measures.

Long silences after each fermata are important, serving to keep the listener guessing what comes next. Never forget that the audience always includes people who are hearing this work for the first time. As I alluded to previously, I have the entire string section play these *Vivo* passages with separate bows two measures before **reh. 12** and at **reh. 13**.

Ravel presents us with a new situation at **reh. 14**. First, the grace note should be played just before the beat, followed by the portamentos in the lower strings. A half note is a long time to make a glissando that creates the eerie sound we are looking for here. For a more unnerving effect, I recommend starting the slide later and giving it the length of an eighth note rather than trying to make it last for an entire half note. I also change bows on each note, which helps emphasize the glissando.

Seven bars later, the bow changes are still in effect, but I also have half of each section play with a tremolo, still within the context of the glissando. It is appropriate for everyone to make a crescendo as the passage comes to an end, with the suspended cymbal (played with a wooden stick) sustaining right up to the whip crack. The *fouet*, or slapstick, comes in various dimensions, and my suggestion is for one of medium size so that the timbre is neither very high nor low. It must be played as loudly as possible, with the idea that it calls a halt to the music that precedes it. You can wait just a bit before starting the Coda at **reh. 15**.

While the solo piano has no problem connecting the phrase that begins at **reh. 15**, Ravel's changes in instrumentation make this slightly difficult. You want the bass clarinet to sound similar to the bassoon and the double basses to flow into the cello line. The cellos' glissando should have a frightening quality, and therefore I increase the crescendo to *forte*, assigning that same dynamic to the basses when they take over. You will need to take a little rehearsal time here to get it right. Often overlooked is the instruction to gradually make an accelerando, which more than likely should last until two bars before **reh. 18**.

The trill in the horns at **reh. 17** is effective and should be brought out. In the piano version, the third bar of **reh. 17** is marked *Sempre vivo*, though the musical notation implies slowing down two bars later. We usually hold the tempo back and conduct the two bars before **reh. 18** in three. The percussion instrument here is a ratchet.

Ravel deviates from Mussorgsky in his treatment of the pickup to the second bar of **reh. 18**. He writes it as an eighth note, but the original is clearly a quarter. I change it to a quarter note, which makes a huge difference musically, playing it short and then having the strings play all the eighth notes off the string. The dynamic should be *fortissimo*, but save enough to make a crescendo two bars before the end. Unless the musicians can really hear each other clearly, it will take a couple of tries in rehearsal to play this with precision.

## Promenade II

After the horrifying images of the gremlins, we need to take a breath before continuing our walk through the gallery. Since the indication here is *Moderato comodo assai e con delicatezza*, the tempo should be slower than the first movement. Comfortably and delicately is the continued explanation. As opposed to the opening, we need to convey the tempo to the solo horn here. Often, the oboe and clarinets play a bit too loud and cover the tune in the bassoon in the third bar. This is especially true on the last note of the phrase, which is one of the highest on the oboe. My solution is to take out the hairpin for the upper voices and have the bassoon play *espressivo*.

The same applies four bars later, where the orchestration is a bit thicker. In both cases, the last eighth note should be on the long side but with enough space to take a breath. The remainder of this short movement is clear. You might consider starting the violins on an up bow, playing "as it comes" and ending on a down bow to facilitate the diminuendo. Again, the last note should not be short.

## 2. Il vecchio castello (The Old Castle)

Mussorgsky's original tempo indication is a somewhat flowery *Andantino molto cantabile e con dolore*, but Ravel simplifies it to Andante. Granted, the composer is being descriptive, but the discrepancy is notable. In any event, it is not a Largo or Adagio. I believe that this movement must be flowing and, therefore, not too slow.

The introduction works well. The original has the piano playing *pianissimo*, while Ravel changes it to single *piano*. I suspect that the reason has to do with his choice to use the alto saxophone as the protagonist here. Not that it cannot play softly, but the instrument was still relatively new in the orchestral world, and Ravel must have wanted to showcase the sound. It will not be played anywhere else in the piece.

I think it is quite important to hear the continuous streams of eighth notes, another kind of walking motif, whenever they appear. When the English horn takes over two bars after **reh. 21**, the pickup note in the original is an eighth, and here it is a quarter. Depending on the musician's ability to play the tone as smoothly as possible, either way works, but I usually ask the player to change to an eighth note.

Three bars before **reh. 23**, it is a nice touch to lean into the F$^{\times}$ in the second violins. The open string gives a plaintive sound that persists for this picture. At **reh. 23**, I prefer for the first violins to slur each beat, as opposed to separating the notes, to avoid unwanted accents during the bow changes. The same holds true at **reh. 24**. All the expression and dynamic marks in the score are Ravel's, and I find that they work well.

As with the English horn, Ravel alters the rhythm in the viola line two bars after **reh. 25**. The piano version has a dotted-quarter pickup note, but Ravel changes it to a quarter—a small detail but one you might want to consider. Many conductors will continue the basses' pizzicato in the third and fourth measures of **reh. 25**. At this point, I should mention that many of these alterations can be put in the parts, but make sure to arrange this with the library in advance so as not to waste valuable rehearsal time.

Ravel introduces a wonderful color after **reh. 25**, where he doubles the flute with the English horn. You need to balance this to create a moment that sounds like just one instrument is playing. We can call it the "florn." Interestingly, the English horn usually sounds louder on the upper note, so it is helpful to back away from this with a slight diminuendo.

At **reh. 26**, neither Mussorgsky nor Ravel provide a dynamic. Since Ravel takes it down to *pianissimo* at **reh. 27**, perhaps it starts this way as well. In fact, Mussorgsky is quite sparse with his information in this and other pictures; Ravel does his best to notate what works with his orchestration. I follow his lead for this passage but alter it when it reappears later.

Another lovely combination of instruments comes with the pickup to the second bar of **reh. 28**, where the flute is joined by the clarinet ("flarinet"). The unexpected E♮ in the fourth bar is wonderful, although I back away from it with a diminuendo, quite the opposite of what I normally do when a note is so noticeably different.

Ravel basically repeats his dynamics beginning four measures before **reh. 29**, but here I change them. I keep the crescendo going until the third measure and then begin the diminuendo, reaching *pianissimo* five bars before **reh. 30**. When I could sort-of play this piece as a pianist, that is what I used to do, since Mussorgsky does not include dynamic markings.

One bar before **reh. 30**, a set of continually alternating instruments play the quarter/eighth rocking rhythm. This actually started all the way back at the fifth bar of **reh. 25** but here stands out from any other musical idea. The bassoon has the lion's share of the motif, trading it back and forth with the cellos and bass clarinet. Try to make the instruments sound as equal as possible.

The final three bars can be tricky. Make sure you have the attention of the first violins and give them a clear indication for the *pianissimo* pizzicato. What follows has always puzzled me. Ravel has the sax play the upbeat with a portamento. I have heard it done this way a couple of times and even tried it out at a rehearsal. To my ear, it sounds awful and out of character with everything else in this delicate movement. Plus, the piano version has it in octaves. One day, I may put this in the first oboe part, minus the glissando.

Tell the strings to listen for the saxophone upbeat—before which you can take a little time—to know when to enter. Keep the cellos under your eye for their pulsating rhythm and let the soloist end at his or her discretion. With only a few people playing, this can be conducted in two rather than in six. Maintain a still posture during the silence and then give the upbeat for the next section.

## Promenade III

We now have our third different tempo indication, although it appears to be close to the previous one. The piano version specifies *Moderato, non tanto, pesamente*. I have been unable to find a proper translation for *pesamente*, so perhaps it is best to stay with Ravel's choice, *pesante*.

Given that he assigns it to the same instrument that began the piece, perhaps the tempo is closer to the first, rather than the previous, promenade. Once again, Ravel strays from the original, as this opening is in octaves for the piano. It is a bit low to give to the second trumpet but can easily be done by the first trombone, if you wish. This alteration will surprise a lot of people if you do it.

If you stay at single *forte*, that is more than enough volume. Sometimes, the third trombone and tuba overdo it in the third bar, resulting in a coarse sound that drowns out the cellos' and basses' pizzicatos.

A slight danger presents itself at the second bar of **reh. 33**, even with orchestras that know the piece well: A stray lower string player may wish to follow the same rhythmic pattern of the previous three notes and move too soon to the E♯. You can help avoid this by keeping your beat small for the second and third beats of the 6/4 bar.

The ritardando starts before the final bar. Keep still for the first two beats of the last measure and then dictate the two eighth notes, followed by the quarter. I prefer to let the harp and horn hold on to the last note for a bit, even though the piano version only contains an eighth note. The cutoff can serve as a two-beat preparation for the next picture.

## 3. Tuileries (Children Quarreling after Play)

Since this painting is lost, we do not really know if it depicts the famous garden near the Louvre with children added for perspective. Nonetheless, it is the first charming picture of the set. The marking is *Allegretto non troppo, capriccioso*, which seems perfect for the music. The whole movement is in four but contains some tricky passages to navigate.

The actual tempo will be determined by the ability of your musicians, and the woodwinds in particular, to negotiate the articulations provided by Ravel. He clearly understands that the oboe cannot play the sixteenth notes as comfortably as the flute, so he provides slurs against the dots. However, I do not follow his reasoning for phrasing in groups of two notes for the flute, since the piano version is straightforward. One matter to address in the first bar and several thereafter is the length of the eighth note. From my point of view, it can be clipped, but not so much that you do not hear the chord change.

The pizzicatos before **reh. 34** are non-divisi and played arpeggiated, starting with the lower note. In the third bar of **reh. 34**, try to get as much sound as possible from the woodwinds, without diminuendo, and ask the second clarinet to make a crescendo to exaggerate the *subito piano*. The bar before **reh. 35** is effective with a diminuendo for the clarinet but without a ritard. Wait a moment before continuing.

Upon arriving at this short middle section, most conductors will slow down slightly, especially on the third beat, to allow a moment to appreciate the portamento in the first violins. This is one of those places where you must explain what you want. I like to think that almost everything the conductor communicates can and should be done with gestures alone, but this spot is an exception.

You can either continue to hold back or pick up the tempo on the fourth beat. A clear indication to the flute, clarinet, and harp is necessary to coordinate their entrance in the second bar of **reh. 35**. Personally, I don't believe that hesitating a second time two bars before **reh. 36** serves any purpose, but this phrase is often performed that way. Instead, I use it to get back to the tempo of the opening of the movement.

In the three bars leading up to **reh. 37**, the dynamic changes from *forte* to *fortissimo* to *subito piano*. The contrast is difficult to achieve without sacrificing some of the dynamic just before it, but you should give it a try. Mussorgsky slurs the two groups of two notes in the original, and I think it makes sense to change this articulation in the strings one bar before **reh. 37**.

Because the line is moving upwards, it is helpful to ask the clarinet to make a diminuendo just before the last bar. Although it is not indicated and very few conductors seem to do it, I enjoy letting the harp ring after the final chord, but a short note can also be effective.

## 4. Bydło (The Oxcart)

Clearly, Ravel envisions the lumbering beast coming from a distance and therefore starts off softly, making a long crescendo. Mussorgsky must have imagined the picture with the protagonist front and center, staring at you with all its weight and might. It comes as a shock to an audience and orchestra that has heard this many times if you decide to employ the *fortissimo* dynamic of the original.

The tuba used during Ravel's time was a smaller, six-valve instrument, closer to a Wagner tuba than the bass ones played today. The phrase goes quite high for the giant but lies somewhat more comfortably for the older instrument. Consequently, it is now often played on a euphonium or Wagner tuba as a substitute.

When I first began playing the passage at full volume, I used to double the tuba line with the horns. Now I find that the tuba can manage it without the reinforcement. However, I also change the accompaniment lines so everyone is grinding away, with long strokes in the cellos and basses and something close to an accent on each one. Ravel asks that the mutes gradually be removed between **reh. 38** and **reh. 39**, but the louder dynamic eliminates the need to play *con sordino*.

If you are sticking with Ravel, this initial crescendo takes the dynamic from *pianissimo* to *mezzo forte* at **reh. 39**. Gauge the increase by putting in relevant *piano* and *mezzo piano* reference points as you go along. I recommend using two harps rather than just one.

At this point in the Ravel version, the dynamic is a result of the crescendo. On the other hand, if you start *fortissimo*, you must decide whether to drop down or just continue loudly. The nature of the orchestration seems consistent with the single *forte* range, or a little less than the dynamic at which you started off.

You may also wish to consider some differences in note length. For example, at the fourth bar of **reh. 39**, the piano version contains an eighth note on the downbeat rather than Ravel's quarter. There are some slurs in the melodic line as well, but I will leave you to discover these on your own.

The buildup reaches a high point at **reh. 42**. Triple *fortes* abound, generating enough power to light up a city. Still, I double the snare drum to make it even more forceful, starting them at *mezzo forte* and asking them to crescendo to the triple *forte* three measures before **reh. 43**, at which point they make a diminuendo with everyone else. It is always useful to know how many percussionists are utilized for a complete piece. Then, if you identify a spot where you want to reinforce the sound, you can check to see if one of those musicians is free at that time.

Mussorgsky offers another instruction at **reh. 42** that almost every conductor ignores, primarily because Ravel did not include it in his orchestration: *sempre pesante e poco allargando*. With the exception perhaps of the last bar, I do not believe I have heard anyone slow down during these last two pages. From my perspective, it does not make sense as the plodding eighths seem slow enough.

Two harps still can work at **reh. 45** to imitate the bassoons, who played something similar four bars earlier. Four measures before the end, Mussorgsky has a single note on the downbeat, but Ravel changes it to the second beat in the bass clarinet. I have no idea why he chooses to do this. The double-bass notes two bars before the end are still long, and only one harp needs to play here. Very clear indications are needed for the pizzicatos in the last measure. Hold your position with the right arm up during the fermata so that you can bring it down afterward for the two beats of silence that begin the next movement.

## Promenade IV

A new marking for the tempo is *Tranquillo*, which of course is a mood and not a speed. Give two quiet beats and then an ample breath so that the woodwinds can enter together. Even though there are differences between the piano and orchestra versions, I think this short interlude is mostly fine as is. The only comment I have is that if you follow what Ravel writes and do not insert a ritard in the last bar, your tempo must have a direct relationship with what comes next. The brief sixteenth-note group two measures before the end therefore needs to be in the same tempo as the fifth picture. The best way to set this up is to subdivide the third beat so that ♪ = ♩ in the next movement.

## 5. Ballet des poussins dans leurs coques (Ballet of the Chicks in Their Shells)

The tempo of this portrait will vary, depending on the ability of your orchestra. First, we see the unusual word *Scherzino*, followed by *Vivo leggiero*. Although it is certainly possible to start with one beat per bar, I recommend at least starting off in two, just to establish the tempo. The main danger here is rushing, especially with syncopated notes such as those in the oboes starting in the fifth measure.

As with the piano version, most of the piece is to be performed *pianissimo*, with a few crescendos along the way. Be judicious with the tempo; if it is too fast, much of the humor can be lost. Along with the above-mentioned oboes, the violas and second violins tend to move ahead unintentionally when they have their two bars of eighth notes. At **reh. 50**, the one-bar phrases and tradeoffs between instruments make ensemble matters difficult.

The cymbals are sometimes played with a metal beater, but if you have a slightly smaller set, they can be clashed if the sound is dampened right away.

For the fermata, just give one beat and have your right arm in a position to indicate the downbeat of the next measure. This not only serves as the cutoff but also clarifies the placement of the flute's second note. The repeat is essential and should be performed in the same manner as the first time.

Marked *pianissimo*, **reh. 52** is often played with small accents in the violins. I resist this, allowing the short notes in the flutes to provide the attack. Instead, I have the firsts play legato, at the tip, for all seven bars. Although it works fine, I wonder if it was necessary for Ravel to put the final bar of trills in the clarinets.

As opposed to his treatment of repeated material in "Gnomus," Ravel serves the music well by changing the colors when the same music recurs in this movement. Between **reh. 52** and **reh. 53**, he creates a rather fascinating sound world by having the side drum play alternating notes on the drum and with the stick striking the side of the instrument. Keep in mind that during the time when this orchestration was created, the drum had a wood frame, not metal as we have today. You might try it out with both types to see which you prefer.

What appears as a sustained A♮ in the violas is usually changed to the F harmonic, which comes eight bars later. At **reh. 54**, the oboe can come out a little, but ask the musician to play the high note as softly as possible. Ravel once again ignores the original and creates another unique color for us to enjoy instead of repeating eight bars. The first violins get the oboe figure and should also play quietly, but with an audible grace note. The second oboe has a bizarre set of octave-F sixteenths, and the first flute has a short flutter tongue on its notes.

Ravel makes a significant alteration to the ending. The piano version has two additional bars that I find wonderful because they lend even more sarcasm to the last "peeps." He also eliminates the fermata that he had placed the first time.

What to do?

Well, if you stay with what is in the score, your task is pretty straightforward. If you add the fermata, just give a cutoff as preparation for the final two bars. Alternatively, if you decide you like the original, you can either find a version to insert (I use the one by Lucien Cailliet) or better yet, orchestrate it yourself. Every conductor needs to have the ability to do this when confronted with the need to make adjustments.

Acquire the tools necessary to make the proper choices.

## 6. Samuel Goldenberg und Schmuÿle

Among the darkest of the pictures, this one also can be very difficult to conduct. Although it looks straightforward, it requires numerous nuanced decisions regarding length of notes, dynamics, and rhythms.

The piano version gives us a little more information to convey the overall feeling of the movement. Ravel just keeps the Andante indication, but Mussorgsky includes *Grave—energico*. This reveals that the tempo is very deliberate and heavy, so conducting in eight is mandatory, at least for the opening. Give a strong seven/eight preparation, with a lot of weight. At the start, the eighth notes should be played long. The piano version includes several *sforzando* indications that are not in the orchestral score and are worth considering.

I think that this entire opening section must represent the rich man openly mocking the plight of the poor one, complete with exaggerated and rude gestures. In that spirit, rather than return to the single *forte* of the opening after the diminuendo in the bar before **reh. 57**, I end the decrescendo at a dynamic of *piano* on the second beat, after which I add an aggressive *fortissimo* for the next two notes, the second of which is played quite short.

Again, that flaunting of wealth can return in the second bar of **reh. 57**. I extend the diminuendo into this bar, but at the F♮ half note, I add a crescendo back to the loud *forte* of the general dynamic. A very clear beat is needed for the 3/4 bar, where you may wish to hold back the tempo to hear the grace notes clearly.

Both Mussorgsky and Ravel are consistent regarding the length of the last note before **reh. 58**, but I have always wondered why this powerful D♭ is not sustained through the whole measure. Certainly, it would fade a bit on the piano, but the orchestra can hold it all the way through to the end of the bar, and that is exactly the choice many conductors and I make.

The passage depicting the complaining and begging soul requires a trumpeter of great dexterity. As you see, Ravel makes no concession as to any change of instrument, but this is typically performed on a piccolo trumpet, either in D or F. Ravel changes the spelling of the notes for the benefit of the orchestral musician reading the individual part. All the double-flats in the piano version make sense for that instrument, since the pianist can see how this line relates to the rest of the music harmonically. This section is conducted in four.

Ravel neglects to indicate where the soloist should breathe in this lengthy passage. To solve that dilemma, trumpeters will usually have the assistant play the three beats of repeated C♯ that occur every other bar. Unfortunately, the C trumpet has a very different sound than its little brother, and to compensate, the second musician will often underplay the volume. Try to get as much sound as possible with a tone quality that matches the other instrument. On occasion, you will find a soloist who can play the whole line uninterrupted. It is very impressive when it works.

Underneath the trumpet line are sustained chords, which are presented in different configurations of instruments as the passage moves along. Pay particular attention to the long notes in the various clarinets, as they represent pedal points to emphasize the harmonies.

The measure before **reh. 60** contains another rather inexplicable discrepancy between the piano version and the orchestration. Ravel replaces Mussorgsky's two-beat crescendo with a diminuendo for the horns and trumpet, which just does not make any sense to me. I suggest that the louder solution is best here and in the next bar, as well.

A significant change appears in the trumpet part in the second bar of **reh. 60**. Mussorgsky clearly intends for the fourth beat to begin on a G♭ in his original, but Ravel, for whatever reason, alters this to a G♮. In an earlier edition by Boosey & Hawkes that showed the piano solo below Ravel's orchestration, the piano part was also changed from the original. Perhaps Ravel was working from a flawed edition, a theory that might be born out when we come to the next picture. In any event, I think the right thing to do here is to change the trumpet part to match the piano version.

In that same measure, I prefer to have the low strings make what can only be described as a very "Russian" glissando from the half-note D♭ to the E♮ on the last eighth of the bar, continuing in that manner for the next couple of phrases as well. In the viola line, we can also add a B♭ upbeat to **reh. 61** and every time we see this pickup note. Yes, I know that it is out of the line of the lower instruments, but having the violas attack the start of the next measure makes this upbeat sound weak.

Make as much crescendo as possible before **reh. 62**, subdividing at the start of this bar. Some conductors have added a whip to the pizzicato. A very long silence ensues. Stay in eight, but make sure to communicate to the orchestra that your next gesture will indicate the seventh beat in the measure you have just been leading. This is important, as those musicians who do not play the upbeat might come in early, not realizing that others play before them.

Exaggerated crescendos and diminuendos follow the piano version, but Ravel omits the instruction *poco ritard con dolore*. I usually play this Coda just a bit slower than what has come before and perform the *sforzando* note quite loudly. Another brief pause can occur before commencing the next bar.

The final measures illuminate two more important differences between the versions. Once more, Ravel does not sustain all the instruments through the first part of the penultimate bar. This makes no sense to me at all, so I hold them after giving two strong beats in a somewhat quicker tempo, still in eight. Mussorgsky tells us that we should be *a tempo* here, justifying my decision to increase the pace.

In Mussorgsky's piano version, the third note of the triplet is a B♭, which is then repeated as the final pitch, but Ravel and his publisher change this to a C. I can understand the musical logic, but it is a far cry from what the composer intended. I recommend changing it and sustaining the final note.

## Promenade V

What? You do not see it in the score? Of all the changes we have discussed between the piano version and Ravel's orchestration, this is the one that musicians and audience members most often bring up. The omission of this promenade has caused some to surmise that Ravel may have been working from a faulty printing. In this fifth promenade, Mussorgsky makes his final full statement of the opening music. It balances well because the remaining movements lead into each other without pause.

So, what if we want to present the full scope of the composer's vision along with Ravel's orchestration? We can get creative. The majority of this last walk duplicates the opening movement, so keeping the instrumentation and orchestration the same works just fine. The beginning features the tune in octaves, like the third promenade, so if you adjusted that one, you could do the same here.

This promenade includes some alterations to the rhythmic scheme, but most of those have appeared elsewhere and can be duplicated. The big change is in the last two bars, where the music is extended by half notes rather than quarters. The final note is a solo B♭, and the obvious solution is to have everyone cut off except the solo trumpet, who holds the note. You can either have the player start *forte* and make a diminuendo, as would automatically occur with the piano, or keep the loud sonority and continue without pause into the next portrait.

Alternatively, you can stick with Ravel's decision to omit the movement.

## 7. Limoges—Le Marché
## (The Marketplace in Limoges—Big News)

I don't really get that last part either, but it must have something to do with the folks gossiping as they shop.

In the Ravel as printed, we see a fermata in the final bar of "Samuel Goldenberg und Schmuÿle" that takes place during a silence. Horn players have told me this helps them get settled for the next movement. However, if we orchestrate that last bar of Mussorgsky's promenade such that the horns do not play the final note, then it is certainly possible, and I would argue preferable, to proceed *attacca*. Whichever way you choose to start this, do give three and four as the preparatory beats, showing the horns where to place the sixteenth notes.

The tempo and expressive marking are the same for both versions: *Allegretto vivo, sempre scherzando*. The movement cannot be excessively fast, lest the notes be blurred, and clarity is very important. I think it makes sense to ask the strings to play lightly and off the string, even though Ravel does not put in the dots that are in the piano version. Mussorgsky does not indicate a diminuendo for the piano during the first bar of **reh. 64**, but most conductors will follow Ravel's dynamics to make sure that the softer second measure is heard clearly.

Give a very direct cue to the first violins when they reenter at **reh. 65**. The celesta part at **reh. 66** is important to bring out, requiring the kind of sound that Ravel might have reserved for the glockenspiel. Any doublings of the harp are purely up to you, depending on the acoustic in which the performance takes place.

From **reh. 67** onward, Mussorgsky is rather sparse in his dynamics, but Ravel gives us plenty of alternatives that work very well. Pay close attention to how he has inserted them. He provides a marvelous bit of orchestration during the three bars before **reh. 69**. A crescendo leads us to a *fortissimo*, also noted in the piano edition. But Ravel inserts what Mussorgsky could not—a trill for the piccolo and glockenspiel as well as rolls in the triangle, snare drum, and cymbal.

This movement presents technical difficulties, not so much for the conductor but rather for the orchestra. For example, we must cheat a little to accomplish the downbeat of **reh. 69**. The upper strings cannot do a true glissando in the previous measure and then attack the next bar clearly because they do not have time to reset the bow properly. Nevertheless, we have a trick that works quite well. The seconds and violas can play all the sixteenths as one long glissando while the firsts play the notes individually without a slide, as Ravel has already allowed in the trumpets. The firsts are then in a good position to start the opening figure clearly, and the seconds and violas should be fine because they have repeated notes in a lower register at this point.

The music is the same as the opening until four bars before **reh. 71**. Here, Ravel does utilize the glockenspiel instead of the celesta, so we can hear it quite well. Make as much crescendo as possible before the *Meno mosso*. The tempo depends on the ability of the horns to play the thirty-second notes. I suppose if they cannot accomplish this, sixteenths could work, but the thirty-second notes impart an important color, and you should try to find just the right speed to accommodate them.

Ravel introduces a rather effective accent just after the third beat, albeit only in a few instruments, worth bringing out. Both versions have a *poco accelerando* in the last bar, but you do not need to exaggerate it. Consider introducing a crescendo, which might occur naturally as the line is moving upward here. The transition to the next movement is accomplished better in the orchestra version, as no one playing at the end of this movement begins the following section.

## 8. Catacombae: Sepulcrum Romanum (Catacombs)

This movement presents us with a true dilemma, as it must have for Ravel. Here is the conundrum: In a work that relies on sustained notes, how much time, if any, are we supposed to allow for the decay of sound?

The opening bars contain fermatas in both versions. Obviously, the sound will diminish on the piano, no matter how many tricks we employ other than shortening the lengths of the bars themselves. Mussorgsky did not put in diminuendos, and a couple of times he seeks the impossible by calling for a crescendo on a sustained note.

Let's deal primarily with Ravel's instructions to see how we might best try to conduct them. He does not indicate a diminuendo on the first note, but he wants the musicians who play it to observe a *subito piano* in the second bar. At this point, the horns and contrabassoon enter. I advise sustaining the lower brass instruments at the *piano* dynamic for almost a quarter note to make those who enter during this second bar sound like an echo of what occurred at the outset.

Ravel does not include a crescendo in the second bar but calls for one in the third, although he does not provide an ending dynamic for the horns, at least in some editions. His manuscript is quite different and worth perusing on IMSLP.[3] We can assume that the crescendo peaks at the *fortissimo* level of the new entrants. How long you take between the fermatas really depends on the time that the musicians can sustain the notes.

The same rules apply going forward, with the instrumentalists who observe the *subito piano* markings holding on until the other musicians have entered. My assumption is that Ravel was trying his best to be faithful to the piano version for the next few bars by observing the diminuendos that Mussorgsky wrote, and they work well here.

To make it easier for the trombones and tuba to sustain the next few bars, Ravel seems to indicate that they need to take a breath after the fermata four bars before **reh. 73**. Observe that the first two horns are stopped the bar before **reh. 73**, but Ravel wants the third muted and the fourth open—odd, but it works.

The bars of sustained fermatas at **reh. 73** each need a slight lift, and the eighth-note rest in the final measure allows the brass to regroup for the *subito piano* after the very full sound of the preceding bars. The breaths between the notes also underscore the solemn mood of the tomb and impart a degree of respect for the dead.

The only instruments that change notes after this are the third and second horn, respectively, along with the clarinets. A solo trumpet intones a melody in a color unrelated to anything else, but it is certainly the right choice of timbre for this passage. The crescendo goes to a *dolce forte*.

The upbeat to **reh. 74** should be quite tenuto. The original has fermatas on the dotted half notes, but Ravel's choice to eliminate those is probably correct. Interestingly, Mussorgsky specifies the second one as a *subito piano*, whereas Ravel starts it *fortissimo* and places a diminuendo over the remainder of the bar.

A long diminuendo follows, and it can be helpful to put in the dynamic *mezzo forte* at the second bar and *pianissimo* by the fourth bar. The fourth horn has an important moving line before a jolting *fortissimo* and extended diminuendo bring the movement to a close. The indication for the double basses is equivalent to *sul tasto*.

Here is a Slatkinism, meaning that as far as I know, I am the only one who does it, but there still might be other alternatives out there. Since I think of the movements starting with that omitted promenade as being performed without pause, I have the first violins begin the tremolo that starts the next movement during the fermata while the musicians are holding the last note of "Catacombs." This is done in a way that is virtually inaudible until the cutoff. Hopefully, it creates an effect a bit eerier than the audience might normally hear.

## 9. Cum mortuis in lingua mortua (With the Dead in a Dead Language)

The cutoff of the previous movement, as laid out by Ravel, would indeed give us a true silence before commencing the next piece. My thought is that the release becomes the downbeat of the first bar. However, I let the tam-tam ring through so that the combination of high and low sounds resonate together.

Six small beats start the movement, and it can help to breathe on the first beat of the second bar, just to show the oboes where to come in. In the fourth bar, the first violins do not reattack the second beat; I just have them release the tremolo immediately after the other upper strings enter. The nature of the orchestration may automatically make the lower voices a bit stronger than you might like. If that is the case, simply ask them to play *pianissimo*.

Musicians can get confused at **reh. 76** because most of them cannot see in the parts where the fermata takes place; they only see the marking over the whole bar. Give the first three beats clearly and then indicate the fourth with your right hand to the left-center of your body. You want to show that the next gesture will really represent the fourth beat, when a few instruments release what they have been playing, and inform the others that you will reiterate that fourth beat as a preparation for those entering on five. But keep your left hand available to prevent the first violins from moving one beat too soon. Try to do this once without saying anything, but it is tricky, so you may need to clarify verbally.

A small musical point, and one that you might not agree with, follows: Since I have done this phrasing earlier in the work, I insert a little separation in the woodwinds after the fermata in between the slurs, except I do connect the last two in the middle of the third bar. The same applies to the lower instruments three measures before **reh. 77**.

At this point, Ravel adds some lovely touches, starting at **reh. 77** with the double basses' pizzicato and in the next bar, the harp's fifths. I am always surprised that he did not continue the upward line after putting it in the cellos. Perhaps he believed that the harp could clearly be heard for the last three notes, but this is not the case all the time. You can double this if needed, but make sure that all the other instruments are *pianissimo* rather than the printed single *piano*.

Find a nice balance between the clarinet and horn at **reh. 78**. There is no dynamic indication for the lower division of cellos and basses in the second bar, but I think this distinctive Russian sound should come forward a bit. The following two bars are the same, but now the muted horn is with the muted solo trumpet.

Doubling the harps is almost mandatory two bars before the end unless you increase the dynamic in the solo instrument. The final bar shows two flutes playing harmonics. As with some brass instruments, this is done by altering the embouchure and adjusting the air flow to produce a different color. It can be difficult to get in tune.

This is, of course, quite different than what the strings have in the same measure, which contains not only "natural" harmonics but "artificial" ones as well. These are very important for the conductor to know about, especially in French music. Often the result is nothing like what appears on the page. Learn them well.

Some instruments in this last bar conclude after the first beat and others cut off after the second or third beat, but the harmonics last right through the end, including the fermata. I can almost guarantee that if an orchestra has not played this work before, most musicians will stop when they hear the flutes cut off. See if you can coordinate it correctly the first time around by looking clearly at those who continue with harmonics while giving the ending indications for the other instruments. Good luck.

## 10. La Cabane sur des pattes de poule (The Hut on Fowl's Legs; Baba Yaga's Hut)

As almost a bookend to "Gnomus," this depiction of the witch is harrowing and therefore must come as a disruption to the end of the last piece. It is certainly possible to delay the shock with a silence, but I find that a two-beat preparation following the F♯ cutoff works well. Although this movement can be conducted in one, two seems more effective, at least at the beginning. I am not quite sure why Ravel chooses to have the timpani only play the first note of the piece and not continue with a G on the second beat. Many of us add this here and in the measures that follow.

Although not indicated by Ravel, a slight crescendo can be made during the four notes preceding **reh. 81**, followed by a subito *mezzo forte* and then an eight-bar crescendo. It certainly works, especially if you make the pizzicatos strong during the crescendo.

Conductors often make an alteration at **reh. 83**, adding a slur between the two notes in the brass. I have done it and found it effective, but these days, I tend to follow what both composers wrote. At **reh. 84**, the balance between the half notes in the horns and those in the trombone should, in theory, sound equal. But even outnumbered four to one, the solo instrument's bell is facing toward the audience, while the horns' bells are pointing in the opposite direction; getting them just right is important here. You can add a crescendo when they meet up two bars before **reh. 86.**

Everything works very well from this point until we get to what I consider to be a complete miscalculation on the part of Ravel, one that I do not understand to this day. Why does he write a diminuendo in the winds the bar before **reh. 88**? The only possible justification is that he thought the strings' glissando would not carry through, but at the expense of diminishing the almost octave leap, it seems like an unnecessary touch. I have never heard it done but would be interested to learn if it could work or not. I make a crescendo in the bar before **reh. 88** for all instruments.

At this point, it is certainly easy enough, and perhaps desirable, to go into one. The ten-bar phrase between **reh. 88** and **reh. 89** is followed by more pounding Gs, as we had at the start of this picture. Once again, Ravel makes an unnecessary alteration. The piano edition has four quarters before the next section commences, but in the orchestral version, with different colors due to mutes, there are eight. You might choose to remove two of the bars. You can decide whether to eliminate the muted or open notes. Personally, I like the muted notes, as they set up the new color ahead.

The flutes, with their alternating sextuplet figure, determine the speed of this section. Most conductors make this part a bit more mournful with a slower tempo. No matter how you choose to do it, it is crucial that the flutes stay in the same tempo as they begin. In addition, you must balance the two musicians to sound like one voice, with continuous figurations speaking at the same volume.

The bassoon and double basses are marked *non legato*, but here it really means that their quarter notes are short. The half notes, on the other hand, remain at full length. Clarinets take over for the flutes at **reh. 91**, with the same balances in play. Do not let this section slow down; when the flutes reenter, the tempo must be the same as at **reh. 90**.

You have some interesting choices at this point. Several conductors, including me, add the upper-octave G to the xylophone part to match the line of the pizzicato strings, flutes, and celeste. One of the alternate orchestrations, that by Gorchakov, includes a wonderful effect.[4] He asks the lower strings to play their pizzicatos *sul pont*, or to pluck the strings almost right on top of the bridge. The result is quite chilling, and I have used it from the time I first learned of it. The basses don't like doing it because they have to bend over a bit more, but it really is worth considering. I continue this effect all the way to **reh. 93**.

One of the most difficult spots for balance occurs here. I can understand what Ravel was attempting to accomplish with the two-bar contrabassoon passage, considering that he wrote extended solos for this instrument in his Piano Concerto for the Left Hand and opera *L'heure espagnole*. However, the contrabassoon's *forte* cannot match the tuba that precedes it, and often I have to adjust the other instruments down to accommodate. Lately I have wondered what would happen if the tuba and contrabassoon parts were reversed here, and perhaps on my next go-round with the work, I will give it a try.

The sixteenth-note pickup in the upper instruments three bars before **reh. 94** requires an ultra-clear beat and attention from the musicians to achieve a sense of ensemble. Hold the quarter note for its full length, perhaps louder than single *forte*. The tam-tam stroke can certainly be louder than *pianissimo*.

We now repeat the first part of the piece, with a few variations. The piano version implies that Mussorgsky wanted a full sonority, so many conductors change Ravel's pizzicato indications to arco here. The phrasing is a bit different for the first few bars but becomes more or less the same four measures before **reh. 95**, including that strange diminuendo, which is now also included in the strings one bar before **reh. 101**.

As before, conduct in one at **reh. 101**, where that ten-bar phrase is still in place. Then, the Coda commences. Be prudent regarding the suspended cymbal dynamic when only the lower instruments are playing; dropping the dynamic down a little is certainly justified here.

In the piano version, *poco ritard* is printed over the final three bars. While this seems to work well for the single instrument, I find it to be a difficult effect to pull off, perhaps because of the dramatic change in color for the orchestra. I do, however, recommend making a crescendo over the last six bars or so.

## 11. La grande porte de Kiev (The Great Gate of Kiev)

I wonder if we will be changing the spelling of the Ukrainian capital to Kyiv for future performances.

Many conductors charge into this movement *fortissimo*, and their enthusiasm is understandable. The full sonority of the brass, with the chords perfectly balanced, can create a powerful effect. But the single *forte* marking in both the piano and orchestral versions is so much more satisfying to me because it acknowledges that we have not yet reached the sonic height and corresponding payoff that are, quite naturally, the highlight of the entire set of pictures.

Think of the tempo of the opening in terms of how you intend to conclude, as there are statements as you go along that must be slower than the previous ones. Once more, Ravel does not include metronome marks but provides the perfect wording of "*Allegro alla breve. Maestoso. Con grandezza.*" It is that first instruction that conductors often ignore, causing tempos to grind to a halting pace as the piece progresses.

Remember to give some thought to where everyone should breathe, as you did for the trumpet line in the first promenade. Try not to shorten too many of the last notes of any given group to maintain the feeling of an extremely long phrase. The single *forte* remains in place at **reh. 104**, but you might need to adjust the volume of the brass to bring out the woodwinds before the *subito* dynamic changes a few bars later. Some conductors lead into this with a diminuendo. Do pay attention to the instruments that are marked *piano* while the others are at a stronger dynamic at this point.

Ravel creates the equivalent of the indicated *fortissimo* through his dense orchestration, so you do not have to force the volume at **reh. 105**. Grace notes should be on the beat, and I ask the strings to take two bows per bar, which is certainly natural for the violins here.

Consider adding a slight lift before the chorale at **reh. 106** to ensure that the fullness of the orchestration does not impinge on the *subito piano* in the woodwinds. *Senza espressione* most likely means that no gradations of dynamics are to take place. This works better in the orchestra than on the piano, and by asking the musicians to play without vibrato, the effect can be even greater. The little hairpin in the sixth bar allows for some color, but aside from that, I tend to keep the whole passage without any nuance.

It is also possible to play this section a bit more slowly and solemnly, but we must get back to the tempo somewhere. That place is one bar before **reh. 107**. I have the clarinets and bassoons put very discreet accents on the two notes and go back to the opening tempo here.

The return of the opening material at **reh. 107** is another place where it is difficult to understand why Ravel makes certain decisions. In the piano version, the full chordal effect of the tune is part of the texture, and yet in Ravel's orchestration, only the horns provide the harmonies. Certainly, the trombones could have also filled them out. Consequently, I am left with the feeling that something is missing.

Ravel fleshes out the orchestral texture at **reh. 108**, and with the brass at single *forte*, everything feels right at this point. The big buildup to **reh. 109** ends with a comma, and that is certainly necessary for Ravel to accomplish what he does. Mussorgsky stays at *fortissimo* for this reiteration of the chorale, but the Frenchman returns to *piano* to match the first occurrence. This is a major change from the original intention, but I can see why he did it. Nonetheless, even without changing the orchestration, you can play this *fortissimo*, potentially shocking the audience members who know the work well.

If you choose to do so, please be advised that some of the woodwinds will be reluctant to give their all at first, as they are simply not used to it. Once you get to the diminuendo before **reh. 110**, return to the indicated dynamics. At this point, Ravel is starting to pull out all the stops and deviating quite often from the piano version, mostly by adding elements, including cymbals and a tam-tam, as well as accents and more back-and-forth between the lower instruments.

Although this section is marked to begin at *mezzo forte*, it is probably better to start around *piano* to get a more subtle crescendo going. Depending on whether you prefer a wispier sound or more tonal clarity, the slurs in the strings at the 6/4 can be played as written or with one bow per bar. Four measures before **reh. 112**, Ravel instructs most instruments to enter or decrease to *piano*, and therefore we can easily justify playing the previous passage at that dynamic level as well.

A crescendo leads us to the fantastic reintroduction of the promenade tune. I take the liberty of having the glockenspiel play in octaves. From my perspective, the addition of the lower voice enhances the tune's "Russian" quality. To help the harps project their glissando three bars before **reh. 113**, you can ask one of the musicians to play as written and the other to enter halfway through the bar, starting with the low B♭. It is also possible for both musicians to retake the glissando at some point. However, I have found that one long glissando is inadequate to cut through the texture of the orchestra.

At **reh. 114**, Ravel goes to extraordinary lengths to stretch out Mussorgsky's descending E♭ scale, reminding me of the transition in Tchaikovsky's "1812 Overture." In my opinion, this idea requires cosmetic surgery. If you do not want to go through the trouble of rewriting the whole passage, you might consider having the brass make a *forte-piano*, just so the other instruments with scales can be heard.

Numerous possibilities present themselves regarding the sixteenth notes. You can divide the slurred bowings into groups of four or eight notes. Alternatively, you can ask half of the section to play the slurs and the other half to use separate bows. It is an awkward place at best. When it ends, you can either observe the hairpin as printed or simply let the brass make the crescendo without a diminuendo, which can be quite dramatic.

Maintain as long a silence as you can possibly muster to keep everyone guessing what comes next. Take a very big breath and feel the upcoming triplet rhythm. The tempo should be on the slow side, but keep in mind that you will need to hold back even more later. This part works very well exactly as Ravel orchestrates it, but remember that even though it is marked *fortissimo*, we still have more forceful spots ahead.

Depending on what tempo you choose, it might be necessary to move forward at **reh. 118** but not by too much. Bring out the various moving notes in the brass as we approach the last set of major differences between the two versions.

At the third bar of **reh. 120**, every fiber of my being screams that even though there is a rallentando over the whole passage, the two notes need to be stretched out, almost to the point that each of them is equal to one full bar. This is a personal decision based purely on instinct, but I feel that the printed rhythm of the piano version belies a more logical setup for the conclusion. At the same time, the introduction of a three-bar phrase feels uncomfortable. Perhaps that is what Mussorgsky had in mind.

If you follow the written letter of the score, stay in one until the bar before **reh. 121**. It is worth noting that Ravel alters the time signature for this last passage, opting for 2/2 instead of the previous 6/4, when the brass were playing dotted half notes. If you wish to extend this phrase, my suggestion is to start conducting in three at **reh. 120**, switch to two for the third bar, then switch back to three for the next two measures, and then once again to two for the bar before **reh. 121**.

Some pianists add a tremolo to fill what can feel like a gaping hole before the final statement of the piece. The brass must take a breath, of course, but that leaves us with nothing prior to the downbeat other than silence, perhaps brief. I suggest a simple solution that feels natural but is not what Ravel wrote at all. Ask the timpanist to roll on a B$\flat$ starting in the middle of the bar before **reh. 121** and connect it to the downbeat of the next measure. A crescendo puts the icing on the cake.

Surprisingly, Ravel omits the composer's instruction of *Grave, sempre allargando* for the last twenty-one bars. Wait a minute! Look at the piano version, and you will see that only thirteen bars remain. Mussorgsky writes these in 4/4 and presents quite a different conclusion than the showy ending for the orchestra. I feel that Ravel's conclusive crescendo offers much more than Mussorgsky's single tremolo in the left hand.

I stay in two for this Coda and bring out a few nuances, such as the bell and tam-tam. The horns contribute an interesting dissonance if they really play a *molto fortissimo* on the E$\flat$ in the bar before **reh. 122**. I can recommend a truly creative way to make the crescendo during the last five bars. Almost every conductor will begin at a lesser dynamic here, to accomplish just that.

I grade the increase by section, with the strings starting to get louder in the first bar, then the woodwinds in the next, followed by the brass, and finally, the percussion. Meanwhile, the tam-tam stays loud throughout. Hang on to the note just before the last bar and give a very sharp downbeat for a strongly accented and short last note.

I suspect that of all the pieces in this series, *Pictures at an Exhibition* has the most interpretive leeway, simply because we are dealing with an orchestration rather than an original composition. How you choose to approach the work is a purely personal matter, but it helps to seek and obtain as much information as possible. Do not just settle on the Ravel because it is the one everybody is used to hearing. You can glean a lot of insight through intense research, and who knows? Perhaps you might create your own version someday.

## Conductor's Etiquette

The Ravel orchestration lends itself to the following bows, usually in this order: solo trumpet (allow plenty of time for that musician to acknowledge the applause), then the tuba, followed by the saxophone. If you wish to recognize the sections, start with percussion, followed by brass, then woodwinds, and finally strings, including harp.

*** 

"Art is not an end in itself, but a means of addressing humanity."

—Modest Mussorgsky

## Notes

1. Modest Mussorgsky, *Pictures at an Exhibition*, in *Complete Collected Works, Volume VIII, Series 2*, ed. Paul Lamm (Moscow: Muzgiz, 1931; reprinted New York: E. F. Kalmus, n.d.), https://s9.imslp.org/files/imglnks/usimg/8/83/IMSLP107727-PMLP03722-Mussorgsky_Werke_Kalmus_Band_VIII_Folge_2_Tableaux_d_une_Exposition_filter.pdf.

2. Modest Moussorgsky, *Pictures at an Exhibition*, orch. Maurice Ravel (London: Boosey & Hawkes Music Publishers Ltd., 1922).

3. Modest Mussorgsky, *Pictures at an Exhibition*, orch. Maurice Ravel (Paris: Editions Russes de Musique, 1929), https://imslp.hk/files/imglnks/euimg/1/1a/IMSLP741261-PMLP3722-115525.pdf.

4. Modest Mussorgsky, *Pictures at an Exhibition*, orch. Sergei Gorchakov (Berlin: Sikorski, 1954).

# Hector Berlioz: *Symphonie fantastique*

"It is not enough that the artist should be well prepared for the public. The public must be well prepared for what it is going to hear."

—Hector Berlioz

Émile Signol, Public domain, via Wikimedia Commons

He was supposed to be a doctor. His instrument was the guitar. He rebelled against the French musical conventions of the time. Hector Berlioz became one of the most creative forces in the artistic world.

Many of you will remember the first time you heard the *Symphonie fantastique*. More than likely, the first three movements seemed a bit boring, but you perked up with the "March to the Scaffold" and "Dream of a Witches' Sabbath," upon hearing all those drums, two tubas, offstage bells, and strings using the wooden part of the bow rather than the hair.

Now you are confronting the piece on a different level. So much goes into executing this totally unique work that we could spend this entire book analyzing it. I always remind myself that *Symphonie fantastique* was written in 1830, only three years after the death of Beethoven. We know how much Berlioz admired the German genius, yet there are very few traces of his influence in this imaginative and original composition. As additional timeline points, Brahms began composing his First Symphony twenty-five years after *Symphonie fantastique*, and the very advanced structures of the Liszt Piano Sonata also came almost a quarter century later. Liszt attended the premiere of *Symphonie fantastique* and immediately changed his compositional style.

How radical was *Symphonie fantastique* for its time? Other notable pieces written in 1830 include the First Piano Concerto of Chopin, Mendelssohn's "Reformation" Symphony, and the "Abegg" Variations by Schumann. Clearly, Berlioz was leaps and bounds ahead of the prevailing musical languages of his era.

Berlioz made two versions of *Symphonie fantastique*, but his changes were mostly about the program and story behind the work. Its autobiographical nature was unique and, in some ways, the piece is like a connected set of symphonic poems, a form devised by Carl Loewe in 1828 and perfected by Liszt. Berlioz, however, had already made his mark, elevating programmatic music with this and subsequent works.

The Bärenreiter New Berlioz Edition contains a wealth of material, from early sketches and facsimiles to critical commentary.[1] The score is similar to the one offered by Breitkopf & Härtel.[2] I will reference the Bärenreiter edition, which is available on IMSLP (albeit without supplemental material) and includes both rehearsal figures and measure numbers.[3]

As Norman del Mar points out in his book *Conducting Berlioz*, this is one of the most complicated works in terms of rehearsal planning.[4] Each movement is scored for different forces—instruments are added and subtracted as if each movement were a separate work. Depending on how many rehearsals you have, it is probably a good idea to know when you want to work on any given movement. Still, unless you are on a very limited schedule, try to play through the whole work the first time you are together. I will deal with the various rehearsal orders as we go along.

In the meantime, here is the complete instrumentation list: two flutes (one doubling piccolo), two oboes (one doubling English horn), two clarinets (one doubling E♭ clarinet), four bassoons, four horns, two cornets, two trumpets, three trombones, two ophicleides (modern performances use tubas), four timpani (played by four players), cymbals, snare drum, bass drum, bells in C and G (or several pianos), two harps (at least), fifteen first violins, fifteen second violins, ten violas, eleven cellos, and nine double basses.

In addition, Berlioz provides supplemental information through specific annotations in the score. For example, the number of string players is the minimum, as he says, "at least."[5] In the second movement, he includes an obligato trumpet part, added for one performance with the great virtuoso Jean-Baptiste Arban. The composer also includes this note in the score: "If it is not possible to find two bells low enough for one of the three Cs and one of the three Gs written, it would be better to use several pianos downstage, playing the bell part in double octaves, as written."[6] That would be something to see and hear.

Performance time varies, depending on whether repeats are taken, but the usual length is somewhere between forty-five and fifty minutes.

## First Movement (Rêveries—Passions)

Among the many details to note are the various keys in which the wind instruments are playing: clarinets in B♭, horns in E♭ and C, trumpets in C, and cornets in G. The conductor's transposition skills are put to the test right away. However, the four trumpets will not enter until two minutes or so before the end of the movement.

This is one of the longest introductions in the symphonic repertoire, and the musical material has seemingly little to do with the main portion of the movement or anything else in the piece. Berlioz is a master of sound and color, utilizing his prodigious gifts to create exactly what the movement title says: dreams. Still, some of them are nightmares, and the composer explores this contrast in the opening section.

The indication Largo and metronome marking ♩ = 56 seem about right. It is vitally important for the conductor to feel the triplet figure when giving the upbeat. Get this fully integrated into your breath, giving beats three and four as the preparation. The notes are equally separated in all instruments.

At the end of the first bar, the conductor already encounters difficulty. Having started *pianissimo*, you must create a *subito pianississimo* on the downbeat of the second measure, even as new instruments enter. These entries provide a clue about how to achieve the desired effect. You can ask the upper woodwinds to make a slight crescendo, giving them enough room to drop down in volume for the second bar. Some conductors take a very slight break before the downbeat, but be aware of the horn entrance at that point.

Ask the muted violins to play with a hint of vibrato when they enter in the third bar. Although the basic beat for the majority of this introduction is four, subdividing the first beat is not a bad idea, just to coordinate the single sixteenth note. That sixteenth is preceded by a short breath for the sake of articulative clarity. The fourth bar can present a slight technical challenge. The firsts are the only section to change notes on the third beat. If we play it too short, the audience does not hear the subtle harmonic change.

Starting the phrase after the fermata can also be tricky, and this is where solid, independent use of both arms comes into play. Sustain all the instruments with a single gesture at the beginning of the measure with the right hand. Do not move it at all. Use your left hand to show the firsts when to change to the D. It is not necessary to show the second beat. Then, indicate the cutoff to everyone but hold on to that sixteenth just a bit. The same motions you use for the first half of the fourth bar also apply to the sixth. Your third beat should be a little more to the left than usual to allow you to repeat that gesture after the fermata. The musicians have a tendency to react late and slow down, so be aware of this and listen carefully to what they do.

The diminuendo signs in the fifth bar, and at several points in the symphony, are more like sighs rather than changes in volume because no dynamic is indicated. When you start the seventh measure, subdivide the first beat and focus on the violas and cellos to synchronize the pizzicato—at *piano*, not *pianissimo*.

At **reh. A**, or **m. 11**, the first violins warm up their sound, but the other strings stay quite soft. I prefer to have the two eighth notes in the lower strings both played down bow. The next bar sees the first entry of the double basses, which is *pianissimo* but must be audible and in tempo. Pay attention to when all the other string instruments cut off.

One of the defining characteristics of Berlioz as a composer is his use of exaggeration, especially when it comes to dynamics. He often includes five or six different manifestations of dynamic markings within just a bar or two. For example, after the fermata, the first violins have a one-beat diminuendo, followed by a one-beat crescendo, a two-beat decrescendo, and a continued relaxation in the next measure. Perhaps a little more sound on the first note is called for here, followed by a light swooping for the crescendo. The basses can defy the usual guideline of keeping the *sforzando* within the context of a preexisting dynamic. I think the first couple of notes are most effective if they are intrusive and then fade away.

More exaggeration occurs after the fermata in **m. 14**. Again, I interpret these hairpins as sighs of yearning, followed by a retreat inward, as if expressing embarrassment. The lower strings have a crescendo, and the violas join in with an accented note at *mezzo forte*. Since **m. 17** is *forte*, we can assume that the crescendo continues right through the bar.

Note that **reh. B** is not a *forte-piano*. You must go into eight here, being very clear and precise with the first four beats. Turn your attention away from the G in the lower strings and make sure that the first violins fully understand the tempo you choose through your distinct beats. The *plus vite* instruction is not an actual speed, so you can decide how fast this passage goes, depending on the capabilities of your orchestra. Part of that decision rests on how you interpret the *animez* and *un peu plus vite* that follow. In any event, **m. 17** cannot start so quickly that you have nowhere to go.

Berlioz gives us advice about how to rehearse this passage. If your orchestra is unfamiliar with the piece, rehearsing the first violins separately a couple of times is indeed a good idea but may not be necessary with experienced orchestras if you are clear with your beats.

Violin sections of any experience level will find the indication *a punta d'arco*—at the tip of the bow—problematic. Common sense suggests spiccato bowing for the staccato notes at **reh. B**, but adhering to Berlioz's instruction about bow placement makes that stroke impossible. Although off-the-string playing was still unusual during Berlioz's time, I believe these notes should indeed be spiccato; however, make sure that the first violins do not play too far off the string. Controlling the tempo is crucial here.

At some point, probably when the first horn makes its entry, you can go into four. This keeps the established tempo moving as more instruments join in and you progress from *animez* to *un peu plus vite*. I ask the strings to continue to play off the string at the *mezzo forte* marking.

Starting in the bar before **reh. C**, the question of how long the ritard should last comes into play. Berlioz writes that this single measure slows down slightly, but right after that, he asks us to continue to slow down until we reach **reh. D**. I have often heard conductors take a somewhat more drastic ritard before **reh. C** and then stay in a slower tempo, making yet another drawn-out ritenuto in the last bar. However, I believe the composer is telling us that when we commence the ritard one bar before **reh. C**, he wants us to think of the next five bars as a continual slowing down, though not by too much, as we are returning to the basic tempo of the introduction. This ensures greater continuity within the lengthy opening section and helps us keep a flowing tempo. I advise conducting the bar before **reh. D** in twelve, mostly to secure the pizzicatos.

We now come to one of the most notorious passages for balance in the entire symphony. While the violins have the tune, each of the melodic strands has its own degree of importance. For example, although not a melody per se, the lower strings have a counter line that provides sustained mild dissonance, and the flute and clarinet also have moving notes, marked *dolce*. Those two instruments must be heard distinctly all the way until **reh. E**, but the dense textures surrounding them make this almost impossible. Berlioz is among the first composers to create slightly obscured moments in which notes seem to disappear only to reemerge. You can follow all the dynamic shifts and still hear the sextuplets if you stay within the *piano* dynamic for the strings where indicated. It is also helpful to adjust the horns, as their sustained notes can often cover moving ones.

Berlioz depicts his restless state of mind at **reh. E** through further exaggerations, specifically the ups and downs in the string dynamics. In the fourth bar, this unease is even more pronounced; the *forte* in the lower strings feels as though a large group of people is ganging up on the firsts. The yearning violins in **m. 40** give way to an extraordinary harmonic moment two-and-a-half bars later, where the eighth note interjections by the winds should be played at full value.

Resist any temptation to slightly separate the syncopations in the strings, especially at the bar line of **m. 44**. The clash of harmonies between the woodwinds and strings is shocking and needs to be emphasized with the *subito forte*. Throughout this passage, keep the *molto legato* line going, minimizing the feeling of the beat. You can stretch out the upbeat to **m. 46** to create a more dramatic *sforzando*. At first glance, you might think that the winds' quarter note before **reh. F** should mirror the strings' pizzicato in length; however, holding it for full value is far more effective, providing a contrast between the two groups.

The next section appears to be simple but is, in fact, one of the most difficult to get just right due to contrasting dynamics, starting with the *espressivo* first notes of the second violins. The legato notes in the flutes and clarinets should be played very quietly, whereas the violas' pizzicatos, marked *mezzo forte*, should stand out. In the second bar of **reh. F**, I suggest conducting in eight, but only for the first quarter of the bar, to make sure that the horn and first violin start together as well as to establish the pulse for the ensuing sixteenth notes. Tell the violins not to play too far off the string here and for the next five two-bar sequences, paying careful attention to intonation during the final two of these.

Three bars before **reh. H**, Berlioz again writes at the extremes, with highly exaggerated reverse hairpins followed by two beats of a furious *fortissimo* and a sudden shift to *subito pianissississimo*. We like to believe that the conductor is only leading the musicians, but the audience also sees and experiences this dramatic moment. Think of the loud portion as a fermata; you don't have to show the two beats. Then, with a quick flick of the wrist and expression change in your face, give the *pianississimo*, thinking of these two beats as another fermata.

Berlioz indicates ♩ = 132 for the Allegro tempo at **reh. H**, which seems about right. But in a footnote, he adds that a whole measure of this new tempo is equal to the quarter note of the opening, which is confusing because the metronome markings of the two sections do not have a direct relationship.

I think he means that the eighth note in the bar before **reh. H** becomes the half note of the new tempo. Just before you start this measure, get the tempo of the Allegro in your head and increase your speed accordingly. Keep in mind that the strings have to get from arco to pizzicato somewhat quickly and then back again within the measure. If they play the first note on an up bow, they will be in the best position to do that. The woodwind notes should be played as a counter to the strings' pizzicatos and therefore short.

Depending on the acoustics of the venue, the quarter notes in the first four bars of the Allegro can be obscured, and I have found that sustaining these notes is an effective solution. After a *mezzo forte* pizzicato in **m. 69**, the strings return to an ultra-soft spiccato bowing before we arrive at the exposition proper.

What you do next will be determined by whether you take the repeat. Remember that this piece was written just three years after the death of Beethoven, and the function of the repeat was primarily to familiarize audience with the material to be developed. Now that most listeners have heard the work several times, it may not be necessary to play this section twice, but if you do (I always do), there is the possibility of doing a few things differently the second time around.

First, let us examine what is on the page. The initial statement of the *idée fixe* appears in the first violins and flute. Berlioz marks several crescendos, but what do they really indicate? For example, **mm. 73–74** can either be interpreted as one continuous buildup leading to the *poco sforzando* or as swells that return to the *piano* dynamic each time the indication appears. Recently, I have taken a cue from the storyline, represented here by the title of this section: "Passions." I opt for the smoother increase the first time and then the undulating, almost stop-and-start feeling of multiple crescendos on the repeat. Interestingly, the composer puts dots on the notes in **mm. 78–79** for the lower strings but not for the seconds and violas. It is hard to imagine this being anything other than an omission.

The passion heats up at **reh. J**, where Berlioz's repeated use of the instruction *animez* suggests an exaggerated acceleration. Meanwhile, we also make a crescendo to *forte*. Physically, our inclination is to increase the size of the beat as music get faster, but for flexibility purposes, the opposite should occur. Start with a large beat and, as the tempo increases, make the gestures smaller, keeping your arms closer to the rest of your body. The reverse is true when slowing down.

The *a tempo* should not be too slow because we have another two-bar ritard to contend with a few bars later. At **m. 108**, Berlioz provides us with another opportunity to show off how our orchestra can turn on a dime when it comes to dynamic contrasts. I use a little technical trick for the next two measures, where the *un peu retenu* following the pizzicatos in the bass line can often catch the conductor off guard. Conduct in two, and when you arrive at the fermata, do not let your arms go too high. Show the basses the second pizzicato with a subdivided beat, keeping your arms more or less at the middle of your body, which then allows you to give the downbeat of **m. 110** clearly. Go back into two, subdividing again for the last quarter note. A flurry of notes at **reh. K** brings us to the *fortissimo*.

At **m. 119**, you can either follow what Berlioz writes, *un peu retenu*, or slightly slow down immediately, if you wish. At **reh. M**, he makes dramatic use of *forte-piano* dynamics, which should sound like sudden shocks. Have the upper strings pull their bows to the tip quickly; meanwhile, the lower instruments should play off the string. At **m. 137**, you can surprise the audience by being as soft as possible from the first note.

The slightly dissonant E♭ pitches in the cellos at **m. 146** are unique to their part and therefore nice to hear clearly. Staying with the cellos, I have found that the last few notes of the triplets at **reh. O**, and at corresponding points, are lost to the listeners, so I eliminate the diminuendo.

After observing a series of pungent *sforzandos*, we arrive at **reh. P**, where it can be difficult to hear all the notes in the violas and cellos. To compensate, you can break up the slurs into two strokes, or they can be played off the string, separately, depending on what works best for the acoustics of the hall. If you decide to take the first ending, I suggest increasing the dynamic for the opening of the repeat and slightly overplaying the various markings, particularly the *sforzando* indications, to heighten the feeling of anxiety.

Whatever exaggerations you did during the exposition should be even more pronounced from the second ending onward, almost to the end of the movement. During this passage, ensure that the whole notes tied over the bar lines are played sostenuto, without a letdown in dynamics. Hearing the eighth-note upbeats to each of these is also critical. Be especially cognizant of the bassoons and lower strings starting in **m. 179**, as each crescendo needs to reach *forte* for maximum effect. The violins do not have a *forte-piano* but rather a half-bar diminuendo to *piano* followed by a *subito forte* in each bar. Most conductors play the four bars at **reh. R** short and off the string, despite the absence of staccato markings. I have been doing the opposite over the last fifteen years or so.

At **reh. S**, Berlioz presents us with one of the most dramatic passages in the movement. Very few conductors observe the *mezzo forte* on the first note, but we all try to create a menacing feeling for the chromatic crescendo that follows. Each phrase should begin quite softly, with clipped notes that start in the middle of the bow and move toward the frog as we approach each *fortissimo*. The six bars that commence at **m. 221** can continue the crescendo, culminating in an intense and very loud thwack from the timpani.

At this moment, no one, including the conductor, should move. Only the third horn needs to prepare for **reh. U**. Once you explain to the orchestra that the horn comes in at that point, everyone will know when they enter. Give a slight emphasis to the first note of the two-note groups in the second violins. When the first violins come in, both sections should be at the very tip of the bow. The *idée fixe* returns; however, Berlioz does not specify a dynamic. Since it is marked *dolce*, we can assume it is *piano*, with a long note as the upbeat. The same crescendos we had in the first violins at the opening of the Allegro reappear, and I will leave it up to you to decide how to interpret them.

Meanwhile, one of the most difficult spots for ensemble occurs in the cellos and double basses in **m. 238**, where they come in with syncopations at a dynamic of *mezzo forte*. This is almost always a problem for any orchestra; so far, the only advice I have found helpful is to tell the section to "feel" the two eighths during the rests. This section requires a lot of concentration, so take care not to ignore those lower voices. In addition, all the musicians have a crescendo and slight accelerando starting at **m. 254**, which only complicates matters.

Berlioz includes a delicious dissonance in the first horn just after the entrance at **reh. V** until midway through the third bar, where the concert E♭ of the horn clashes nicely with the D in the other instruments. The diminuendo you see here can be interpreted as an accent, considering the corresponding crescendo indication. But it is also possible to think that each phrase begins successively louder, in which case a little decrescendo is certainly allowable.

A bit of a conundrum pops up between **reh. V** and **reh. W**. When this material is first presented at **reh. J**, the indication is *animez*, and here it is *en serrant un peu*, the meaning of which is somewhat vague. Plus, the ritard that leads into the *a tempo* in the exposition does not appear at this point in the Bärenreiter edition. Nevertheless, most conductors will play the passage in the same manner both times.

Beginning in **m. 275**, the cellos have an interesting chromatic line worth bringing out. The *sforzandos* at **reh. Y** serve as strong accents, exaggerating the syncopation. At **m. 297**, the majority of the strings play in a similar manner as they did at **reh. R**. Whichever way you chose to play it then should apply here as well. At **m. 304**, every *fortissimo* should start with down bows; retakes help with the diminuendo.

Do not overdo the *sforzandos* starting at **reh. A1**; a *dolce* feeling is more elegant here. Since several ritenuto instructions lead into **reh. E1**, we must remain in tempo at **reh. C1**. Although he had it at his disposal, Berlioz opted not to have the basses go down to the low C♯ at **m. 354**, presumably because the continuation of the line would have ended with two unavailable notes.

A sort-of-new tune in the oboe commences at **reh. E1**. Although played *espressivo*, the *idée fixe* in the violas and cellos must always be clear. Sustaining the whole note and tied quarter is imperative here, just as it was after the second ending; otherwise, the tension of this counter line is lost. The first violin line can be played either on or off the string, but off-the-string strokes do not permit as much flexibility if you decide to add a little rubato. Several rises and falls of dynamics help create the impression of Berlioz's passion overflowing. The second violins eventually take over for the violas, allowing the latter to double the winds and later the cellos.

Finally, after about ten minutes or so, the trumpets and cornets get to play, although their first entries are not obvious. You can give them a little look or warning at **reh. I1**, but make sure you know which two of the four are making the first entrance. If you are leading a seasoned orchestra, your brass players will know when to come in, but first-timers never seem to get it right. Berlioz has the wisdom to keep all four of them at single *forte* when everyone else in the orchestra is going full blast. The composer was also one of the first to specify the type of mallet to be used by the timpanist, alternating between three different kinds of sticks. You can learn more about their use in this piece in an excellent article by Andrew P. Simco.[7]

At **reh. L1**, the *animez* can also be construed as an accelerando, and it is wise to have the strings play a bit softer than *mezzo forte* to allow the counter rhythm in the winds to sound equal to the bassoons and double basses. Most conductors slow down right away at **reh. M1** rather than observe the gradual ritard Berlioz indicates. I find it interesting that he keeps the pizzicatos at *fortissimo* before **reh. P1** and then returns to *piano* for the arco.

The oboe has an almost Mahlerian moment when the line goes down a half step from E to E♭. I actually add a slight crescendo into it. Despite the dots on the six notes before **reh. Q1**, the ritard makes it more logical to play these on the string. I go one step further by playing the last note a bit longer than those preceding it, as if it were an upbeat to the next bar and thereby emulating the general line of the *idée fixe*.

To conclude, Berlioz gives us an expressive mark, *Religiosamente*, rather than a tempo. Some conductors favor *non vibrato* for the strings, but I think that a dead sound is not what the composer had in mind. What a stroke of genius to have the piccolo play in the lower register rather than use two flutes in octaves! This provides a very special color for a very special moment.

## Second Movement (Un Bal)

Although Berlioz originally conceived of "Un Bal" as the third movement, he was certainly correct in placing it second. After the tumult of "Passions," some respite is needed, and this fills the bill.

Right away, we notice that the composer specifies the need for at least two harps on each part. This is the only movement in which they play, so he likely wanted to amplify their impact. If you are fortunate to have four harps, then you can have some fun with instrument placement by separating the two parts to achieve the intended antiphonal effect. Yes, it is tricky to coordinate, but I guarantee that this is a great solution. However, most budgets cannot afford this luxury, so we will assume that you are conducting just a pair of harps with the duo placed next to each other.

Written in 3/8 time, this waltz is marked *Allegro non troppo* with a metronome indication of ♩. = 60, which seems just about right. Except for a couple of moments, the movement is conducted in one. The opening string sound is almost a tremolo and needs to be mysterious. The double-bass line works best if the players start on an up bow and switch to a down bow on the *sforzando*. Since the harps both start in a lower register, it probably makes sense for them to begin a bit louder than *pianissimo* to ensure the audibility of their first few notes. Take into consideration, however, that the lack of a dynamic marking in **m. 11** implies an overall volume of *pianissimo* throughout this opening.

The crescendo builds until the harps take the lead at **m. 30**, at which point everyone reaches *fortissimo*. I have found that unless the harpists are experienced, these measures are often not in sync, usually due to a lack of coordination at the downbeat of **m. 32**. If possible, isolate this phrase in rehearsal and have the harpists practice it together a few times.

At **reh. B**, the waltz begins. To establish an elegant mood, I have the second violins and violas play on the string, avoiding any Viennese influence in the rhythm. If you wish, going into three for the rallentando can work, as long as the tempo does not get too slow. The glissando at the *a tempo* should sound graceful and be played closer to the landing note rather than start at the beginning of the measure.

The mood changes a little at **reh. C**, with slightly more activity in the accompaniment. It is now possible and desirable for the sixteenths to be played off the string. Assuming you have one harp at your disposal, an interesting option is to have the second harp double the first for seven bars and then move to the other part. This might be one reason Berlioz wanted at least two on a part, not simply for the spectacle but for the volume. The woodwind scale just before **reh. D** should conclude at single *forte*, with the dynamic level of the horn entry adjusted to match their volume.

Give a very precise downbeat in the second bar of **reh. D** to obtain a slight release before the spiccato sixteenth notes. In **m. 75**, Berlioz indicates a *subito pianissimo* for the strings but not for the woodwinds. He also includes a hairpin for the winds, and many conductors will add this in the strings as well, making their *sforzando* gentle. The interplay between the woodwinds and horns is a matter of balance. Higher notes tend to sound louder and more defined, so take care to make these equal.

At **reh. F**, make sure that the trill in the first violins and cellos stops and the tied-over sixteenth note is not reattacked, a small but nevertheless important detail. There is a nice exchange between all the instruments except the first violins at **reh. G**. You can decide whether the eighth notes should be long or short, but in either case, they must be played the same way by everyone. I suggest you rehearse this once without the firsts. The directive *sans retenir* reminds me that Berlioz was a gifted conductor, one of the first, and anticipates a negative instruction worthy of Mahler's approval. Again, experienced orchestras know what to do here, but those coming to the work for the first time will always slow down.

We have a very fast diminuendo to make at **reh. I**, followed by a surprising chromatic scale in the cellos. I suppose that the notes in the upper strings can be played as written, but they are more often interpreted as a tremolo, in keeping with Berlioz's instruction *presque rien*, meaning almost nothing. With the return of the *idée fixe*, we find a rhythmic figure in the cellos and basses. For the first half of the twentieth century, this was almost always played with thirty-second notes. But conductors eventually came to understand that this should sound like a group of four very-short sixteenths.

While the woodwinds are busy with the tune after **reh. J**, the upper strings are trying to disrupt with fragments of this movement's main theme. Since there is a huge discrepancy between the two editions, you can decide how loud or soft these intrusions should be. It is a magical moment in the piece. In the bar before **reh. L**, the flute has no indication of a dynamic change, but in the corresponding passage three measures later, the first violins have a *subito piano*, so I think it makes sense to do the same earlier.

Establish an agreed-upon length for the sixteenth notes in the equal dialogue between winds and strings that commences in the fourth bar of **reh. L**. Light, off-the-string playing works well here. Note that these instruments have a diminuendo that takes them to *pianissimo*. At the same time, the horns go in the opposite direction and arrive at *fortissimo*, covering up the rest of the orchestra. This is intentional, so do not try to either lessen the horns or bring up the others. Even if they cannot be heard, the eighth notes three bars before **reh. M** should be played at full value.

I have found it effective to take a little time at **reh. M** to relax the tension of the previous section. Imagine the shortest of fermatas on the diminuendo before commencing with the sixteenth notes. It looks like Berlioz did not want the audience to hear the first violins, considering their dynamic marking, but I think this charming figuration needs to come up a bit. In **m. 183** and onward, you can again double the harps. The final notes of the first violin before **reh. N** can be played with a slightly exaggerated crescendo, especially effective if the subsequent eighth note is sustained.

After **reh. O**, the composer wants us to bring out the pizzicatos, and this works well. Since they are in upper registers, a slightly dry sound is appropriate. The typical placement of the second violins and violas onstage makes it harder to hear the inner voices in this passage, so strive for equal balance. The second flute must switch instruments quickly in **mm. 228–30**, but they usually manage it in time. Get as much diminuendo as possible in these measures and then amplify the brief crescendo to *mezzo forte*.

Next, stay perfectly still and instruct the orchestra to do the same during the measure of rest one bar before **reh. R**. This pause can be dramatic and slightly extended, keeping the listener guessing what comes next.

This is the one place where the added cornet part is quite lovely, but I still would not use it. Pay attention to the accents in the horns. The violins' sixteenth notes are played off the string but not overly short.

Two bars before **reh. S**, you can go into three, but I recommend not making too much out of this rallentando, saving it for the next occurrence before **reh. T**. In both cases, the last note of the phrase needs to be elongated, in line with the ritard, so that it does not disappear. Next, revert to the main tempo.

At **reh. T**, the *animez* is *subito* and only a little faster. We will continue to move forward as the Coda builds. There has always been some controversy about the length of the upbeat to the second bar. If you look at similar places in the music that follows, it is written as a thirty-second note. Most of us change the first one to match the others, but I suppose you could make them all sixteenths if you prefer. This is a surprisingly difficult transition to align precisely. I suggest starting at the *animez*, asking the winds to listen for the cellos and basses. In addition, you might need to tell them that the first violins have a note before they enter. Once you have established the tempo, go back three bars and rehearse the transition.

Seven measures before **reh. U**, observe the *subito mezzo forte* in the first violins. Even at that dynamic, the music should still convey a lightness of character. During this passage, many conductors will speed up, gaining momentum as we move toward **reh. W**. Starting in **m. 279**, Berlioz includes a rare example of a hemiola. Because it is conducted in one, we cannot really show this. To give this rhythmic figure some prominence, you can put a slight accent over each group of three notes and point it out to the musicians involved.

Since only the solo clarinet is playing the final statement of the *idée fixe* at **reh. W**, there is no need to go into three. For the rallentando before **reh. X**, I usually cut off the horns and let the two clarinetists play on their own. The *a tempo con fuoco* is traditionally taken at a faster pace than the *animez* that preceded it. Now the lower instruments get their turn with the hemiola after **reh. Y**, so use the same bowing. The word *serrez* at **reh. Z** has several meanings; for musical purposes, it indicates moving ahead, and this lasts right until the last bar.

Although marked with a *sforzando* and double *forte*, the final measures should not be overly aggressive. All the instruments play the last note longer than the eighths, with one full bow length usually sufficing. I go one step further and ask the harps to let the chords ring. This is their final contribution to the piece, so it seems fitting to give them the last word.

## Third Movement (Scène aux Champs)

In my youth, I did not care for this part of the symphony, finding it too lengthy of an interruption before the good stuff. I would bet that many of you reading this only warmed up to the first three movements as you grew older and gained experience as both a listener and performer. Now, I cannot wait to lead this part; it has become the literal centerpiece of *Symphonie fantastique* for me.

Berlioz adds three players to the timpani mix. Usually, these parts are played by the percussionists who will be present in the section for the final two movements. The musician assigned the second part continues playing timpani the rest of the way.

The logistics of the opening present us with several possibilities. Berlioz only employs one oboe in the waltz for good reason: he wants the second player to have time to prepare for the switch to English horn. However, if there are only two oboists total, the first will have to leave the stage and take his or her place in some distant location. This is awkward, and these days, most orchestras have the *cor anglais*—neither a horn nor English—performed by the musician hired for that specific purpose as a member of the ensemble. This frees up the second oboe to go offstage during the waltz. If your orchestra has four players in the oboe section, then there is no need for a change of scenery.

But where should the offstage oboe go? Berlioz says, *"derriere la scene,"* which means behind the stage. Most people interpret this as just offstage on whichever side is practical. In any event, the oboe and English horn need to be able to hear each other. This is a dialogue between two shepherds tending to their flocks on separate fields. The two musicians need to agree on the phrasing and note lengths. If the acoustics make it possible, and you have the benefit of a video monitor, it is not necessary to conduct anything until the second measure of **reh. A**. Despite the marking of Adagio, $\eighthnote = 84$, this opening section should not really convey a feeling of tempo.

I should add that I almost always select a different placement option for the oboe. Since this conversation, in theory, involves the two protagonists being able to see each other, I place the musician in the upper balcony. This provides a more intimate view of the discussion, although those who sit nearby will have a very different point of reference than most of the audience.

After **reh. A**, all you really need to do is nod to the violas to indicate their entrance. However, once they come in, the two soloists may not be able to hear each other clearly, in which case you will need to beat time, discreetly, without drawing the attention of the audience. In **m. 14** and **m. 16**, we find the first *rinforzando* references in the violas. This represents a sudden, almost violent interruption of what has been going on beforehand. Some conductors have interpreted this as a *forte-piano*, but it really is a strong accent followed by a six-beat diminuendo. The English horn player, as well as the oboist two bars later, must give as much as possible here. The sheep are restless.

All the movements in the symphony are dreams, and perhaps that is why this incredible part of the work seems a bit scattered in terms of formal structure. We move from the two shepherds calling from afar to the unbearable loneliness of the solitary English horn at the conclusion. As before, exaggeration is a major part of the unique character in this piece.

When the two reed players have ended their conversation, a unison tune appears in the first violins and solo flute. Ask the musicians who enter at **reh. B** to match the color they have been hearing. The F is the same for all the instrumentalists, so this is usually possible. A little bit of vibrato helps. All the *sforzandos* are relative to the dynamic being played prior to that indication. I aim for a maximum of *mezzo forte* for the overall crescendo in **mm. 28–31**.

Berlioz did not indicate the dynamic for the pizzicatos in the lower strings before **reh. D**, but I recommend asking for these to be plucked gently, as if just touching the string. Be sure to have the lower line of the basses play out a bit at **m. 44**; this fundamental note makes the inversion interesting. One bar before **reh. E**, all strings should play on the string.

If you have not moved the tempo yet, **reh. E** is a good place to pick it up a bit. Notice that the *forte* phrase in the second bar does not contain a diminuendo, making the *piano* dynamic in the third bar *subito*. The strings have little sighs in the fourth and fifth bars. For the undulating rhythm in the strings at **m. 59**, you can either take slight separations between the eighth notes, as I do, or play this all legato.

In the context of the overall diminuendo just before **reh. G**, each crescendo should become gradually less intense. At **reh. G**, keep the tempo moving along, and notice the three differing dynamics for the solo winds. The cellos and lower division of violas have the tune at **m. 69**, and I recommend that the first two or three stands of violas play the melody. Bring out the *sforzando* pizzicatos and perhaps raise the volume of the first violins so that their passagework does not get covered up. This is not an accompaniment but rather an obbligato line that can be played expressively. In the bar before **reh. H**, I do a slight diminuendo on the first note, then come back up on the third beat. I separate the three groups of two notes with a diminuendo at the end. Because the violins are being asked to play in the upper register of the instrument at the third bar of **reh. H**, you might need to consider some alternate bowings to ensure that nothing sounds pinched.

In the middle of the bar before **reh. I**, we have to consider the acoustics of the room, which may cause the first notes after the sixteenth-note rest to be obscured. If this is the case, make sure that the last notes of the violins are as short as possible but on the string. Perhaps the violas and cellos will need to increase their dynamic slightly as well. A *dolce* accent is a nice touch on the first note of each group in the woodwinds, both times.

I truly do not understand the diminuendo indication before **reh. J**. If Berlioz had just stuck with the single *forte* tremolo, then that would be clear. However, he writes *très serré*, which roughly translates to very tight, or rough. That indicates *fortissimo*, which he does put in for the next utterance at **m. 92**. Along with most conductors, I add a crescendo into the tremolo for everyone, putting as much force as possible into the lower strings and bassoons. In addition, I speed up slightly so that I can return to the calmer tempo when the voice of the lover, the *idée fixe*, returns.

As the protagonist dreams of lovemaking, the music evokes a dynamic of dominance against submission or possible reluctance. The dissonance in his music, usually punctuated with a *sforzando*, contrasts with the relaxed nature of hers. The couple begins a closer dialogue three bars before **reh. K**, where they seem to answer each other's desires. The duo gets in sync by the time the *animez un peu* commences, when it becomes clear what is going on. They reach the climax at **reh. L**, but Berlioz misleads the strings with his notation. After the tremolo on the fourth beat, I think they need to match the phrasing in the winds. You can add a slur to indicate a release point, but avoid reattacking the fifth beat of the bar. The eighth notes that end the tremolos can be either long or short; I prefer them clipped.

All these sixteenth notes should be played on the string, starting marcato. Then, as the rallentando and diminuendo begin, the notes get a bit longer. I ask for all up bows in **m. 110** and two down bows followed by two up bows in **m. 111**. After that, we have one of the boldest strokes in the entire work. No one could have foreseen this D♭ coming. It is best to wait a little bit before giving this cue to the cellos. The cooldown period has started, and since the woodwinds have an ascending line, the crescendo will occur automatically. I prefer to create one continuous line rather than asking the flutes and oboes to drop to a *subito piano* two bars before **reh. M**. The firsts have a trill that connects to the next bar.

A brief side note: I remember very well that on my old LPs, this is the point in the piece that the orchestra would play the resolution on the downbeat and then stop altogether. I had to flip the record over to hear the remainder of the movement.

**Rehearsal M** begins with a triple *piano* pizzicato that softens to quadruple *piano* six bars later. The sound the conductor hears on the podium can be quite different than that which extends to the rear of the concert hall. For that reason, I cannot suggest a proper level for these notes to be played. You must judge for yourself, preferably with the help of someone listening from various vantage points. Dynamics can look good on the page, and even sound fine onstage, but the effect is diluted if the music is inaudible to some in the audience.

The clarinet intones a phrase that seems to reflect the opening violin motif of the movement, while the underlying pizzicatos are a decorated variation of the violin melody. This instrumental voicing is wonderful in its simplicity. I urge you to avoid making a ritenuto at **reh. O**, where we have some marvelous, inventive ideas going on. My preference is to follow what Berlioz asks for in terms of notes played on and off the string. I follow a simple rule: If there are no dots, keep the bow on the string. Observing the first beat *mezzo forte* gives the *subito piano* on the next beat extra meaning. Berlioz indicates another quadruple *piano* before **reh. P**, but this should simply be played softer than what has come before.

At **m. 139**, each *sforzando* in the winds should increase in volume along with the crescendo. At **reh. Q**, we encounter the last loud moment in this movement. The next few minutes will be spent winding the material down. Take care not to overdo the rallentando two bars before **reh. R**, as it should lead to the *a tempo* rather than go past it.

At **reh. R**, two motifs come to the fore simultaneously, and each bar imbues them with a different color. The diminuendo at **m. 155** can be difficult to bring off, and orchestras often reach the *piano* dynamic way too early. I have found that sustaining the *forte* for three beats before relaxing works well. Since Berlioz does not specify a dynamic in the next bar, it is up to the conductor to ensure that the first pizzicato notes are audible. The sudden *sforzandos* can fall within the *forte* range, anticipating the coming storm.

Some conductors, including me, have placed these timpani offstage. This means you need a second set of drums, so it may not be practical for every orchestra. The first entry of the timpani, back at **reh. L**, should come from the stage, as it is feasible for just one person to play those two notes. Then, that musician leaves the stage to join the others. Another possibility is that the four percussionists play the offstage timpani so that the principal does not have to leave at all.

What is the reasoning behind the offstage placement of the drums? To answer that, we have to look ahead to the Coda, when the solitary English horn is no longer answered by the oboe. Programmatically, I assume that the thunder is coming from somewhere near where that shepherd was at the start. The prospect of a deluge has prompted him to hide with the flock. It also gives a more ominous tone to the proceedings. I think that the conductor should keep this in mind if the timpani are onstage. If they are in the wings, a video monitor focused on the conductor, or an assistant positioned backstage, is usually the order of the day.

The *idée fixe* returns in an abbreviated form at **reh. S**, with a series of triplets as a counterpoint. Those are clear until we get to **m. 163**, when they are played by the double basses. Having them start a little louder can help. The rhythmic pattern that we played legato a few times earlier in the movement can be performed in that manner once again. This creates some interesting mild dissonances.

Starting at the third bar of **reh. T**, the cellos need to be heard clearly until they stop their pizzicatos. Berlioz could have ended the movement here with a couple of F-major chords, but instead, he gives us one of the most remarkable passages in all orchestral music. There are many ways to interpret the Coda, and how you deal with it will depend entirely on your vision of this moment. I will share mine with you.

If it is possible to position the timpani offstage, then the effect of the rolling thunder in the distance is easily achieved. As with the opening of the movement, the English horn does not need to be conducted. Neither do the timpani. I have the percussionist playing the F♮ serve as an assistant, not only performing on the drum but also giving entrance and cutoff cues to the others. It looks rather silly for the person on the podium to beat time when the audience cannot see anyone being led. A similar plan can work if the instruments are onstage. However, if they really want a conductor, you can indicate the entries without giving all six beats in the measure because the parts usually show what all four are doing.

Throughout, the kettledrums should underplay the dynamics to give the illusion that the sound is coming from the distance. The English horn can wait just a bit before each entrance. There should be nothing metronomic about this section. Two bars after **reh. V**, the crescendo can go almost to *forte* and cut off abruptly, as if the shepherd were distressed at not receiving an answer to his queries. It can be spellbinding for the whole section from **reh. U** until three measures before the end to be performed with no motion at all from the conductor.

I am pretty certain that Berlioz's intention was not harmonically based when he chose those particular notes for the timpani; it is a sound effect. But some conductors have changed the note for the fourth drum to A♮ in the third bar of **reh. W**. When I was young, this was my choice as well, but now I find it disruptive.

Discreetly raise your arms during the final drum roll, waiting to bring in the strings and second horn until after the timpani have concluded. It is not necessary to beat the whole bar. Observe the length of the final three notes, and when you arrive at the last bar, gently cut off the strings but allow the horn to hang on a little longer, enough for the listener to know that the ending is indefinite.

## Fourth Movement (Marche au Supplice)

The first few times I heard this symphony, I could not wait for the march to begin. Everything that came before it seemed so pale and tame that I wished the last two movements comprised the whole work. I feel differently now, of course, but this dramatic moment still brings chills if conveyed with the menace it deserves.

After the tranquil conclusion of the previous movement, I recommend waiting a little while before giving the downbeat here. There are practical considerations, as well. For example, one of the musicians who played a timpani part needs to move back to the percussion section. All in all, you need six people to cover the parts. In addition, no matter where you placed the offstage oboist, that musician needs time to get back. Since the first time they play is at **m. 39**, it is possible, but not ideal, for them to enter while the opening of the march is in progress.

At the outset, we have an unusual indication of *Allegretto non troppo*, ♩ = 72. As with the second movement of Beethoven's Seventh Symphony, the word Allegretto contradicts what is normally interpreted as a lighthearted movement. Once again, we have seen some performers take a fairly brisk pace, but a statelier tempo corresponds more appropriately with the solemnity of the storyline. It also allows the two timpanists to utilize the mallets as Berlioz indicates—both sticks on the downbeat and only the stick in the right hand on the other five beats. It is difficult, and most players don't do it, but with the right people playing it, the effect can work.

The divisi pizzicato line in the double basses is very important in terms of balance. This movement is in G minor, and therefore the tonic note, both at the top and bottom of this divisi, must be heard to establish that key.

Often, the B♭ of the first timpani dominates and gives the impression that this movement starts in a major key, even though there is no F♮ in the chord.

With each pair of horns set in different keys, clearly Berlioz is trying to get all the notes to sound alike. He also imparts a sinister quality by having the musicians put their hands in the bells. This nasal texture is mitigated when the bassoons enter four bars later. The conductor must decide when the stopped notes become open, as the composer does not indicate this. Perhaps the least disruptive solution is to remove the hand from the instrument four bars before **reh. B**, since the lower brass come in at that point. You can also wait until **reh. B** itself.

Along with the third trombone, one of the ophicleides enters. This instrument was in wide use during Berlioz's lifetime, but today, tubas are used. Sometimes one is slightly smaller than the other. This will be important a bit later. Since the strings all have a *forte* pizzicato two bars before **reh. B**, be sure that the crescendo in the winds and timpani does not cover this up. On the downbeat of the climax, it seems like a miscalculation to have some instruments at single *forte* and others *fortissimo*, as well as some playing an eighth note and the rest a quarter note. I prefer for all to play the downbeat as an eighth and as loudly as possible.

The violas' dynamic at **m. 25** may need to be adjusted to allow the four bassoons to come to the fore. A nice effect occurs at **m. 34** as one group begins a long diminuendo while the other makes an abrupt crescendo. The bar before **reh. D** should wake up anyone in the audience who may have nodded off during the third movement. Play it aggressively, almost unmusically.

Another great moment for the four bassoons arises at **reh. E**. Inject an air of sarcasm into this passage, one of many opportunities to do so in this movement. When the quartet comes to their divisi harmonic shift in **m. 59**, do not let the dynamic drop. The octaves in the tuba line before **reh. F** can sound amazing if played cleanly.

At single *forte*, the march at **reh. F** is not bombastic. How to perform the accented notes in terms of length is a matter of preference; I ask for the first two to be played slightly long and the third one short. Each time it happens, the first instance being one measure before **reh. G**, I prefer for the quarter note to almost go into the next bar.

Scholars do not entirely understand why Berlioz put in a repeat. Some think this idea came from the publisher. Aside from recordings, it is usually omitted in performance.

To really hear the woodwinds' answer at **reh. H**, consider reversing the dynamics between them and the brass. Add an accent for the brass in the second bar and then drop down a little, or just have the woodwinds play as loudly as possible.

At **m. 82**, it is helpful to think of one continuous line by imagining that just one instrumental group, including the percussion, was playing the whole phrase. Bring out the accents on the first notes of each timpani so that you can clearly hear the ascending pitches.

The strings are now added to the march, but it is not so easy to hear them at the start, so I suggest raising the dynamic a bit. Berlioz's intention for the double basses remains a mystery to me. I try to bring them out by changing bow direction every beat, but this is rarely noticeable. Aside from these additional instruments, Berlioz keeps everything else consistent with **reh. F**.

Changes begin at **reh. L**, where three separate ideas are going on. The strings' *fortissimo* can be enhanced by sustaining the quarter notes. While the double basses are the only group not to have the grace notes, I do not recommend adding them. The lower brass begins *mezzo forte* and eventually overtakes virtually all the other instruments before **reh. M**. Sadly, the audience rarely hears the woodwinds, but these quick notes are worth bringing out, if possible. The winds should play as loudly as possible for the final sextuplet. I also think that the indicated diminuendo in the brass and low strings at **m. 122** should function as an accent over the quarter note and should not come down in volume.

At this point, many conductors reduce the tempo slightly, giving a weightier feeling to the passage. I tend to agree with this interpretation. Berlioz reminds us to pay attention to the different dynamics for the cymbals and bass drums while simultaneously observing the significant diminuendo for the rest of the orchestra. I ask the strings to employ a heavy spiccato played near the frog at **m. 135**. Berlioz does not specify how softly the diminuendo ends at **reh. O**. I bring down the volume almost to *pianissimo* to underscore the bizarre nature of the execution ahead.

The dotted eighths of the winds and brass should contrast with the length of the sixteenth notes that follow—in other words, sustained dotted notes and short sixteenths. Despite the lack of dots over the *fortissimo* quarter notes, I think they sound best when played short. Beginning three measures before **reh. P**, conductors often continue the same bowing pattern as the previous phrase. Surprisingly often, they eliminate the slur. This is a shame because the effect of the slurred notes followed by the short ones is quite dramatic.

The two bars of eighth notes at **reh. P** can either be performed with the bowing "as it comes" or, more persuasively, using all down bows, which also looks great. In the third bar, Berlioz affirms that these notes are not a mistake. The idea that tritone chords would occur this close to each other was quite new for the time and could easily have been misconstrued. The two bars before **reh. Q** continue the diminuendo and are followed by a loud outburst from the orchestra. I slightly underplay this explosion and make a crescendo to the second bar.

All the quarter notes before **reh. R** are short, but I do sustain the last one to create the feeling that the clarinet solo is emerging rather than suddenly there. You do not have to conduct this solo, and I recommend that you see what the player wants to do with it before commenting. It represents the protagonist's last look at his beloved before the blade drops, so there are all manner of options. The *fortissimo* needs to be jarring, and going into four for this one bar helps. To do this, you have to change the tempo a bit, and I suggest playing the pizzicatos stronger than *mezzo forte*.

The three timpanists and the tambour, played without snares, announce the end. Even though Berlioz says solo for the latter, it is quite okay to use more than one, but don't start them at the volume level of the timpani. Note that everyone else is just single *forte* until the upper strings enter. The last bar, for most of the musicians, is a *subito fortissimo*, but you can have the tambours make a crescendo with the timpani. There is a reason the composer puts a fermata after this final note. He is asking for a bit of silence before continuing.

## Fifth Movement (Songe d'une Nuit du Sabbat)

While the first four movements are unique in their own right, Berlioz saved his greatest innovations for the Finale. Yet, despite how often the work is played, there remain numerous technical and musical challenges for every conductor.

The instruction Larghetto seems to belie the ominous nature of the introduction. With the metronome at $\droit = 63$, you would think that the opening would be conducted in four. That works some of the time, but not always. The three-part divisi in the upper strings is dependent on whether you want the listeners to hear each note in the chord equally. Even though it appears that these notes are measured, a slightly slower tremolo achieves the desired atmosphere. I give a purposely vague and small upbeat, with no real indication of tempo, and I don't start the lower strings until the sound is just right to my ears.

Because of the way it appears on the page, many musicians are not sure how to subdivide the sextuplet. From my perspective, it should be three groups of two notes, the last of which is a sixteenth rest. I think of a triplet when I finally give the upbeat to the cellos and basses. Starting a little below *piano* can make this passage even more eerie, but be sure to increase to at least *mezzo forte* as Berlioz specifies.

Now comes a very tricky bit: The third measure should be conducted in eight. Since the upbeat to this bar is a quarter note, you can divide your beat into two eighth notes, giving the strings a chance to feel the rhythm coming up. At the end of **m. 3**, go back to the quarter-note beat for the second half of the measure. You have established the rhythm, so nothing really changes, but this gives the musicians space to begin thinking about the next bar. It is efficient to rehearse each of these measures separately to show the strings how they fit together. I realize this seems like a lot to take in, but it is the best way to utilize rehearsal time.

Two bars before **reh. A**, go back to beating in eight. The sextuplets in the low strings are played as if they were two groups of three notes. The sound is like a growl. The next measure is more like the devil mocking the latest entrant into the underworld. I think of it as a musical imitation of "ha, ha, ha." Conductors often overlook the staccato marks and when they end. I start with short notes and lengthen them as we go along.

The downbeat of **reh. A** can be quite strong, but it is not a *forte-piano*. Play it as it looks, a quarter-note diminuendo. We are also back in four at this point. In the third bar, Berlioz uses perhaps the most unconventional orchestral technique in the entire symphony. He writes an octave descent in the woodwinds as a glissando, but he is not clear on how to accomplish it. There are two possibilities: The first and easiest way is a chromatic scale played quickly and as close to the next bar as possible. The second and better option is a "bend" or "lip" glissando. Although none of the instruments can play all the descending notes, they can hit enough of them to make the effect work. This slide also needs to occur near the end of the bar as opposed to beginning it when the initial C is played.

Three bars before **reh. B**, Berlioz gives us some more novel sounds, which must have come as quite a surprise at the first performances. First, the two bass drums, each placed with the flat side up, are played as if they were timpani. The third horn uses a hand stop to imitate the woodwinds and then, although not indicated, can also add a lip glissando down to the low C.

The measure before **reh. B** is conducted in eight as everyone makes a crescendo. However, the downbeat of the next bar is unusual. Notice that the strings return to the tremolo of the opening and have an immediate *pianissimo*. In contrast, the woodwinds continue to increase the volume, creating the impression that the bowed notes are emerging out of nowhere. As with the first bar of the movement, I wait until the *pianissimo* has set in before cueing the cellos and basses. The *sforzando* in the strings should be discreet but audible at **m. 15**, followed two notes later by a *subito piano*. Stay in eight for **m. 16** to coordinate the rhythm in the upper strings. A wonderful note change in the first two bassoons and third trombone occurs three bars before **reh. C**.

The Allegro is not too fast, setting up the furious tempo that will come nine bars later. You do not find too many C clarinets around these days, although this instrument imparts quite a different color than its brothers and sisters. Today, this line is usually played on the B♭ clarinet. Berlioz wants it to sound very distant, with just a little crescendo. The metronome speed of ♩. = 112 works well. Some conductors ask the strings to use the ricochet bow stroke at **m. 25**. This can work but makes it harder to accomplish the crescendo. I advise against making an accelerando.

The outburst at the *Allegro assai* needs to be as fast as possible. The metronome marking is o = 76, implying that this passage is beat in one. Nonetheless, this is impractical with so much going on. You can accomplish the same effect by staying in two at a speed of ♩ = 152. Give an extra kick to the last note.

Whether you choose to take some time before starting **reh. E** depends on the acoustics of the hall. I think that most of the sound from the previous measure should dissipate before you recommence; however, be cognizant of taking too much time. The oboes and C clarinet play in a folksy manner with a slightly nasal quality. In a complete nose-thumbing of the *idée fixe*, Berlioz is at his cheekiest with the E♭ clarinet. Note that the tempo indication is slightly slower than at **reh. C**. The grace notes are quick, but audible, and I like playing the quarter notes on the longer side with a singular exception: In **m. 46**, I always ask the musician to play the two highest notes quite short, adding what I hope is even more sarcasm to the passage.

The four bassoons join in the fun with a four-note figure that almost seems out of place. Next, the violas and cellos start imperceptibly with sixteenth notes that will not be heard but were probably intended as a visual effect. You can bring them up a little if you prefer. At **reh. F**, after the entrance of the horns, who are not stopped at this point, the first violins pick up the tune and continue the crescendo.

Everyone has a *fortissimo* indicated at **m. 65**, but I have found it best to limit the horns' volume to single *forte*. Three bars before **reh. G**, I ask the brass entering on the second beat to change their dynamic to *forte* as well. Then, I have them all make a crescendo the measure before **reh. G**, returning to single *forte* for the eighth notes. This gives the chromatic lines a better chance of emerging.

The tendency for players to rush four bars before **reh. H** has always presented problems for orchestras and conductors. Musicians often want to race ahead at the start of each subsequent measure without waiting for the full length of what amounts to a quarter note to occur. Rehearse this a couple of times and, once the pitches are accurate, ask them to play it without looking at the music, but watching you. Give very strong downbeats. The measure before **reh. H** is also susceptible to rushing. Make sure that the strings understand that the winds play on the downbeat. You can also mention that everyone plays together on the second beat of each bar.

The sixteenth notes at **reh. H** are usually played off the string. Exaggerate the dynamics in the first two bars. The last note at **m. 85** will come on a down bow if you take the bowings as they come, and that will facilitate a strong *sforzando* on the eighth. However, the cellos must play the same note up bow. The tension seems to be winding down, but the tempo should not. I like to delineate between the two Cs at the end of this passage with a very slight lift between the two notes.

Scholars have many theories about what kind of bells Berlioz wanted and where they should be placed. We know that he requested large cast-bronze church bells. Only a few orchestras have these, but they can be rented if you want the real thing. Otherwise, chimes usually serve as a substitute. However, since there are just two notes, you can also obtain a close kinship to the sound of church bells with synthesized replicas. They are surprisingly effective if the playback system is good. In any case, the sound of the bells comes from a distance, offstage. The percussionist can see the conductor either directly or by television monitor. However, since these two notes are very loud, hearing the orchestra can be difficult.

The first orchestral entry is in the violas, with a very significant *subito forte* on the last note. This will become an accent and an important feature later in the movement. At the second bar of **reh. J**, having the trombones play a long, *fortissimo* quarter note creates a stunning effect. In the next bar, in addition to the accent on the upbeat, I recommend making a diminuendo, allowing the soft bell note to be heard clearly. Try to line this up exactly, as you can get an oddly uncomfortable dissonance between the bell's C and the C♯ in the strings. The *subito pianissimo* marking at **m. 123** is almost impossible to achieve on the large bells, and very few even attempt it.

We now come to the *dies irae*, a very popular tune used by Liszt, Rachmaninov, and others, but rarely for religious reasons. The unusual timbre of the four bassoons and two tubas is striking, and we must always be careful to observe the single *forte*, lest the former be obliterated by the latter. Berlioz once again surprises us by writing the second-to-last note as a syncopation when he could have very easily placed it on the second beat of the bar. At **reh. L**, balancing the chorale with the bells can be problematic, depending on where the bells are positioned. It is always helpful to have someone in the hall listening, as what we hear on the podium often differs from that which is emanating to the audience. Note that the brass usually need to take a breath in the middle of **m. 151**.

The woodwinds and strings enter at **m. 157**, and since they play the same music, the length of the winds' notes should be closer to that of the pizzicatos. It is not worth the rehearsal time required to achieve precision with the rhythm of the scale before **reh. M**; just allow the six fast notes to be played the same. The landing-note C can also be elongated. Next, the lower strings have an aggressive pizzicato that answers the tune. Then, the bells begin a series of entries that are not coincidental with the phrase structure of the tune, but the melody is notated in the part to help the percussionist follow along. The trumpets join in at **m. 176** but should just be part of the texture and not prominent.

The strange rhythmic utterances continue at **reh. O**, with the *dies irae* on the beat, an immediate answer from the cellos and basses, and then outbursts from the bass drum on the second beat. These three groups must be equal in sound on each attack. The bar before **reh. Q** brings back the second bass drum, and the two musicians should begin with just enough volume to be clearly heard. Sometimes the duo is placed next to each other and other times on opposite sides of the stage; either option can work effectively.

The last time we were given a metronome marking was back at **reh. E**, and that instruction, ♩. = 104, is repeated at **reh. R**. Berlioz writes that if the tempo has changed, you can get back during the *animez* that begins at **m. 223**. With any luck, you have not altered the tempo and have no need to observe this instruction. The lower strings should take the bowing as it comes, starting with a down bow on the slurred triplets at the end of **m. 225**. This places the *sforzando* on a down bow, and we will see this pattern repeat several times in the next section. The buildup continues with everyone getting quite loud, including the bass drums. The two cornets, flutes, and oboes change notes before the double bar, so make sure they are heard clearly.

The final portion of the symphony is the *Ronde du Sabbat*, sometimes referred to as the "Witch's Sabbath." Despite the steady tempo, many unusual effects give an unearthly meaning to this romp. A somewhat jazzy syncopation interrupts the proceedings, first heard in the brass at **m. 247**. The bowing I mentioned earlier, which places the *sforzando* in **m. 242** on a down bow, applies to every appearance of that motif. Note that the indication for the slurred trills at **m. 244** is not meant as a reattack but rather a continuation of the trill, with a release before the fifth eighth note in the bar.

By **reh. T**, Berlioz has put the theme into the woodwinds, but the accent still applies. A variant of that syncopated rhythm is tossed around by the strings starting at **reh. U** and should be placed at the fore each time it appears. A huge contrast of dynamics occurs in the first six bars of **reh. V**. One measure before **reh. W** does not really represent a diminuendo but rather a strong accent on the two slurred groups. You might need to drop the string dynamic a little after that to allow the woodwinds to emerge through the dense texture.

**Rehearsal Y** presents one of the most difficult patches for ensemble in the entire symphony. The notes and rhythms are not complicated, but where they are placed is often confusing for the musicians. For example, in the third bar, the violins either come in early (with the first note of the woodwinds) or late (having waited too long for the winds to finish playing the two-note groups). This can happen with the finest of orchestras and has to do with not understanding the rhythm of the woodwinds.

Each conductor will have a different way of rehearsing this passage. I usually have the violins play their figuration alone a couple of times so that they understand and feel the three notes starting on the beat. Next, I ask the flute and oboe to play their grouping. Then, I put these instruments together, a bit under tempo, until everyone gets it. Gradually, I speed it up and then go back to **reh. Y** to put it in context. The cello and bass lines tend to get obscured by the timpani and bass drums. To hear the notes clearly, quickly reduce the volume of the rolls. The slurred sign for the strings, along with the accents at **reh. Z**, make no sense, so consider doing these two notes separately.

The third utterance in this section changes the rhythmic structure and is much easier to coordinate. Note that there is no diminuendo for the pizzicatos, but the woodwinds do diminish the sound. This little motif makes its final and most complicated appearance at **m. 320**. The winds play on the beat for the first time and have a diminuendo. Meanwhile, the seconds and violas continue playing *fortissimo*. The firsts have a *pianissimo* trill, and the bass drums fill in the third eighth note where the winds have a rest. I advise rehearsing this slowly, with everyone playing softly. Gradually increase the tempo until it all works, then go back to **reh. Y** and play the whole passage up to **reh. A1**. You might need to do this a couple of times.

Apply a firm accent at **m. 329** in the horns. At **reh. B1**, we can interpret the *poco forte* as *mezzo forte*. However, this inference is up for grabs, as the composer does not use *mezzo piano* as a dynamic indication. Berlioz probably felt that the first F in the basses would not be heard clearly if played in the lower octave, which looks logical. The canon in the bassoons needs to balance with the low strings, but the intrusions from the horns, including the low one, should sound rude.

The next section begins with a *subito mezzo forte* tremolo in the upper strings. The second and fourth horns, along with the cellos, play the *dies irae* with each note accented. After it fades away, conductors often interject their own drama into the proceedings. Berlioz has thrown many orchestral effects at us so far, but this one is not to be found in the score. The violas are sometimes asked to play **reh. E1** as close to the bridge as possible, on the string, and *poco marcato*. This produces an ominous tone, suitable for Halloween. Of course, you do not have to do this, but I find it effective.

The horns and double basses interrupt with five more notes of the chant, followed by the violas playing *normale*, but off the string, for all the notes just before **reh. F1**. A solo bass drum takes over, and if you wish, each successive string entrance can be done *sul ponticello*. If you opt for this effect, ensure that everyone is playing almost on top of the bridge; otherwise, the result is halfhearted. Each of these string entries begins a hair louder than the preceding one. The hand-stopped horns add another wonderful color. The second bass drum enters at **m. 374**, and the firsts join in *sul ponticello*. About two bars into this, the strings should gradually move to on-the-string playing in *normale* position; everyone needs to be there by **reh. H1**.

**Rehearsal I1** is a place that looks better on the page than it sounds. Assuming the orchestra does not rush, the first four bars usually work because they are simply a rhythmic displacement, and everyone is playing the same thing. However, that changes at **m. 399** when the remaining instruments enter on the beat. I can appreciate the idea, but at the tempo indicated, it is pretty much impossible to achieve, even if the orchestra is playing the passage accurately.

Although I have never tried it, perhaps separating and accenting each note might make the cross rhythm perceptible. But the clash of harmonies makes these four bars really special, and that requires us to blur the sonorities. The best advice I can offer is to rehearse the two rhythmic cells separately, put them together, emphasize the downbeats so that no one pushes forward, and hope for the best.

The two tunes come together at **reh. K1**, but the dynamics make it difficult to hear the strings. The best solution is to have the brass play each note with a strong attack followed by an immediate drop to *mezzo forte*. Avoid making a crescendo until two bars before **reh. L1**, where the orchestra can increase its volume alongside the timpani. Each note of the second violins at **reh. L1** can benefit from the addition of slight accents. At **m. 440**, try to get the first violins and woodwinds to sound equally loud.

The upper strings often complain about **reh. M1**, and some players do not want to do a true *col legno*. Use your most charming skills to get them to be as aggressive as possible. It is also possible to have one desk of each section play *normale* to emphasize the harmonies, but do this discreetly. The tune in the woodwinds and cellos celebrate the trill. The one in the middle of **m. 450** should not be reattacked; slur it from the first one so that the trill is a continuation of what came before. The trills on the eighth notes are more like turns because of the tempo.

**Rehearsal N1** presents an intriguing harmonic mix on virtually every note. *Piano* is an appropriate marking, but sometimes the piccolo entry seems too loud. I add a diminuendo over the last three bars to make the double *forte* as surprising as possible. The single *forte* in the woodwinds after **reh. O1** is interesting, but most conductors play it quite strongly. After the *fortissimo* of **reh. P1**, keep the woodwinds' rush of sixteenth notes aggressive, especially when the line moves downward.

It is always a good idea, even when working with experienced orchestras, to rehearse the separated eighth notes that begin at **m. 480** slowly so that the musicians can hear how they fit into the pattern. The same advice applies to rehearsing the strings, whose passage here never sounds the way it looks on the page. Everyone should make a crescendo two bars before **reh. Q1**. I find that the last note is effective if held for full value.

The bass drums have their moment in the sun here, making an extreme hairpin, but observe that the strings have *subito* dynamics. They will be tempted to make a diminuendo during the *fortissimo*. At **reh. R1**, the *animez* should be very slight; otherwise, the offbeats in the seconds and violas can be difficult to place. Exaggerate the accents on the eighth notes. The two bars starting at **m. 506** are striking if played off the string as strongly as possible.

From here, it is certainly permissible to continue the *animez*, but do not get too fast, lest the final measures be overly difficult for the tuba articulation. At **reh. S1**, a descending line in the lower brass and bassoons alternates with an upward set of scales in the piccolo and E♭ clarinet. If your orchestra employs two flutes as well as the smaller cousin for these performances, then consider doubling the piccolo here.

To cap it off, the final five measures can be made even more impactful if the brass, who have repeated notes at single *forte*, make a crescendo three bars before the end. The instruments that have a moving line, in particular the tubas and bassoons, must be heard distinctly but might be covered near the end. That is okay, as the cumulative effect is one of maximum volume. However, do not make the sonority harsh.

One last note: The cymbal in the final bar is suspended and played with what was then called a sponge stick. Given that one of the percussionists is not playing at the end, I have the extra player add another cymbal to the proceedings. Even better, and quite effective visually, is to have one of these musicians strike two cymbals, one on each side. This gives the most dramatic of symphonies the most dramatic of conclusions.

## Conductor's Etiquette

First and foremost, in terms of solo bows, the English horn stands at the top of the list. Depending on who played the offstage oboe and whether they have returned to the platform, that musician can come next. Following those two, special attention goes to the four timpanists. I then proceed to acknowledge the two tubists, followed by the remainder of the brass section. Next, I recognize the four bassoons, first clarinet, piccolo clarinet, and the rest of the woodwinds. Finally, I acknowledge the two harps and the strings.

***

"It is not enough that the artist should be well prepared for the public. The public must be well prepared for what it is going to hear."

—Hector Berlioz

## Notes

1. Hector Berlioz, *Symphonie fantastique*, ed. Nicholas Temperley (Wiesbaden, Germany: Breitkopf & Härtel Urtext PB 4929, n.d.).

2. Hector Berlioz, *Symphonie fantastique*, ed. Nicholas Temperley (Kassel, Germany: Bärenreiter Urtext of the New Berlioz Edition 16, 1971).

3. "*Symphonie fantastique*, H 48 (Berlioz, Hector)," International Music Score Library Project (IMSLP)/Petrucci Music Library, https://imslp.org/wiki/Symphonie_fantastique,_H_48_(Berlioz,_Hector).

4. Norman del Mar, *Conducting Berlioz* (New York: Oxford University Press, 1997).

5. Berlioz, *Symphonie fantastique*, Bärenreiter Urtext of the New Berlioz Edition, 5.
6. Ibid., 115.
7. Andrew P. Simco, "Performing the Timpani Parts to *Symphonie fantastique*," *Percussive Notes* 36, no. 2 (April 1998): 62–65, http://www.kettledrummer.com/wp-content/uploads/2014/11/Berlioz.pdf.

# Johannes Brahms: Symphony No. 1

"The idea comes to me from outside of me—and is like a gift. I then take the idea and make it my own—that is where the skill lies."

—Johannes Brahms

Fritz Luckhardt, Public domain, via Wikimedia Commons

88   Johannes Brahms: Symphony No. 1

Sometimes the wait is worth it. Brahms, aided by the advice of Robert and Clara Schumann, worked on his First Symphony for more than twenty years before finally presenting a composition in the form that had been so dominated by Beethoven. The shadow of Beethoven's footsteps is among the first sounds we hear in Brahms's initial symphony. Brahms had tried his hand at the symphonic form with some early ventures that eventually turned into his First Piano Concerto. He had also completed exercises that could be considered symphonic, such as the two serenades (Opus 11 and Opus 16). However, when he completed this First Symphony, a new world of orchestral composition was born, and with it, a new set of demands for the still-developing world of conducting.

The general acceptance of the piece was only mitigated by a few critics who found it overly long and, in places, too reminiscent of Beethoven. Once the work established itself, it became beloved by all, except the French, who for a time abhorred the composer.

Bearing an opus number of 68, it falls in the middle of Brahms's compositional output, but there is no trace of naivety in this piece. Rather, it is a wholly original work that stands out from most of the other symphonic writing of the time by any composer.

There are not very many differences among editions of this score. We will reference the Breitkopf & Härtel publication, which contains not only rehearsal letters but measure numbers as well, available on IMSLP.[1] The Breitkopf & Härtel edition is also reprinted in Dover's *Johannes Brahms: Complete Symphonies in Full Score*.[2] The instrumentation is conventional for the time, with woodwinds in pairs, save for the addition of a contrabassoon in the last movement. Four horns, two trumpets, and three trombones (only appearing in the Finale) round out the winds. You can find the key changes for the brass and timpani at the beginning of each movement. The strings are standard, with no indication of how many desks are required.

Today's halls are larger than the ones to which Brahms would have been accustomed. As the size of the venues increased, so did the number of string players. By the start of the twentieth century, conductors would often double the woodwinds and sometimes the trumpets and horns in the denser and louder passages. You still see doubling occasionally these days, but more often, the woodwind principals and first horn have someone sitting next to them to take over during some of the longer periods as well as augment the sound.

In the first movement, the horns are divided two apiece in C and E♭. Brahms preferred the sound of the natural instruments and used them in all of his orchestral works. Trumpets are in C, and timpani play C and G, the traditional tonic/dominant notes. These transpositions will change as the movements go forward.

## First Movement: Un poco sostenuto; Allegro

Right from the start, we are presented with a conundrum. Brahms abhorred metronome marks, saying that he was not a machine. Nevertheless, he usually put in something to tell us roughly how fast or slow we might interpret the music. But not here!

*Un poco sostenuto* is not a speed. With the movement being in 6/8, we do not have any idea if this is for a bar in six or in two. Looking at the ending doesn't help either, as all we see is *Meno Allegro*. The best we can do is read the score and listen to what might have been performed by either Brahms himself or those who were close to him. Recorded documentation came well after the point of the first performance, so it is difficult to know if this represents the actual thinking of the time. Most conductors choose tempos in the range of ♪ = 72–88.

There is a fascinating and well-researched book about various approaches to this work, as well as the other three symphonies, called *Conducting the Brahms Symphonies: From Brahms to Boult*, by Christopher Dyment.[3] Written in 2015, it offers a comprehensive view of stylistic interpretations and gives us many clues about how the composer wanted his works to be played. To summarize, the book suggests that nothing should be overdone, but performers should bring a bit of individuality to their conception of the pieces.

Where does that advice leave us, in practical terms, in our discussion about how to conduct the First Symphony? Perhaps the best approach is to discern what is on the page, examine various possibilities, and consider technical advice about how to achieve the desired results. In other words, treat this piece as we would any other.

Everyone agrees that the opening must be in six. There are basically three elements going on simultaneously: the descending line in the winds, the ascending one in the violins and cellos, and those pounding strokes on each eighth note. Let's start with that last element.

Timpani, contrabassoon, and double basses are the instruments of choice, but most of the time, all we hear are the drumbeats. Everyone playing has a dynamic of single *forte*, so Brahms must have wanted a degree of equality among the three forces. This will change dramatically when we get to **m. 25**. I do know of a couple of instances when, in the desire to be "historically informed," conductors have asked that the first timpani stroke be played with one arm and the remaining five strokes with the other.

One way to help determine the tempo is to keep in mind that the winds can only sustain notes so long before running out of breath. The way the slurs are laid out certainly does not help, as there is very little musical logic in having separations between them. But perhaps the fourth bar provides a little clue. It is not possible to maintain the tied note in the flutes, oboes, and bassoons; it has to be rearticulated, so a little breath can occur here. Now it is a question of the wind players having enough air to get through the first three-and-a-half bars at your tempo.

There are several ways to perform the first eight bars when it comes to breathing. You can leave it up to the musicians to decide, tell them where you would like the slight separations, or have different lines breathe at different times. This last approach can work if those breaths are staggered to give the illusion of no breath.

For the strings, the choice is somewhat similar. They have to change bow direction at some point, and you can decide on a uniform bowing or let them play freely, with a few guidelines. If you try to sing the passage, even if you have a terrible voice, it is easier to figure out where those changes should occur.

Balancing the three simultaneous lines sets the tone for the entire symphony, like an announcement that Brahms has arrived. Before you commence, you must have your chosen tempo firmly in your mind and body. The delivery of your first gesture tells everyone the manner of performance you will give.

Make sure that you have allowed enough room to make the crescendo in the 9/8 bar. Having the number of beats change during a movement was highly unusual at the time, although the composer did much the same in the First Serenade and First Piano Concerto. Whether or not you make a slight ritard before **m. 9** is a matter of taste. Regardless, you must allow for just a little time to pass after the downbeat to create enough space for the upper strings to prepare for the pizzicato.

Intonation can be tricky for the woodwinds here. If you need to adjust it, start with the lower instruments first and gradually add the others. The gentle swells in **m. 11** and **m. 12** do not usually present problems unless they are too exaggerated. However, the cellos and basses clearly must separate the repeated notes, somewhat resembling the opening of the piece. I usually ask them to play the last three notes as one continual slur.

Brahms introduces slight differences in the buildup beginning six measures before **reh. A**. Pay attention to the fact that the hairpins disappear after the first two bars. The two eighth notes that occur in the strings two bars before **reh. A** should be heavy and equal. Make as much of a diminuendo as possible so that the next buildup can start mysteriously. The timpani should use somewhat harder sticks to make the heartbeats clear. Prior to the *fortissimo*, make eye contact with the brass and wind players who have upcoming entrances so that they come in right on the beat.

Consider holding back slightly just before the downbeat at **m. 25**. This is a spot where the heartbeats are difficult to hear. Some conductors have actually changed the timpani and contrabassoon parts to match the double basses. I ask the basses to play all the notes on down bows, with an accent on each. Since the timpani is playing a roll, but only at single *forte*, there is a chance that this shadow of Beethoven can be heard. A slight ritard is customary just before **m. 29**.

As with the strings' pizzicatos, take a little time before commencing with the oboe solo to create a structural likeness with the earlier passage. When the cellos enter, they pick up the fragment and expand on it in a most expressive way. Often, a very discreet portamento is added between the octave Gs; this can create a lovely color if done gently. Then, the two pizzicatos are played just loudly enough to be audible to listeners. Be sure to cut off the upper strings prior to giving the last pizzicato before the Allegro.

As with the rest of the symphony, we are given no clues about how fast or slow the main section of the movement is supposed to go. To determine the upper limits of that tempo, we can look for measures containing steady streams of sixteenth notes. We do not have to look much further than five measures after **reh. B**. As opposed to the similar three-note pattern near the outset (**mm. 48–50**), these are separate notes and not slurred. To hear the sixteenth notes clearly, the suggested metronome mark will probably be somewhere between ♩. = 84 up to possibly ♩. = 100.

It is odd in music by Brahms for some of the musicians to be marked *forte* and others *fortissimo*. All instruments have to be well-balanced so that the third and fourth horns do not dominate. Getting the sixteenths to come through in the third bar of the Allegro takes a little effort. It is best accomplished by letting those players take a breath so that they can attack these notes as aggressively as possible.

Everything you do from this point on must be consistent. If you played a certain quarter note at full value, then when the same phrase recurs and the score indicates nothing to the contrary, you must do it that way again. One of the best examples of this is at **m. 44**. Conductors seem divided as to the length of the first note. Some keep it short, and others try to sustain it, perhaps lending more connectivity to the accented second beat.

The long vs. short issue will come up continuously, especially in this movement. Look at **mm. 51–53**, comparing them to the same material—but written in a different way—in the lower strings starting from the middle of **m. 53**. Consistency is the key here. We must observe the rest after the quarter note, but the question is about the length of that quarter note. I prefer the weightiness of a sustained sound, which then makes the answer more connected.

**Measure 54** provides an example of notation that seems contrary to what is desired. We see this often in Shostakovich as well as other composers: a slur into the eighth note but also a dot. This really means to add a separation just after the quarter note.

As with composers going back to Mozart, the use of *più forte* is usually interpreted as a crescendo rather than a *subito* dynamic. At **m. 63**, we are already *fortissimo*, so you might ask, "How much louder should it get?" The additional instruments a few bars later help us understand that the G7 chord before **reh. B** is the high point of this passage. Keep everything before that chord under control so that this moment can be powerful.

Sometimes lost in the sonority of the long notes are the slightly off-kilter eighths in the upper strings and timpani at this point. I place a little accent on the first note of each to emphasize the unusual syncopation, but not so much as to distract from the melodic line. Make sure to observe the *sforzando* indications at **m. 82** and **m. 83**. In **mm. 84–86**, the woodwinds must play as loudly as possible for their sixteenth notes to be audible against the sustained strings.

The long/short dilemma reappears in a different guise beginning at **m. 90**. An alternation between strings and winds should be observed, even at the quickest of tempos. Brahms would not have spent so much time and energy writing in this way if he did not intend it.

Seven bars after **reh. C**, there are both slurs and dots in the violins. Some conductors very carefully slow down to emphasize this bar, but I think all you have to do is ask the musicians to play this on the string and slightly separated. Soon enough, you will have the opportunity to hold back. In **m. 106**, listen for the series of repeated eighths in the cellos; as much as you might wish to pay attention to the pizzicato, it is equally important to focus on this rhythmic element so that the tempo does not slacken.

Again, other interpreters hold back slightly at **m. 110** but run the risk of interrupting the structure of the movement. Plus, that cello figure is still going on a few bars later. This changes to a slurred sequence four bars before **reh. D**, which is a good place to take a bit of time. (At **reh. D**, I find it interesting that Brahms marks both *espressivo* in the winds and *dolce* in the strings; his intention is unclear to me.) The slight holding back needs to be just that—slight. You should readjust at **m. 130** and either stay in the slower tempo or pick it back up. In any event, the violas have now taken over the repeated eighth notes, but with a slur over each group of six, presumably to show that these should be played on the string.

Lots of back and forth occurs from **m. 137**, but this cannot be under the spell of a ritenuto. Brahms's notation is a little confusing at **m. 143** and **m. 144**, as he has left out the slurs in the violas. It is hard to imagine playing these bars differently than the previous ones. The *pianissimo* in the strings is most effective if played *molto legato*.

Purists are going to object to what I am about to suggest. (You are warned!) The motif for the third horn in **m. 154** is clear, but jump forward to **m. 426**. Brahms continues here, with the horns in octaves as in the preceding measures. So, why didn't he do the same earlier? The second E♭ horn had these notes available. Maybe he thought that extra notes would be too loud, but then, why bother to put them in the next two bars?

Is it sacrilegious to add the lower octave at **m. 154**? You will have to decide for yourself. All I will say is that when you examine the later passage, you may find other discrepancies to address. Brahms is nothing if not careful about structure, and since we cannot speak with him about this, the best we can do is speculate.

Another seeming contradiction occurs in the violas at **m. 157**. There are dots on the notes but also the indication *marc*. The tradition is to play these two bars like the ones that follow—off the string. There is also an accent on the first note. I continue to place one on each of the string entries to clarify the rhythmic syncopations.

Although I have discussed the value of performing the various notes at the length that Brahms writes, there is also a matter of when to release some of them. Starting at **reh. E**, it is tempting to take very short breaths after the dotted quarters. However, Brahms includes fascinating clashes of harmonies that can only be discerned when the notes are held for their full length. But what about, for instance, the second bar in the low instruments, or the fifth measure on the downbeat? Musicians have a natural tendency to back away after the initial attack, but this detracts from the tension inherent in the music.

Now we come to the hotly debated matter of the repeat. This is usually thought of as a structural necessity to maintain the sonata-allegro format. But Brahms had a thought on the matter. In a letter to Dvořák, who was about to conduct the Second Symphony, Brahms said that the piece was now familiar to the audience, so they did not need to hear the exposition twice to understand the material being developed.

We learn from this comment that the repeat not only served the structural integrity of the work but also functioned to serve the listener. Most of the time, at least in the first two symphonies, conductors choose not to perform the music again. Most of us agree that in the First Symphony, the two bars comprising the first ending seem perfunctory and unconvincing, as if Brahms knew that he had to put something in to get back to the Allegro. As conductor Max Rudolf once said, "I don't think the material bears repeating."

The start of the development is unusual for the choice of key, B major. And if you needed any further proof of my obsession about the length of quarter notes, all you have to do is look at **reh. F**, where we find a dot on the downbeat. Since Brahms has the woodwinds playing an eighth, this appears to be simply an error, as it is going to sound the same in both groups.

An air of mystery fills the next few phrases; observing the *pianissimo* while the bassoon plays more expressively is particularly important. Any material that appears to be the same as in the exposition should be played in a similar manner here.

An interesting contrast of slurred and separate notes commences in **m. 232**. The middle and lower strings have a combination of these, and it is tempting to want to make them all *molto legato*, in line with the first violins. However, Brahms clearly wants the fullness of the sound to reach his listeners, so I do not recommend changing this. But you must drop down a dynamic level at **m. 242** to have more power seven bars later.

The music at **reh. H** represents a highly original use of the introductory material, with the timpani and cellos reprising the pulses of the opening. Do not slacken the tempo so as not to interrupt the flow of the music. When the eighths cease, it is certainly possible, even advisable, to relax, especially before the pickup to **reh. I**. However, do not slow down much, as there will be another opportunity to hold back in about a minute.

You must make a decision at this point regarding the crescendos. Do they signify a continual increase of sound, or do you return to a lesser dynamic at the start of the next phrase? Since these qualify as a rare example of overlapping swells, my feeling is that the dynamic drops back after each crescendo, creating a series of tense moments leading almost all the way to **reh. K**.

The militaristic nature of the horns, trumpet, and timpani presents the possibility of a slight *pesante* here. Some conductors choose to separate the sixteenth notes in the strings, and this is certainly possible, especially if the other instruments overwhelm. Note that Brahms has the horns and trumpets at only single *forte*, but not the timpani.

At one point, the composer went straight from **m. 335** to the recapitulation. The eight measures that now exist make for a much more seamless transition, and we can also use them to get back to the original tempo if it has slackened.

Most everything proceeds as it did previously, with the occasional hairpin or dynamic slightly altered. The dilemma with the horns that appeared at **m. 154** now moves a couple of measures and into the bassoons. Unless you think the low C is too coarse, I see little reason not to ask the second player to put it in five bars before **reh. O**.

I suppose we could call the passage at **m. 462** a pre-Coda. This is one of the most dramatic moments in the symphonic literature. The horns and low bassoons should have an accent, which, if needed, can be played as a *fortepiano*. This depends entirely on the ability of the other instruments to cut through the texture of the long notes. Five bars before **reh. P**, some conductors will lower the dynamic to get maximum effect from the crescendo. If you do this, be discreet.

At **reh. P**, consider asking the strings and bassoons to wait a little longer before beginning. This clears the air for the *subito forte* and adds a bit of tension during the silence. It also allows us to start calming down before the actual Coda. Brahms provides us with a written-out ritard in the cellos, but that is purely rhythmic. We can slow into the *Meno Allegro*.

Originally, this was marked *poco sostenuto*, the same as the very opening of the movement. Should we play it that way or just look at this concluding section as a simple relaxing of the Allegro tempo? Most conductors prefer the latter solution. If you choose this, then the beat stays in two, but if you opt for the former, then going into six makes sense.

The question of long or short quarter notes arises once again in **m. 499** and **m. 501**. To me, it makes more sense to continue the melodic line without interruption by sustaining those notes.

The final five measures can be difficult waters to tread technically. You have to keep the line but also indicate when the various groups cut off. The easy way is to conduct in six, but if you decide to stay in two, then you must use your left hand for those releases and your right hand for the next entry.

The hairpin three bars before the end is also a left-hand gesture. Should the final note in the winds be held or cut off with the pizzicato? In either case, I would advise giving three eighth notes during the second half of the last bar. Why? Because no matter what, the strings will have to release the bow to make the final note possible. Therefore, they come off on the sixth beat. You can then decide if the winds stop on the downbeat or hold on a little longer. Take plenty of time before starting the next movement.

## Second Movement: Andante sostenuto

After the storm of the first movement, we enter a mostly calm sea. In contrast to the C minor-major, Brahms has chosen the somewhat remote key of E major, which more than justifies a pause before commencing.

*Andante sostenuto* is the slightly more apt term for this movement than the composer gives us for the opening. You do not need to conduct this in six, but pay attention to the bassoons by taking a breath before starting. When there is no metronome mark, it is helpful to look at other places in the score to get an indication of how fast or slow will be appropriate. From my point of view, that moment is at the recapitulation after **reh. C** (I will explain later). In any event, a speed between ♩ = 40 and ♩ = 56 will suffice.

We have an indication of *gestopft* in the third bar for the horns. This is to hit the note on a valveless horn, but since we do not use them today, is it still worth doing? Most certainly it changes the color, in line with the *subito piano* of the other instruments. Unless your musicians are truly subtle, perhaps the best course of action is to keep the notes open. Another possibility is to ask them to play it half-stopped, but this can affect the intonation.

As we will see, line is everything in this movement. Keeping the flow, both melodically and rhythmically, is crucial for a successful interpretation. It is easy to fall into a feeling of ritard every two or four bars, but then the connections are lost, and the movement can seem endless.

While there is no break following the dotted quarter note in **m. 9**, I recommend a very slight separation of the eighth notes. Gently hold back these three eighth notes for the first two statements but get back to the tempo for the final one. Conductors can get bogged down in **m. 16**. It is just the concluding bar of a long phrase, and you do not need to wait before starting the viola's last three notes.

Brahms can be so subtle. What is the only difference between the two-bar phrase at **m. 18** and the same phrase at **m. 20**? Just the bassoons, but what a difference they make. Take care to balance the opening melody with the oboe solo five measures before **reh. A**. Three bars later, avoid the danger of waiting too long before having the first violins play their syncopated E.

I advise against speeding up at **reh. A**. Serenity characterizes this passage, and you will have ample opportunity to move forward a bit later. Notice the two-note phrasings in the string parts on the sixteenth notes at **m. 31** and **m. 32**. I give a gentle push on the first of each group to emphasize the syncopation and lend some pungency to a few of the mild dissonances.

Rather than slow down the bar before **reh. B**, you can move forward slightly to imbue the next section with a bit of anxiety. Give a very clear pulse for the benefit of the upper strings and be aware that if your solo oboist is inexperienced, he or she might need guidance on when to place the first sixteenth note. A nice touch is to ask the clarinet to enter *pianissimo* in **m. 42** and then make a slight crescendo as the moving passage comes into view. This should have the feeling of one instrument taking over from the other. Brahms sort of allows for this with the cellos and basses in **m. 46**.

Now the mood starts to get quite restless, and the intensity of the moving notes increases. Observe the dramatic *subito piano* in **m. 53**—as if the bottom has fallen out of the music—but continue the forward momentum.

Depending on your willingness to change what the composer wrote, I can offer an interesting sonic possibility in **m. 55**. The cellos and basses have the same material, but on the second beat, the basses could jump down an octave. Since the lowest note in the upcoming passage is a B♯—C♮ for our purposes—I wonder why the composer did not opt for that. The answer is simple: he did not have it at his disposal. The extension for the instrument was invented the year after Brahms died. The question is, would he have used it?

In this case, I speculate that the answer would have been yes. Here is an option that makes sense and is a combination of what existed then and now: Half the section can play the passage as written, and the others can go down the octave. This can continue all the way through two bars before **reh. C** or end a bit earlier if desired.

If the tempo has increased, we have to figure out when to return to the opening pace. It seems clear that this must occur at the recapitulation, which is on the third beat of **m. 66**. The danger is in breaking up the dialogues between the different instrumental groups in the preceding phrases with unnecessary pauses. I suggest getting back via a very gradual ritard and trying to connect the sections, including the rests. You can wait just a moment before commencing with the *pianissimo*.

For the first time in the movement, the trumpets enter. It is not as easy as it looks. The E can be precarious, so even though it is good to have made eye contact with the two musicians, do not fix your gaze upon them for too long.

Meanwhile, you must think of the triplets in the cellos that will set the tempo in motion. This is where we get the idea for the basic tempo of the movement. I always think of this spot before starting, and it helps me remember the flow of the movement rather than the more static quarter notes that occur right at the beginning. From this point, the music is a variation of the first time this material was played. In **m. 71**, subdivide the final quarter of the bar and stay in six for the next measure. Then, go back into three and, despite what seems to be the anxiety returning, stay within the basic tempo.

At **reh. D**, as with the passage in the ninth measure, you must lightly separate the triplets, and if you wish, hold back just a bit before moving forward at the *dolce* crescendo.

What magic at **reh. E**! The trio of solo oboe, horn, and violin is set against the harmonies that have finally settled down in the remaining instruments. This is almost all about balance. Oboe and horn mirror each other in octaves, and the violin comments with fillagree in the upper registers. Whereas the two wind instruments must stay in tempo, with little room for fluctuation, the violin can be almost *ad lib.*, as if improvising. The concertmaster should always be able to play without forcing the sound, so it can be helpful for either an assistant conductor or even one of the members of the orchestra to go into the hall to listen for the balance. Better yet, let the assistant conduct so that you can hear for yourself.

It is easy to get involved in the beauty of these solo lines, but you must attend to more pressing matters. Once you get to **m. 99**, take care to ensure the rhythmic stability in the triplets that accompany the soloist. Most important to me is the doubled clarinet, the only musicians playing with no rests. If the other instrumentalists can hear them, they will not lag behind.

I introduce what I consider to be a nice touch at **reh. F**. Most of the instruments leading into this have a crescendo, which we can assume goes to single *forte* at the most. The following measure has no specific dynamic in the strings, but they probably take over from the winds at *mezzo piano*. Then, the winds enter slightly softer at *piano*. To continue the falling dynamics, I change the fourth bar to *pianissimo* (but not inaudible). This extended falling line culminates in a silence, which can be slightly prolonged.

As I note in other essays, as well as this one, when a slurred note is connected to another one within the same beat, the latter note might have a dot over it. This means that the previous note is separated from the subsequent one. In **m. 115**, **m. 116**, **m. 121**, and **m. 122**, the flute, clarinet, and bassoon apply this rule over two beats. These are difficult to do effectively, as the last note can sound abrupt if played too short. A subdivision prior to the dotted note can help, but more than likely you will have to say something about how long or short you prefer the note to be played.

The trumpets once again have that slightly perilous E to deal with, so you have to pay attention to the balance. You do not need to conduct in nine for the last five bars, but you might consider subdividing the final three notes in case the timpani and solo violin cannot hear each other. Everyone cuts off before the last bar, save for the violin, and you can wait as long as the concertmaster will allow before bringing in the orchestra for the final note.

### Third Movement: Un poco Allegretto e grazioso

Acting more as an interlude rather than a traditional Scherzo or Minuet, this miniature is very much the calm before the storm. It requires a delicate touch from the conductor and orchestra. I do not think of it as a prelude to the Finale and therefore do not make any connections from this movement to the next. Taking plenty of time after the Andante ends is always a good idea.

As usual, we can only guess at the speed Brahms wished for this piece given the *Un poco Allegretto e grazioso* indication. The word amiable comes to mind as to the character, so Allegretto seems appropriate, with a speed around ♩ = 84–92, for both the main body and the Trio section.

When you give the upbeat, it helps to feel the eighth-note pizzicatos in the cellos to find the tempo, which has to be steady; whatever flexibility or rubato you want to give the clarinet must fit into the pulse. Brahms had an affinity for five-bar phrases, and this is yet another example. We don't really feel it as such because he is such a master of disguise.

The pulse continues in the double basses, but it is also important to create a single line out of the accompaniment in the other strings. You can rehearse this separately. At **reh. A**, the composer has some fun with us by stretching the opening into a seven-bar phrase. Four bars before **reh. B**, he includes a rare triple *piano*.

Most of the time, the rhythmic passage at **reh. B** is played off the string. I have to disagree with that, although for most of my career, I, too, did it that way. Then, I thought about the marking, *dolce*. I suppose it is possible for this agitated part to be played sweetly, but the first time I had the strings do it on the string and at the tip, I knew that this had to be Brahms's intention. It's a little like playing it on the piano with the help of the pedal, particularly effective for highlighting the different dynamic shadings within the syncopations.

The dynamic four bars before **reh. C** is *forte*, something often ignored. The figure in the first violins and violas can be shaped with little hairpins here and there. It most certainly should not be played like an exercise. Another great harmonic shift occurs just before **reh. D**. Brahms takes us from E♭ major to B major with such ease that we hardly notice this unusual harmonic change.

A few conductors slow down for the Trio, but if you find the right tempo for the main portion, this is not necessary. Also, slowing down would interrupt the wonderful transition. There seems to be a discrepancy in the violin phrasing starting at **m. 85**. The horns are slurred, and the separate notes feel a bit contradictory. Opinions vary as to whether to do the same with the violins. All the sixteenth notes should be played on the string.

I know a little trick if your first violins have difficulty negotiating the first part of **m. 103**. Since almost everyone is playing the downbeat, add the upper B♭ to the seconds and place an eighth rest at the start for the first violins—problem solved. I have never heard this movement played without the repeat, but you might ask the horns and trumpets to place a little diminuendo at the first ending to make the transition smoother.

The second ending is another matter altogether. It can feel hasty and slightly aggressive. I have found that a slight *pesante* can work well here. However, it must stay at single *forte* for the brass, even coming down a little on the dotted quarter note so that the woodwinds can answer with something similar. Strong pizzicatos, still held back tempo-wise, work until the bar before **reh. E**, when I ease back to the opening tempo.

The principal reason for insisting on the same tempo for the start of the movement and the Trio becomes evident here, when both rhythms are in play at the same time. I see no harm in making the figuration at **m. 123** a quintuplet. In **m. 126**, make sure that the D♭ in the lower strings is audible against the E♭ in the horns, even though both are marked *pianissimo*.

You will know if your tempo choice is too fast when you arrive at **m. 138**. The sixteenth pizzicatos should not sound like a blur of sound. Also, the first violins need to be loud enough to emerge out of the winds' *forte*. In **m. 150**, the figuration should not sound like triplets. Brahms only wants us to slow down a little for two bars.

For the final nine measures, we get a two-against-three feeling, which can be obscured if your tempo is too quick. Four measures before the end of the movement, you can expand a little, but from there, you have to keep the triplet rhythm in your head, lest the tempo get too slow. I just subdivide the second beat at this point and then refer back to the ending of the first movement. Give a clear indication for the pizzicato and use your left hand to hold the winds and low strings before cutting them off. The walk in the park is over.

## Fourth Movement: Adagio; Più Andante; Allegro non troppo ma con brio

Technically the most difficult, the Finale is regarded as an ideal test for both conductors and orchestras. The somber and dramatic opening could easily be mistaken for a prelude to an opera Brahms never wrote. Even the most experienced orchestras need the leadership of the conductor to guide them through the various traps, be they rhythmic, harmonic, or structural.

I personally don't care for starting the fourth movement immediately; it lacks a thematic relationship with anything that has come before it and has a completely different mood. We might consider the third movement as a palate cleanser.

Ensure that you are physically and mentally prepared to begin. The orchestra needs to see the kind of mystery and intensity you will bring to these first three notes. Make sure that the contrabassoon knows you are aware that this instrument plays with the lower strings. I usually think of this first bar as being somewhat vague in terms of tempo. The indication is Adagio, but that can mean many things. Should we feel this in four or eight? We see on the page that the first note is not *pianissimo*, so it needs some heft. My suggestion is to give a silent downbeat, then cue in the instruments; an upbeat to a quarter rest will do you no good and possibly cause confusion.

Whether you choose eight or four, do not subdivide from the second bar onward. The violins' *forte-piano* can be slightly aggressive. It is not possible to get to the tip of the bow and create a shock because the musicians will run out of bow to continue the phrase in the same stroke. Starting up and then coming down on the *forte-piano* is the best solution.

The fourth and fifth bars present a conundrum. The violin notes are slurred, but if Brahms wanted them to last for a half note, he certainly could have written it that way. My preference is to slightly reattack the two repeated notes and add a small crescendo between them.

Every conductor has their own way of dealing with the pizzicato passage. If there is ultimate trust between the podium and the musicians, it is possible, but not advised, to stay in four. However, most conductors will do this in eight, perhaps starting *pianissimo* and a little slower than the main tempo, which has yet to be established. Balance is crucial in the four bars of stringendo, two with hairpins and two with a crescendo; the dialogue must sound like ominous footsteps.

The timpani downbeat in the sixth bar is a gentle attack, meant to start off the proceedings. The strings tend to rush during the first couple of bars. Try to keep in mind where you want the tempo to end up. It should not sound like a Tom and Jerry cartoon. If you go into four in **m. 10**, save room for the continued acceleration. At the *a tempo* indication, the speed of the quarter note should equal something close to that of the eighth note with which you started the movement.

Depending on the acoustics—or even if the hall is dry—let the D♭ chord settle in before cueing the woodwinds. Everything is now reduced, almost in half: just one bar of slurred/repeated notes, only two bars of stringendo, etc. Insert a very slight pause to let the sound of the final pizzicato die away and allow the string players to reset their bows for the arco two bars before **reh. A**. However, if you extend the pause too long, the tension will be lost.

At the *a tempo*, you can either stay in four for the first two beats or go into eight, but discreetly so as not to give away the ominous thirty-second notes. It is easy to get tangled up in terms of where your arms are, making it difficult to give a proper downbeat. When you give the final quarter of the pizzicatos, do not come all the way up, as you would with a traditional fourth beat. Try to end where the third beat was, allowing more space to give a visible upbeat.

Conduct in eight at **reh. A**. The tempo can also move ahead if you wish. This is very much a *Sturm und Drang* moment, and we must make the most of the restlessness. Brahms clearly was writing for a divided violin section, with the seconds to the conductor's right; that is the only way the passage at **m. 24** makes sense. Even then, while the conductor might hear equality between the sections, the listeners do not because the f-holes of the seconds are facing the opposite direction from the firsts.

This problem will come up in many pieces, and you have to decide if splitting up the violins to obtain a few effects is worth it. Later in this work, we will discover some passages where the massed violins really can make quite a difference. I wonder what Brahms would have thought if he had heard the string range from high to low across the stage?

All these quick notes must be played on the string for maximum power at the start, followed by a controlled diminuendo and very loud *subito forte*. But we still have to save something in terms of the volume. Three bars before **reh. B**, we are building up to the climax of this opening section. The next bar contains three syncopated *sforzandos*, each louder than the next; on the final one, the timpani shatters everything with a tremendous *fortissimo* roll. Right at this moment, shift into four, but since there is not much motion, all you really have to do is give a clear indication for the middle of the measure before **reh. B**.

Meanwhile, the timpani has switched from the tremolo to a measured group of twelve notes. When you arrive at this critical transition point, make eye contact with the drummer. In addition, the diminuendo must allow for audibility of the A♭ in the low instruments. I usually put in a slight crescendo to emphasize this change. At the double bar, the twelve-note grouping changes to six, implying that ♪ = ♩, but we also have a new indication of *Più Andante*. This is a marked difference from the Adagio of the introduction, but I think it is more about mood rather than speed. Just as you are about to give the signal for the timpanist to begin the measured notes, have the tempo of the new section firmly in mind and indicate it with your upbeat.

We are now somewhere in the mountains, and the Alphorns are singing away. This sound can be more aggressive than you would think, so a little bit of brassiness is allowed. The second horn has the difficult job of starting under the first but matching the tone so precisely that it sounds as if only one instrument were playing the whole passage.

The upper strings have the undulating rhythm of the timpani, and violinists frequently opt to play the two-note groups on one string. This is possible for many, but not all, of the figures. Instead, I suggest asking for the second note to be played on the next lower string whenever possible. This results in a very different sound, and while it requires some practice, it also helps avoid a potentially out-of-tune and harsh-sounding open string.

With all this going on, please do not forget that the trombones, who have not played one note in the entire symphony, make their first entrance. They will not need a cue, but a little glance their way is always welcome. The flutes take over the role of the shepherd, striving for the same balance that the horns achieved.

The strings have a difficult transition at **reh. C**. They have to get from arco to pizzicato with seemingly no time to do so. To avoid a frantic scramble and the possibility of a dropped bow, I have found it best to let the strings play the entire bar as is, with no ritard. Just hold on to the fourth beat a bit longer to allow them to play all the notes and get the pizzicato ready. So, the upbeat to **reh. C** is the cutoff for the orchestra. This also gives the winds a chance to catch their breath for the upcoming chorale.

Alternatively, if the violins and violas finish on an up bow, then they are immediately prepared for the pizzicato. And yet a different idea might be to consider letting just half the section play near the end and asking the remainder to prepare the pizzicato. If you wish, the double basses can drop to the low C in the middle of **m. 33** and then return to the printed note at **m. 38**.

If you gauge it just right, the balance between the bassoons and trombones can be magical. Clearly, the main line is in the first trombone, but that musician has not been anywhere near a high A until now. It is hard enough, so don't stare.

The remainder of the introduction proceeds apace, with no need for a ritard at the end. Brahms has already written that out for us with the rhythm in the timpani. There are two ways to begin the main body of the movement: You can either cut off the brass and timpani, with that constituting the preparatory beat for the next section, or you can wait a little before commencing after the cutoff.

What does *Allegro non troppo, ma con brio* mean? Beats me. Not too fast but with life? Brahms himself changed the tempo markings several times. You have to look ahead to understand. The *animato* at **reh. D**, one of several to come, is only indicated in the violin part, but it tells us that this great tune should not be hurried. I will refrain from suggesting a metronome mark because they can vary so wildly.

A nice, robust *mezzo forte* always feels about right for the melody. Here is one of the places where amassing the violins together creates a marvelous sound. Be aware that the half note to quarter in **m. 65** is reiterated. This should be somewhat exaggerated to allow the final note of the bar to appear as a pickup. I add a slur in the violins and violas on the half note going into **m. 73**. It gives the diminuendo a little more elegance, but unless you really believe in it, do not try it. To help justify this emendation, it is written that way for the winds four bars before **reh. D**.

The *animato* can be tricky to pull off if you try to do it as a *subito* tempo. I wonder why Brahms did not put that indication on the previous beat? Certainly, we need to be quicker here. Make an accelerando to **reh. D**, but don't overdo it, as there are lots of notes coming up.

We have another of those pesky controversies starting at **m. 97**. The strings have accents, and many conductors over the years have played these with a strong marcato. I can suggest another option, and it will come in handy later on. You can sustain the notes and still accent them. (This will become apparent in a few minutes.) Try to get the lower instruments to play as forcefully as possible from **m. 102** so that the rhythmic counterpoint with the others is clear.

As we have already seen, dots do not always mean off the string. Such is the case again at **m. 107**. All these notes should be marcato. Isn't it interesting that Brahms slurs the woodwinds' sixteenths but not the strings' sixteenths? A second *animato* follows at **m. 118**, and this is also a place where you can go into two beats per measure. How to phrase these next ten bars is up to you. Some conductors separate slightly before each group of eighth notes; others do not.

It is probably a good idea to go into four starting three bars after **reh. F**, but just for these two bars, because the next transition is difficult. The traditional approach, and one I observe, is to go back into two at **m. 132** and slightly delay the second note of the violas. In other words, insert a tiny *meno mosso* here.

For the sake of imitation, I alter the slurs in the cellos and basses at **m. 136** so that the quarter connects to the dotted half. At least to me, this seems logical as a counter to the oboes. Go back into four at **m. 142** but resist the urge to want to play this louder than *piano*. Let the buildup take care of itself.

I return to conducting in two at **m. 146**. At this point, you might be wondering, "Is it really a good idea to switch back and forth that often?" One of my key philosophies is that the way we appear physically must reflect how the music sounds. It also helps communicate more contrast. With that in mind, go back into four at **m. 156**, mostly to help the violas with each entrance. Sometimes you may need to remind them to start the first note from the string.

The accented quarters return at **m. 169**, and these really seem to be fuller when played as long notes. A little dynamic adjustment is needed at **m. 176** and in subsequent passages. The moving line is in the woodwinds and can be obscured, at least for the first few notes, by almost everyone else. I encourage you to start the second beat at *mezzo forte*, maximum, and then make a crescendo as the wind line moves upward.

I could write an entire chapter devoted to the next problem we are about to face. I am speaking again about accents, but these are different because we have no idea what they meant in Brahms's lifetime. In **m. 177**, you will find what looks like an exclamation point, sort of. Most definitions of this marking say that it represents *staccatissimo*, or the very shortest note possible. Well, if that is true, then why would Brahms put it over quarter notes? I have lost sleep over this. I have varied how they are played over the course of my career, all the while questioning what that indication really means. Maybe it means to emphasize sustained accents. I have taken that approach the last few times I have performed this symphony.

Perhaps something interesting, and I suspect controversial, can be done here. What if the strings play each of the notes down bow? This could be worth a try, at least in rehearsal—your call. Still, as the passage continues and the winds are added to the mix, I am not sure it is a good idea.

As with composers before him, Brahms plays around with the sonata-allegro form in the Finale. The fourth bar of **reh. H** almost has the feeling of a repeat following what might have been a first ending, but there are enough differences to tell us that this is not the case. Highlighting those helps us to understand that this is developmental material rather than a recapitulation.

The winds are the key element when the tune starts. Most everything is phrased in a similar manner as before, save for an important difference between **m. 197** and the corresponding passage at **m. 73**. This time, the score only indicates a diminuendo for a couple of instruments. Did Brahms really want a sustained *sforzando* here, or was this simply an accidental omission? Since this section contains significant alterations to the original statements of the material, I am inclined to think that he wanted the difference.

I can name a few moments in works by Brahms that I would have given anything to have written myself. One of them occurs three bars before **reh. I**, when the composer gives us one of the most incredible key transformations ever penned. Treat this transition from C major to E♭ major with love. A clever reintroduction of the pizzicato material from the introduction is another brilliant stroke of genius and helps us understand how Brahms is trying to distance himself from Beethoven.

Once more, we must decide how to get into the *animato* at **reh. K**. Whatever you did the first time must be repeated, as must all the other inflections you made earlier.

I would also like to draw your attention to an important feature worth trying. Beginning at **m. 234**, which of the quarters are connected to the phrase that has just occurred and which are pickups to the next one? Look at the first example, the last note of **m. 233**. On the page, it seems that this is just the end of the previous phrase. But doesn't it feel as if it is the upbeat to the next section? I usually play this seemingly isolated note a little stronger to make it function as a true pickup. I continue this strategy all the way through **m. 241**.

Also, take note of the different indications for the length of the quarter notes: the winds have dots on the quarters, but the strings just have accents. I actually think this works, even though it looks strange.

At **reh. L**, since the tempo has been well established, you can go back into two for a while. Continue the diminuendo right until the end of **m. 256**, as if the music were dying away. Then, wait for a brief moment before diving into the *forte*, and at which point you should go back into four.

Here we have one possible indication as to how long the quarters with accents are to be played. But this is only written in the bassoon part, which says marcato. Can it be applied to all the similar places in the entire symphony? Maybe, but factors such as ability, acoustics, and logic will inform any decisions.

Leading into **reh. M**, many conductors pull back the tempo slightly. Over the years, I have changed my mind about this, and staying in tempo is now my preferred method of presentation here. This is because I look ahead to **m. 279**, which certainly requires some time. If I hold back too soon, this effect is diminished.

Almost as far back as the time that valved horns became commonplace, conductors have asked the first two horns to continue the line established by the woodwinds at **reh. M**. This takes place over the first four measures, after which point they return to the printed material. The tension builds as we come to the syncopated figures at **m. 279**. Strong first and third beats are needed here, but back off the second and fourth, as you need to have the orchestra's full attention to set up what is to come.

When you arrive at the end of the bar before **reh. N**, freeze the fourth beat, as if a video were suddenly put on pause, before giving the silent downbeat. It is customary to broaden the tempo, but the shock is the silence itself. Moreover, the way you look when doing this is almost as important as the sound. Balance is difficult here because only the first violins have a melodic line. To keep the power of this diminished chord and still get the tune to carry through, I have the second violins play the same music as the firsts for four bars. This idea did not originate with me. Because the volume is so strong when this begins, not much is lost by eliminating the second violins' repeated notes, and if you wish, you can add those to the viola part.

The timpani triplets four bars later show us that we should not be too slow. However, you should keep the tempo steady once it starts. It might be a good idea for the timpanist to have choices of sticks available so that you can decide on the articulation and sonority. Hearing this G clearly is truly significant in the middle of **m. 290**, as the G now becomes a dissonance with the A♭ in the cellos.

At the calando indication, the bowing for the violas and cellos at first appears counterintuitive. Often, conductors will adjust and tie the eighth note to the dotted quarter for each of the next four bars. I have come to believe that playing it as written is quite wonderful and gives some unusual flavor to this passage. You can stretch out **m. 300** a little. When you feel that the diminuendo has reached the level you want, go back into two for the *animato*. The principles of beating and phrasing that we established for this material the first time all apply here as well.

From **reh. Q**, we begin the remarkable transition to the Coda. It is very possible to go into two from here, but you might want to consider conducting the first two bars in four, just to establish the pulse. Violas can be off the string, which should help keep the rhythm steady. Rehearse the various pyramids that create the chords with just those musicians moving from one note to the next to establish an even balance. I go so far as to introduce a slur into the cellos and basses at **m. 372**, connecting the two notes so that they are similar in intent to the winds.

Keep in mind that this buildup must start softly from **m. 375**. Violins are on the string, but the crescendos are gradual, with the *sforzandos* in the dynamic we have been playing. The climax of this crescendo does not occur until the indication *Più Allegro*. The stringendo itself is not easy to bring off.

I have found it helpful to rehearse the eight bars before *Più Allegro* with the different rhythmic groups separately. Start with the woodwinds, cellos, and basses. This is the easiest group to keep together as you accelerate. Next, rehearse the seconds and violas. You can do this one time without making the accelerando, just to reinforce that these two instrumental groups play the same music. Then, put these two parts together, without the rest of the orchestra. Add the first violins, still with no increase in tempo, and then play it a second time with the increase in speed. Now you can put the whole passage together.

One more obvious but important matter: Only in the final two bars do all the instruments play together rhythmically. If any musicians feel that they are not quite in sync, they will look to the conductor for a really strong downbeat two measures before the double bar.

How fast does this final section go? Much will depend on what you want to do with the chorale at **m. 407**. A nice touch is to have the cellos and basses play the four notes in the fourth measure all down bow. No matter what you do, the strings will always seem stronger in the back-and-forth with the winds a few bars later. Do the best you can, which usually entails having the strings drop down a little when the winds enter and then come back up each time they have the one-bar subject.

Should we slow down for the chorale at **m. 407**? For me, it is a matter of taste. I know that I will take a slightly faster tempo anyway for **m. 417**, so I only hold back slightly—noble, yes, but lugubrious, no. Many conductors alter the disposition of the notes in the brass, but the only one that makes sense is for the first trumpet to play the high A right at the start. Do not mess with the timpani part by adding notes and rolls; it is just fine as written.

Since **m. 413** brings the woodwinds back, but only at single *forte*, I ask the brass to give a little accent to this as well as the note two bars later. Then, I have them crescendo until the release, with the strings coming in full force. As mentioned, I usually push forward a little bit at **m. 419** but not so much that the quick notes are obscured.

Although I have not done this, others have: The second violins, to reinforce the firsts, can continue to play the same as their colleagues from **m. 425**, but obviously an octave lower. The timpani has a very dramatic moment that can be emphasized by adding a crescendo to the end of **m. 434** and **m. 438**. If you wish, you can introduce a slight delay of the entrance just after those two measures. Very short, punctuated chords lead to the stretch run.

Some dynamic adjustment might be needed to bring out the low woodwinds, bass trombone, cellos, and basses in their ascending arpeggio. As to whether to slow down for the last five bars, the thinking today is only to wait a moment before the last measure. It can be effective to play the second-to-last bar slightly longer.

The final question we have to answer is, "To sting or not to sting?" This is a term that comes up all the time, and it can apply to any instrument. In this case, it is about the timpani. The final roll can either simply end with the orchestra cutoff or, when that signal comes, the musician can give an attack for the conclusion. This can be either strong or gentle. It is akin to adding a period to a sentence.

Most certainly, we should not let the sound level decrease in this bar. The strings can take two bows, ending on an up bow, which not only sounds dramatic but looks good as well. This also generates an automatic feeling of crescendo, which is why a little button in the timpani seems fitting. We begin in ominous territory and conclude in victory, which of course does not belong to us but rather to Brahms himself.

## Conductor's Etiquette

When you return to the stage after the initial group bow, it is appropriate to acknowledge some of the solo players. In this symphony, the concertmaster gets the first one, followed by the oboe and then the horn. I usually do not give the timpanist any special attention here but have seen it done a couple of times.

\*\*\*

"Study Bach. There you will find everything."

—Johannes Brahms

## Notes

1. Johannes Brahms, *Symphony No. 1, Op. 68*, ed. Hans Gál (Leipzig: Breitkopf & Härtel, 1926-1927, Plate J.B. 1), https://imslp.org/wiki/Symphony_No.1,_Op.68_(Brahms,_Johannes).

2. Johannes Brahms, *Complete Symphonies in Full Orchestral Score*, ed. Hans Gal (New York: Dover Publications, 1974).

3. Christopher Dyment, *Conducting the Brahms Symphonies: From Brahms to Boult* (Woodbridge, Suffolk, UK: The Boydell Press, 2016).

# Antonín Dvořák: Symphony No. 9, "From the New World"

"It cannot be emphasized too strongly that art, as such, does not 'pay,' to use an American expression—at least, not in the beginning—and that the art that has to pay its own way is apt to become vitiated and cheap."

—Antonín Dvořák

Portrait of Antonín Dvořák, Public domain, via Wikimedia Commons

Familiarity breeds ennui. Due to the popularity of the final symphony by the Czech master, it often receives minimal rehearsal time. Nevertheless, conductors can make a myriad of discoveries upon close examination of the score.

Before approaching the actual music, I would like to consider a few questions that musicians have pondered ever since the work was premiered: "Is it American?" "Where did the tune in the slow movement come from?" "Why does the symphony end softly?" I will address these as we go through the work, but the first question needs some clarification.

Dvořák was invited to the United States in 1892 at the request of arts patron Jeanette Thurber, who was in the process of founding the National Conservatory in New York and needed a director. Dvořák's music had already found a foothold here, and he could not resist the opportunity to explore what must have seemed like a completely foreign musical world.

To his dismay, he discovered that American music, at least that which was described as "classical," was a rehashing of the styles and sounds prevalent in Europe. Since Dvořák had a keen interest in the folk music of his native Bohemia, he spent some time investigating the indigenous music of America.

"I am now satisfied," the composer said in an interview with the *New York Herald*, "that the future music of this country must be founded upon what are called the negro melodies. This must be the real foundation of any serious and original school of composition to be developed in the United States."[1]

Dvořák was easily the most prophetic of commentators when it came to identifying nationalistic styles. The impact of those words, as well as other comments, is finally being taken seriously, and more attention is now paid to composers of diverse backgrounds.

Over the course of more than three years, Dvořák wrote at least eleven works in the United States. Several are somewhat forgettable, but three masterpieces were created in that timespan: the String Quartet No. 12, "American"; the Cello Concerto; and, of course, the Ninth Symphony. But the question still lingers—are these works American or Czech, or possibly a combination of the two?

For the piece we will be focusing on, only one thing matters: It is simply called Symphony No. 9. The subtitle is "From the New World," as if it were a postcard being sent home. As with any work that utilizes the word "symphony," structure is the key, and the goal is to get from beginning to end in what should seem like a continuous line. We use every technical and expressive tool at our disposal to convey the moods and emotions of the piece.

It is helpful to study other works by Dvořák, particularly those in which his Czech nationalism is on display, such as the *Slavonic Dances* or the scherzos of previous symphonies. I had the good fortune to work on the Ninth Symphony with one of my teachers, the Czech-born and Czech-trained Walter Susskind. He offered insight into the performance traditions and traits found in the work. His guidance, coupled with the nearly two hundred performances of the symphony I have led over the years, has informed my thoughts on how to bring this extraordinary work to life.

Several editions of the "New World" Symphony have been published, but the basics remain pretty much the same. In 1955, the State Library in Prague issued what was then considered to be the authoritative version, and it is the copy that I still use.[2] However, the New York Philharmonic's digital archive contains the actual parts that were used for the premiere.[3] Although he did not conduct, Dvořák was on hand to supervise the proceedings. Recently, scholar Jonathan del Mar published an edition that incorporates his findings of discrepancies between the original and the revised.[4]

Early editions call the piece Symphony No. 5, reflecting the publishing order rather than the chronological sequence of composition. Most of the parts and scores contain rehearsal numbers as well as bar numbers. Both are helpful when rehearsing this piece.

The size of the orchestra is traditional for the late Romantic period, with woodwinds in pairs, other than the famous English horn solo in the second movement. The second flute also takes up the piccolo for four bars. Sometimes, the actual piccolo player for the orchestra will play this line and then assist in doubling the flute part on occasion.

The clarinets are in A for most of the piece, and bassoons are notated as usual. There are four horns, the first and second starting in E and the third and fourth playing in C. At the time the symphony was written, valveless instruments were still in use, and these transpositions were commonplace. At different points in the piece, the horns will be asked to switch to another key, although these days, of course, it is all done on the same instrument.

The two trumpets are in E but switch to C in the last movement. The first and second trombone parts are notated in alto clef. Most of the published parts retain this, but some rewrite them in bass and tenor clefs. The bass trombone and tuba are set out as usual. I should point out that at least one edition includes indications for the tuba to play passages in both the Scherzo and Finale.

The timpani will utilize many pitches, but there were no pedals for quick changes when the symphony was written. The timpanist will alternate between three drums.

The score is laid out in the traditional way, with woodwinds at the top, brass in the middle, followed by timpani, percussion, and finally the strings.

Each movement has an added instrument that did not play in the previous movements, and these instruments only appear in the list at the beginning of the movements in which they are utilized.

The Czech publication lists the timing of the movements, which total forty minutes. Of course, this depends on the conductor and whether the repeat in the first movement is observed. My performances tend to last closer to forty-three minutes.

## First Movement: Adagio; Allegro molto

With a marking of Adagio, we know it will begin slowly. In the original manuscript, Dvořák provided metronome indications as well, which are more than helpful for the opening of the work. While it is written in 4/8 time, the beat is in sixteenth notes at ♪ = 126, which seems too fast. The conductor's job is to try to get the feeling of four beats to the bar while showing eight. It is certainly permissible to give two preparatory gestures before commencing.

An unusual feature of this opening is the independent role of the double basses. While establishing the *pianissimo*, make sure that this line is audible.

The question of phrasing comes into play right away. Some conductors take a little breath before the second bar, while others aim for the longer line. It might depend on the capabilities of the woodwinds, who have the same phrase starting in the sixth bar. I prefer to connect the first three measures. The third bar presents an opportunity for a breath when the sixteenth notes commence. Even though dots appear on these sixteenths in the strings, there is no such indication for the low woodwinds when they enter, and therefore I recommend not playing them too short.

One of the most highly argued points in the score occurs in the fourth bar. Different editions notate the rhythm of the horns in two ways—the rest at the beginning of the measure is either a double-dotted eighth note or a sixteenth. The original manuscript indicates the former, so the thirty-second-note upbeat is just before the fifth beat from the conductor. This has been debated forever, and to some extent, you can decide what you think is best.

However, Dvořák does not indicate a dynamic for that upbeat, and although we have a *sforzando* indication on the main note, it is unclear if this is meant to be loud or just signifies a little accent. The overwhelming majority of conductors play it strongly and strive for as much diminuendo as possible, no matter which of the two options they have selected for the length of the note.

Once you give the cutoff for the horns, it is unnecessary to beat the remainder of the measure. Nevertheless, giving the flutes and oboes two preparatory beats can be helpful in securing this entrance. I remain in eight, but some conductors switch over to four. As with the low strings, the winds can either play the phrase in one breath or take a slight pause after the sixth bar. In either event, Dvořák adds a crescendo to deal with, leading to another *sforzando*. If you choose to interpret the phrase as one continuous line, you must decide on a dynamic at that point. This will affect the bassoon entrance, which must blend into the established texture.

The length of the note at **m. 9** is different from its counterpart in **m. 4**. After the cutoff, remain quite still. Do not give anything away by beating through the measure, as this prompts the audience to anticipate what is coming. Then, give a strong beat to elicit as much power as possible from the strings. In some editions, **m. 10** is also indicated as **reh. A**.

At this point, I slightly increase the tempo, primarily for dramatic reasons. Most timpanists will start around *forte* and make the indicated crescendo. The balance between the upper woodwinds and horns can be tricky, with the latter usually sounding more prominent. Taking them down to single *forte* is one solution, but you can decide this at rehearsal because you never know exactly what will happen. I recommend holding the quarter note for full value.

One of my favorite sudden dynamic changes in the entire repertoire occurs at **m. 13**. Each orchestra has its own way of playing a *forte-piano*, which can be interpreted as a quick diminuendo or a shocking, immediate drop. I prefer the latter here, as the preceding bars are full of *Sturm und Drang*. Ask the cellos and basses to pull the bow across the string very quickly, getting to the tip early. This is a spot where you want to startle the listener, always keeping in mind that some audience members are hearing the piece for the first time.

Conducted in eight, **m. 15** presents an interesting phrase structure. The first three notes of the upper woodwinds do not have dots, but all the remaining thirty-second notes do. Playing these early ones legato and then switching to something lighter creates a lovely effect. The key to achieving this is to emphasize the eighth notes in the basses. Slight separations between the notes and the addition of a little accent enhance the drama.

The next bar includes another contradiction in note length, with dots in the horns but not in the violas and cellos. Since it anticipates the melody of the Allegro, which gives no indication of short notes, I think this must be a long phrase. Therefore, do not add a separation before the *forte*. This idea will hold throughout the movement. Do, however, exaggerate the hairpin.

From my point of view, **m. 18** is just a single crescendo for the whole bar. Clearly, Dvořák must have meant for the crescendo to lead to the next measure, and the idea of a *subito forte* is not one I have ever heard from any conductor. The thirty-second notes played by most of the instruments are short, ensuring that the second violins and violas can be heard upon their entries. This is also the first time the trumpets and trombones play. Pay particular attention to the C♯ in the low instruments at **m. 20**.

In the next measure, Dvořák writes an interesting rhythmic figure that usually goes unheard. While everyone is playing a duple rhythm, the low horns, cellos, and basses have a triplet at the end of the bar that the crescendo tends to obscure. I change the last note of the horns to A♯ to match the other bass instruments. These notes should all be played quite marcato.

Along with the dispute about the horn rhythm in **m. 4**, an equally contentious set of opinions surrounds the timpani roll in **m. 22**. Some conductors reattack the two Bs and others make it one continuous sound. Since the trill indication is present and goes into the next bar as well, I think Dvořák wanted the syncopation, and therefore I do not have the timpanist play the note again.

Remember the *forte-piano* in the cellos and basses? Here it is again, but this time in the violins. They also go immediately to *pianissimo* and have a fast tremolo. Ask for a strong pull of the bow, starting at the frog and getting to the tip as quickly as possible. You do not need to conduct after this downbeat, but you should observe the length of the bar before getting to the Allegro.

Here, the metronome is ♩ = 136, slightly faster than the tempo you have been leading for most of the introduction. Generally, unless you exaggerate, it feels the same as that which has been heard earlier. The horns in C should play the four bars in one continuous line, setting up all the other times this pattern will occur. You can make a little crescendo in the upper strings going into the fourth bar. The pickup to m. 28 in the woodwinds is short, even though there is no indication of that.

I ask the first violins to play a bit *espressivo* for their sixteenth notes in **m. 31** and to put in the accent on the landing. Note the lack of a crescendo prior to **m. 39**. At this point, it can be helpful to look at the corresponding passage in the recapitulation. There are several differences, and you must decide whether the composer and publisher might have erred one way or the other. This moment, however, seems clear.

It would be nice to have an unlimited number of strings at **m. 39** to allow the winds and timpani to play *fortissimo* without fear of covering up their colleagues. Unfortunately, since that is most likely not the case, you will have to either ask the brass to play single *forte* or drop them down after the entrance. The strings should use full, long bows, making sure to connect the second bar to the next one.

Antonín Dvořák: Symphony No. 9, "From the New World"   117

The dynamic at **m. 47** is a *subito forte*, which I usually take down to *mezzo forte*. This makes sense, as the crescendo that comes four bars later arrives at *fortissimo* and is not *subito*. The unusual *sforzando* at **m. 53** puts the rhythmic structure out of whack in the lower strings.

Two bars before **reh. 1**, bringing out the moving line is important. Immediately after the downbeat, decrease the volume of those playing repeated eighths or sixteenths to *mezzo forte* but keep the rest at *fortissimo*. Then, just follow the crescendo indication.

Because the trombones also have the tune, they can play with the specified dynamics. I suppose an argument could be made for rearticulating the timpani in each bar, but that does not really make sense to me. However, I do suggest changing the notes for that instrument starting in **m. 67**; they should be the same as the bass trombone until **m. 73**. Purists will object, but many great maestros have made this alteration.

Right at **m. 73**, try to get the second violins to make a crescendo that lasts until the end of the bar. We also have a phrasing issue in the next measure that may need some clarity; it can be helpful to slightly separate the two B♮s and then the B♭s two bars later.

At **reh. 2**, the only instrument that plays *mezzo forte* is the first violin. However, I find it equally important to be able to hear the clarinet and bassoon clearly. It remains a mystery to me why Dvořák did not choose to have the bassoon play the phrase in full. In any event, by the time you get to **m. 80**, these two instruments now serve a melodic function.

Tradition has it that we slow down slightly one bar before **reh. 3**. You do not have to, but this music seems to want us to take time. Another debatable point concerns the dynamics in the flute and oboe, which have a *sforzando* on the first note of the second bar. Does it apply to just that note or the whole measure? I opt for the latter. Then, at **m. 95**, I bring out the clarinet to imbue this four-bar passage with another color.

The dynamic in **m. 99** is triple *piano*, and the second violins now have the tune. Dvořák writes a slur over the bar, so I do not separate the two B♭s this time, but you might consider asking them to rearticulate the second one on the same bow. Bring out the second flute and oboe on the note change. The cellos can play their pizzicato *non divisi* with open strings. In addition, they may choose to do this with just the left hand.

At **m. 107**, make sure that the lower strings clearly articulate all the notes, which can become muddy here. While the sound diminishes to *piano* in **m. 111**, the final note for the first violins must sustain until the end of the bar. Since the tempo is steady, it is certainly possible, even elegant, to go into one for a few bars beginning at **m. 115**. Balance the cellos' pizzicatos with the double basses' rhythm here.

Go back into two at **reh. 4**. The dynamic is only single *forte*, and Dvořák is quite clever here. He starts the diminuendo in the winds a bar before letting the strings decrease their volume. At **m. 125**, the violas should play the sextuplet off the string and quite short so that it can be heard clearly. Meanwhile, the woodwinds have a mordent that should be played on the beat.

Here is a nice bowing that Walter Susskind showed me when I studied the work with him: At **m. 129**, the violins start on an up bow for the first two notes, followed by a down bow on the second beat. Take the following bar as it comes, resulting in an up bow on the quarter note. Then, slur that into the next measure and do two up bows on the eighth notes. The elegance of this bowing is lovely and breaks the dramatic tension. Once you have established this phrasing, turn your attention to the triplets in the lower strings.

You will have to ask the violins to retake the down bow at **m. 133** to duplicate the way you played this passage the first time. The double basses have an independent line to start here and are joined by the bassoons a bar later. Although it isn't a melody, the counter line in the cellos is worth bringing out. I start the cellos' crescendo in **m. 137** at the beginning of the bar so that the G is clearly audible. This time, that triplet figure is just in the basses. If you are planning to relax the tempo at **reh. 5**, do not slow down until those triplets have concluded.

Usually, I find that the flute solo projects over the strings, but some conductors reduce the number of string players here. Note the rhythm in **m. 153**, which changes when this passage recurs in the recap. Even though a breath might be needed, this phrase should extend over eight bars. The violins imitate the flute, and to keep the longer line, I suggest this bowing: Play **m. 160** with a down bow. Slur this into the next bar, all on a down bow, to make the diminuendo even more effective. If you have slowed down for the flute solo, the place to get back to tempo begins at **m. 170** or possibly a few measures earlier.

Speaking of holding back during the flute solo, Dvořák does not indicate that we should do it, and some literal-minded conductors do not relax the tempo there. From my point of view, the contrast between the two themes is essential. Taking time gives you more flexibility, especially if you wish to ease up on the two eight notes in the third bar of **reh. 5** as well as the corresponding spot in the violin line.

When I first listened to this piece as a youngster, before I ever thought of being a conductor, almost every recording omitted the first-movement repeat. Today, it seems indispensable, not because the listener needs to be reminded of the material to be developed but rather because going straight into the second ending feels abrupt.

Moving along to the second ending, emphasize the cellos and basses here, sustaining the half note in the second bar. You might need to lower the violin and viola dynamic after the *sforzando* to help with the balance. I think Dvořák implies that the diminuendo that starts in **m. 189** is meant to continue until the horn solo. Bringing out the triplet rhythm in the clarinets adds a nice touch.

As you can see, the second flute is asked to switch to piccolo and play only four bars on that instrument. In some orchestras, this is considered doubling and entitles the musician to extra payment. To counter that, a few orchestras ask the designated piccolo player to do this short passage. The piccolo player then sits there for the rest of the piece, unless the first flute wants some relief, in which case the piccolo player puts down that instrument and takes up the flute. It feels a bit petty.

In **m. 201**, the main point of interest is in the oboes and not the violins. The cellos take over in **m. 203** with answers to the flute and oboe. A crescendo takes place, and therefore, the *forte-pianos* are played at varying dynamics. I suggest that the first violins play this passage on the string, which allows them to increase the volume more evenly. The trumpets should continue to crescendo through the measure leading into **reh. 7**.

The rhythmic figure in the double basses at **reh. 7** can be effective if you can somehow get it to be heard. As a reminder, **m. 217** is a four-bar phrase that should sound connected. I recommend sustaining the dotted eighth note in **m. 229**, advice that holds true for the instruments that have the same figure at **m. 233**. You can ask the strings to really dig in near the frog at **m. 236**.

To bolster the violin line that starts in **m. 241**, I suggest changing the bowing to two bows per bar. At **reh. 8**, the timpanist can make a slight crescendo in the second bar and then come back down in the next measure. The music at **m. 249** duplicates what came before it, so I change the violin bowing here as well. I also like to bring out the newly introduced timpani figuration.

At **m. 261**, the trombones have a *forte-piano*, which should not be too aggressive, followed by a four-bar diminuendo. Sometimes the conductor asks for a breath here; however, I prefer that the musicians connect through the chord change while slightly changing the color. The second and first violins will trade a short phrase, but to complement the dynamic in the trombones, the first violins should play more gently.

Balance issues can arise at **m. 269**. I am not sure why Dvořák assigned this passage to the second flute, but nonetheless, that musician must play with soloistic flair. Keep the strings down as much as possible and ask the basses to bring out the pizzicato. To gauge the crescendo that leads back into the recapitulation, some conductors double the flute and clarinet line four bars before **reh. 9**. You may only need to do this for two bars, if at all.

Most of the section before the Coda is the same as the first time around, but the composer creates some significant structural differences. Our first challenge is to try to get the flute and clarinet to come through clearly on the downbeat with those three notes. As previously pointed out, a crescendo leads into **m. 292**, which is not the case earlier.

Dvořák manages a clever shift by altering the key at **m. 296** and then writing the phrase four bars later as a seventh chord. He then has many options for how to proceed. During this transitional passage, I suggest that the low strings play the phrase legato to counter the bouncy musings of the violins and violas. Four bars later, these two ideas are switched; the upper strings play legato while the lower strings dance. Stay in tempo until this rhythm ends, and if you want to make a slight ritard, contain it to two bars before the flute solo.

Once again, the composer assigns an extended solo to the second flute, this time in the lower register of the instrument. To achieve balance, tell the strings that if they cannot hear the flute, then they are too loud. The pizzicatos in the double basses are important, particularly the second of the two notes.

Notice that, as opposed to the first time back at **reh. 3**, the flute does not have a *sforzando* in the second measure, and a lively counter line for the second horn begins at **m. 324**. From there until four bars before **reh. 13**, the music progresses much as it did earlier. Be aware of the rhythmic differences between **m. 378** and **m. 386**.

Two bars before the Coda, you can consider expanding the tempo, but to accomplish that, you must deal with the continual sixteenth notes in the upper strings. I tell them to simply add one or two, depending on how long I stretch this out. Balancing the trumpets and trombones is very important at **reh. 13**. When you arrive at **m. 408**, take the brass dynamic down to single *forte*. At **m. 412**, you can ask for a strong attack in the brass and timpani, but immediately go back to *forte*, possibly *mezzo forte*. Two bars later, the trumpets should exaggerate the accent on the reattack. Then, insert a crescendo to lead into **m. 416**.

Susskind showed me an interesting idea for the trumpets that I find very effective: Ask them to play the ascending notes in **m. 416** quite strongly and then drop back after the accent on the second beat. In the next measure, put in a crescendo, and then repeat this for the next three phrases.

The brass and timpani should come down to single *forte* at **m. 424**; ensure that they hold the notes for full value to contrast with what comes four bars later. The trumpets have an important *sforzando* at **m. 442**.

This next suggestion is a luxury but worth considering if you have the resources. When I was much younger, it was common to double the woodwinds in much of the repertoire from the Romantic era. This was not only to reinforce the loud moments but also to clarify places that might not be heard easily. I did not want to present this analysis with doubling in mind, but you can use it to spectacular effect for the trills at **m. 444**. At the same place, the trumpets have a complex rhythmic figure that is nice to hear.

To close out the movement, go straight ahead with no ritard or accelerando. The last three bars should sound equal. When the final chord is played, hold your position and ask the orchestra to do the same, if only for a couple of seconds. The silence creates tension and can also possibly prevent premature applause.

## Second Movement: Largo

In this most famous of musical works, mood is everything. It is arguably even more important than the tune. Establishing the temperament of this movement must start with the type of sound you achieve at the beginning.

The scoring for the introduction is marvelous. Dvořák introduces the tuba, which only plays a total of fourteen notes at the beginning and the end, all of which double the pitches in the bass trombone. Why would he do this? Remember that in the first movement, he utilizes the piccolo for just four bars. In the Finale, he assigns only one note to the cymbals. These brief additions tell us that the composer understands the value of color in orchestrating the work.

Starting this movement is one of the most difficult moments for any conductor. The tempo marking is Largo, ♩ = 52. Since it is very slow, the key is taking a breath. I am not only speaking about the winds but the conductor as well. Although it can be done, I advise against trying to do the four bars in one breath and recommend inserting a lift after the second bar.

You can try conducting two preparatory quarter-note beats, but it can be dangerous for ensemble if you convey any hesitation. I have found it works best to give two eighth-note indications and then go into four when the piece starts. However, you must give these with an air of calmness.

If you have the music on the stand during the performance, you might consider putting your baton down to conduct this movement, which requires very few angular gestures. Even if you are doing it from memory, you can discreetly slide the baton between the music and stand of the instrumentalists sitting to your right.

To get into the third bar, you must give a cutoff in the previous measure. This usually lasts for about an eighth note. Does that mean that the last half note of the second measure gets shortchanged? No. Hold on to it for the full length and make a slight ritard before starting the third measure.

The crescendo goes to single *forte*, but the timpani entrance is marked *fortissimo* in some editions. I underplay these dynamics to connote gentleness, asking the timpanist to use a soft mallet that takes the edge off the strong entrance. Some of you may opt for a more aggressive sound.

In the fifth bar, the muted strings can make their entrance while the brass are still playing. This creates a wonderful moment: as the winds conclude, the strings are already there. Give the bowed instruments a cue to enter but use your left hand to sustain the winds until the strings have come in (and they should do so with vibrato).

You will need to separate the two notes in the fifth bar, but what happens next is open to interpretation. The slurs going into **m. 6** normally tell us not to reattack the downbeat; however, there is a line over the note as well—clearly contradictory. I believe this is a matter of choice for the conductor, but these days, I tend to view the line as the defining matter here. In recent performances, I have reiterated the first note of **m. 6**.

Even though the dynamic is triple *piano*, you can still make a diminuendo on the dotted half note, simply because the strings will run out of bow. When you feel you have established the proper atmosphere, it is time for the English horn to sing. This instrument, unlike the piccolo in the first movement, cannot be played by the second oboist, as that musician has a separate part. The original intent was for the first oboe to take over the solo, but that does not happen today.

Compromise can be an important part of the music-making process. Here, the tempo you might have in mind may not be the same as that which the soloist imagines. Unless you meet for a few moments before the first rehearsal, you cannot know how fast or slow the English horn player wants to do this, but this tempo is critical because it represents the speed upon which all your decisions will be based.

You can be a little vague with your beat upon this entrance, waiting to learn what speed falls in the musician's comfort zone. It is possible that the soloist might stop and say, "That's a little too slow for me," or "Can we hold the tempo back." For the time being, just go with what the soloist proposes. You can meet during the rehearsal break and come to a mutual understanding.

This familiar melody can be phrased a couple of different ways. Certainly, the first two bars should be done in one breath, but it is also possible to extend the phrase over four bars. No matter which you do, there is a question of the breath at the end of **m. 10**. The English horn needs one, but should the strings also take it? This is a decision you will have to make on your own, but if you choose to insert one, do not take too much time.

The clarinets, who have changed to B♭, enter without upsetting the balance. However, balance issues can arise at the *forte* three bars before **reh. 1**, where the strings, even though they are muted, tend to overwhelm the climax of the English horn. Take a little breath just before **m. 18** and then again before **m. 19**.

Getting from **reh. 1** into the second bar must be accomplished smoothly. Connect the triplets in the cellos to those in the flutes, and continue the slur into the second bar, with the second flute reattacking the downbeat. As with the opening, two bars in one breath are in order here. Be sure to make a crescendo over the last two beats of the third measure.

The dynamic at which the music should culminate in **m. 25** will depend on your overall concept of the movement. It can certainly be done at a true *fortissimo*, but I prefer to keep the sound more *dolce*, including the brass entrance in the middle of the bar. This moment can be one of the most beautiful in the whole symphony if you observe the cutoffs carefully. The woodwinds stop, leaving the brass to make a diminuendo. I ask the brass and timpani to change their final note to a quarter, allowing the strings to sneak in as they did in **m. 5**.

At this point, I ask the strings to play *sul tasto* but with a bit of vibrato. Communicate to the violins that in **m. 27**, the cellos have two eighth notes and therefore a different rhythm. In **m. 30**, emphasize the syncopation in the second violins. I ask the strings to reduce their dynamic to create an echo in the next bar, just as another coloration. Then, I increase the volume and move the tempo ahead for the next two measures, slowing down again at the 2/4 bar. Bringing out the sustained F in the second violins lends a bit of dissonance to the passage.

Dvořák presents new material at **m. 42**, with the muted horns creating a distant ambiance. Before **reh. 2**, do not cut off the cellos and basses until the horn has played the sixteenth.

We now arrive at a remarkable sonic moment that requires great sensitivity. The solo flute and oboe play in the same register, and if you balance this passage correctly, you have essentially invented a new musical device: the floboe. Listeners should not be able to discern which instruments are playing. In **m. 52**, I ask the two soloists to play the quintuplet at the same speed as the sixteenths that begin the bar so that the notes do not sound rushed.

Transitioning to the *Poco meno mosso* tempo works well if the cellos do not make too large a diminuendo when they take over the triplets from the violas. The metronome mark shows that this section is a little faster than the opening. The almost jazzlike walking bass line stabilizes the tempo, while the first violins have a figuration akin to something you might hear from a cimbalom. I usually ask them to place a subtle tenuto on the first note, each time, for emphasis. Make eye contact with the second violins for the two pizzicatos in **m. 58**.

Some editions have a diminuendo for the winds at **m. 60**, but the source material does not, so the *subito piano* in the next bar should be dramatic. Pay attention to the first violins in the bar before **reh. 3**. I take out the diminuendo written in this bar and add a little crescendo on the last four notes. You do not need to speed up or slow down; just catch the top note and settle into the same tempo you established at **reh. 2**.

Once the section at **reh. 3** commences, all usually proceeds without incident until **m. 72**. The dynamic is clear, but the diminuendo is rarely observed because of the *forte-piano* in the next bar. I insert a quick crescendo in its place and a portamento between the B♯ and the F♯.

In the bar before the *Meno*, I take a slight breath with the first violins after the first beat, almost as if the ensuing notes were a pickup to the *Meno* itself. At this point, I recommend that you pay particular attention to the offbeat pizzicatos in the second violins. At **m. 82**, you can ask the cellos to play a bit louder from the second eighth note; the first violins can breathe before the two eighth notes at the end of the bar.

For the continuing calm, I insert a slight hairpin in the strings in **m. 87** and a diminuendo in the next bar. One measure before **reh. 4**, you can take some time on the triplet and ask the upper line of the violas to make a small crescendo to shift the minor key to major. Let the sound fade away and begin with the oboe, conducting in eight.

Here we have a series of canons in which one group starts off and gets imitated by other instruments, in this case over six bars. Try to balance these so that they are heard equally throughout. Recently, and against what is written, I have begun to have the clarinets play short sextuplets, as the oboe does in the previous measure. The word *leggiero* appears here, and this seems to contradict the slurs. Often, the final canon in the cellos and basses can get overwhelmed by the violins playing in a much higher register.

The loud climax of the movement is at **m. 96**. Some conductors will make a slight ritard here, but I prefer to go into four for the second half of **m. 96** and then stay in four, in tempo, until the ritard that leads into **reh. 5**.

The double bar presents a real problem if played as written because the composer includes an instruction for the strings to reduce to just four players starting on the downbeat. If we take this literally, there is no resolution, harmonically, for the rest of the section. My solution is to have everyone play these notes—but just for the length of a quarter note and with a continued diminuendo—and then fade away, leaving the small group as a result.

Take note that the clarinets are changing back to the instruments in B♭, and the trumpets are hanging on through the start of the third beat. The strings further reduce to duets at **m. 105**. The second violins should slightly separate their notes, or at least give a little push on each one. Since this passage only involves a few players, all of whom are in front of you, your beat can be small here.

The bars that contain fermatas can be tricky in terms of the second-violin cutoffs. I prefer to hang on to these notes and make sure that all the musicians are in contact with each other to better coordinate the phrase endings.

As far as where to place the beat, your fourth beat in **m. 107** should be angled somewhat downward so that you have room to give a true upbeat. In the next bar, stop your motion in the middle, in between what would normally be your second and third beats. Again, this is to ensure that you have enough space to give the pickup to the next measure. Sustain that last note in **m. 108** for its full value. The pattern for the third fermata bar is similar to **m. 107**.

The three solo instrumentalists at **m. 110** can play a little louder than the indicated *pianissimo*. The viola's long D♭ is important and should balance equally with the melodic lines.

The full string sections return in **m. 111**, but the question is, should it sound like they have suddenly entered, or should they come in discreetly? I favor the latter, and I accomplish this by asking the solo instruments to make a slight crescendo at the end of their phrase. Meanwhile, the other instruments come in softly. With any luck, the audience will not perceive it as an intrusion.

Until the *a tempo*, you must continue to beat minimally. Specifically, when you get to **m. 117**, use your right hand to cut off the winds and conduct the next three bars with only the left. The two mordents should be played slowly and before the beat.

I continue the diminuendo right through the ritardando, with each note marginally softer than the preceding one. Just as at the start of the movement, I give two beats of preparation for the brass and bassoon entrance. In other words, the last note in the first violins will already be in the opening tempo. If I feel like making a more significant ritard, I might give the indication for the violin note and then a separate seven/eight for the next passage.

The crescendo that starts at the midpoint of **m. 121** should only go to single *forte*. This is really a gentle dynamic, reflective of what has occurred previously. All the brass, bassoons, and timpani (whose *sforzando* clearly is in relation to the other instruments) should reduce their volume right away to allow the cellos to come through.

When contemplating a bowing, sometimes it is more helpful to look at where you want to wind up rather than how you start. Certainly, the triple *pianissimo* would benefit from a down bow, thereby making the bar before it an up bow. However, playing the seven eighth notes in one bow can sound pinched and unexpressive. I prefer that the violins take two bows in this bar, but I stagger the change to preserve the long line. I ask all the violins to start down bow, with the outside players slurring the first four notes and the inside players slurring the first three before changing direction. Meanwhile, make sure that you indicate a breath for the entrance of the two flutes. Everyone cuts off together, and you can wait a bit before turning to the double basses.

Here we have a divisi problem, depending on how many basses you have available to you. With the minimum number of four players, the division is straightforward. If you have five, I suggest the extra player take the higher $D^\flat$. With six musicians, bolster the middle two notes, and with seven, the top three, asking the person playing the low $D^\flat$ to be louder. If you have eight bassists, I recommend that you assign each stand the same note because this is better for intonation.

The final note can be even more effective with this little nuance: Ask the basses to start with some vibrato. Then, as you indicate a diminuendo, they should stop vibrating while softly sustaining the note. However, they should not all discontinue the vibrato at the same time. It really does work.

Maintain the silence by keeping very still and only move a few seconds later, as if the note were still lingering. Take plenty of time before continuing with the symphony. As Victor Borge put it, "People who have never coughed in their lives will do so here."

### Third Movement: Molto vivace

Dvořák commonly replaced the traditional Minuet or Scherzo movement with a rhythmic dance known as a Furiant. This is a quick piece in 3/4 time and characterized by hemiolas, which combine two consecutive bars and place the accents on every other beat. One wag pointed out that since this is Dvořák, they should be called Bohemiolas.

## Antonín Dvořák: Symphony No. 9, "From the New World" 127

With an indication of *Molto vivace*, $\dot{\phantom{o}}$. = 80, it is indeed quite fast and furious. The conductor has the option to show one beat to the bar or shape it as a four-bar phrase; the orchestra will not get confused. Dvořák adds a prominent part for the triangle in this movement, emulating Brahms, who inserted the instrument in the third movement of his Fourth Symphony. Right from the start, the triangle must be loud and disruptive.

The woodwinds begin with short unison notes and a figuration that will dominate the movement, with the horns joining in on the second eighth note. I wonder why Dvořák didn't just have the horns play the whole phrase, but it does give the other winds the chance to play clearly on the downbeat.

Traditionally, in **m. 5**, the basses are asked to take a down bow and then another in the following measure. However, that creates a hole, so I have them play the solo figure as it comes and then connect the bars with no break. I ask the violas to do the same, starting with an up bow. In this way, both instrumental groups will be in a better position to make a crescendo into the *sforzando* of **m. 8**.

Give a very clearly punctuated downbeat in the following bar for the benefit of the first violins and cellos. These repeated notes should be played off the string but not so far off that they are not together. The woodwind canon that begins at **m. 13** usually balances well, but make sure you note that the second flute is playing. Few mistakes are as embarrassing as giving a cue to the wrong musician.

The pattern changes ever so slightly in **m. 20** for the first violins. Since it breaks the sequence, you might want to bring it out. Before **m. 21**, the violas will need time to get into position for the pizzicato of the next bar. At this point, the counter line in the seconds can come to the fore, as we have had plenty of time to digest the main theme. The timpani should be played with relatively hard sticks throughout the first part of the movement.

I should also note that the clarinets have *sforzando*s on each of their dotted halves, but Dvořák does not indicate a dynamic. They must be loud enough to be heard clearly, especially at **m. 24** and **m. 28**. You can help the violas' pizzicatos to project by asking them to pluck the second note a bit louder than the first. This is often the case when pizzicatos are written in octaves and the second note is lower.

A sudden change in dynamics occurs at **m. 29**, followed by a very big crescendo in the strings, who continue to use spiccato bowing. The hard sticks of the timpani can make quite an impression at **m. 33**; however, be careful that the strings do not rush the two preceding bars and that the timpani stays in tempo for these intrusions. For the *fortissimo*, all instruments should play on the rough side, near the frog and off the string.

Balance problems arise at **m. 41**. The tune in the first violins is answered by the upper woodwinds a bar later. The horns have the hemiola, but interestingly, delayed by a beat. The conductor must grab their attention to prevent them from entering late and getting behind the other instruments. I know that some conductors have all the woodwinds play just the upper octave to balance them with the strings. I have never tried it but perhaps might one day, just to see if it works.

The balance issues get more complicated at **reh. 1**. Now the tune is in the lower instruments, which do not have the power to cut through the shrill tones of some of the other voices. I find it interesting to place an accent on the A in the second violins and violas in **m. 2** and to bring out their notes in the next bar. Since it serves the function of a Scherzo, the repeat is mandatory.

The transition to the *Poco sostenuto* presents some problems. I don't think I have ever heard, even in my own performances, the indicated dynamics in the first violins at **m. 60**. It might be effective to play the two eighth notes *forte* followed by a *subito piano*. The overriding question is whether we make a ritard going into that next section or suddenly shift the tempo.

To me, changing the pulse that the middle strings establish at **m. 64** feels abrupt and out of character. Like many other conductors, I move the *Poco sostenuto* back four bars and just hold back very slightly. If you listen to some older recordings, you will discover that they often played this rhythmic figure as if the first note were a sixteenth note instead of an eighth. This does not occur very frequently these days, but we still play the first note with a little emphasis.

If they are comfortable with it, the flute and oboe should try to do the eight-bar phrase in one breath. The same goes for the clarinets, but the high notes can present some intonation problems. Because the first is in the stratosphere, it is not necessary for the musician to play loudly. Don't forget about the triangle.

At **m. 84**, you will have to decide how strong the *sforzando* should be in the accompanying strings. How is it different from the *forte-piano* that appears four bars later? My preference is to play the latter as an echo of the first phrase, so the accent is gentle. The winds should also reduce their dynamics.

Depending on your tempo of choice, it might be preferable to go into three for the passage at **m. 92**. If the horn is seated near the woodwinds, you could opt to stay in one, but I have found that letting the orchestra see the difference makes the sudden transition to the opening tempo at **reh. 2** feel a bit more natural.

Isn't it interesting that Dvořák does not have the basses playing on the downbeat here? Perhaps his aim is to allow a smoother transition from pizzicato to arco. To make sure it sounds purposeful, I place a very slight accent on the E. As with most passages that have soft, quick, staccato notes, staying close to the string is paramount to ensure ensemble. If you find yourself a little too slow at **reh. 2**, use the time starting at **m. 113** to make an accelerando, being careful not to overdo it.

Build this long crescendo carefully to ensure that the triple *forte* really is the climax. The third and fourth horns almost always try to steal the show four bars before **reh. 3**, but the bassoons and low strings have the same passage. It can be helpful to rehearse these instruments separately. Be careful that the timpani does not overwhelm the proceedings.

Speaking of the horns and bass instruments, the musicians will have to drop down after an accent on the downbeat at the double bar. The first and second horns are the only instruments at **reh. 3** that have a contrasting rhythm, so try to amplify this.

Several interpretive possibilities exist at **m. 138**, four bars before the Trio. We don't know what dynamic Dvořák intended, so the diminuendo can be exaggerated or just slight. I have even heard performances in which the conductor kept the whole phrase loud. The violins can retake the down bow in the third measure, especially if you interpret the diminuendo literally, or you can ask them to change bow somewhere in the second bar if you prefer to keep the intensity.

The first twelve bars of the Trio are an extended diminuendo and, as such, each entry needs to be softer than the previous one. Since it starts with only flute and two oboes, the timpani must blend in, accenting the entrance only as much as needed. All the strings should play spiccato.

The bar before **reh. 4** can be done one of two ways: The first choice is to consider that the cello notes lead to the downbeat and mimic the pattern all the other instruments have played to this point. The other option, and one I prefer, is to take a little breath before starting the legato phrase, stopping the beat for a moment before continuing. To my ear, this helps differentiate the short notes from the upcoming long phrases. You have to rehearse it with the cellos alone a couple of times.

A very interesting group of three notes passes from one instrument to the other. If we assume that the fifth bar of **reh. 4** is the start of an eight-measure phrase, then the implied harmonic structure is divided as three bars followed by five. However, it can also be thought of as 3 + 2 + 3. There are other combinations as well. No matter how you choose to think of it, make sure you are aware of who is playing, especially when reading through the piece.

We confront another famous dilemma just before the double bar. Actually, we have several decisions to make, the first of which is the tempo. Should this main portion of the Trio be slower than the bulk of the Scherzo? Tradition dictates that it should, but times have changed. More and more conductors adhere to staying in the same tempo, with no ritardando preceding it. I personally think a hint of relaxation is needed, especially if you take the earlier portion at a good clip.

What has really changed over the years is how we tackle the "long and short" of it. Let me explain. To achieve a more dancelike feeling, conductors of the past would play the passage starting at the double bar with crisp articulation, including the upbeat. But those examining the score would argue that this is incorrect. The endings of the two-bar phrases hold a key for us. Notice the eighth-note rest in the first two measures and the lack of a rest in the similar rhythmic passage at **m. 180**. I think a nice compromise is to play the opening phrase lightly and then the next phrase *espressivo*.

An exchange between the low strings and timpani underpins this passage. It doesn't hurt to rehearse this interplay once, as even the most experienced orchestras often do not know that it is going on. As far as the triangle is concerned, I believe that the opening salvos and those throughout the Scherzo should be played on a full-sized instrument. For this delicate passage in the Trio, a smaller triangle with a very light metal stick works well.

The repeat is mandatory and should be played the same as it was the first time around. When you arrive at the second ending, you must make another decision. Is the last note a pickup to **reh. 5** or just the conclusion of the previous phrase? The dot over that note seems to indicate that it is part of what comes next, even though it does not appear just before the repeat sign. That is the opinion of most conductors, who also play it at the *mezzo forte* dynamic indicated in the following bar.

In fact, most of my colleagues go up to *forte* for the passage, probably to create more contrast for the *subito piano*. You can do the same thing with the woodwinds instead of having them play all eight bars at the same dynamic. The trills should be fast and last as long as possible, almost connecting to the next note. Although it would seem logical to have the violas and cellos perform the triplets spiccato at **m. 201**, I think it is better to play them on the string at the tip of the bow.

The first violin figure at **m. 209** is sometimes played with a "Viennese" lift. In other words, the first beat is slightly rushed, and the other two beats are held back. It certainly works if it is not exaggerated, but the other string instruments need to be made aware of this so that they do not come in early on the second or third beat. At **m. 216**, you can either have the orchestra play the printed dynamics, or you can start a bit louder and make a diminuendo over eight bars. Please note that the clarinets change from long notes to a sextuplet.

Remember the alternating phrasing at the double bar? Starting at **m. 224**, Dvořák presents basically the same material, but this time, he always includes a rest at the end. What to do? Should we perform it as we did earlier or observe the printed text? I will leave this one up to you. Build the crescendo and take the repeat, where everything should proceed in a manner similar to the first time.

The transition back to the Scherzo sometimes produces a little chaos at the initial rehearsal. We have gotten used to four-bar phrases, but **reh. 6** is only a two-bar phrase, and then the seconds and violas change notes. At first reading, some musicians will assume otherwise. I put a small accent in the lower line of the violas to make sure that this critical difference is heard clearly.

If you have chosen to do the Trio at a relaxed pace, use the last five bars before the D.C. to get back to the opening tempo. Everything is played as it was before, minus the repeat. I suppose you could consider having another go at the opening material, but it does not seem necessary.

The Coda begins quite dramatically. I make a cutoff in the violins before commencing and also extend the beat to increase the tension. All the strings should start playing as powerfully as possible and make the three-bar diminuendo. Just like in the first movement, the motif in the horns should be played in one breath as a four-bar phrase.

The dynamic at **m. 261** is most likely a reminder and not any kind of new shading other than a change of key. Be careful that the tremolo does not overtake the woodwinds before **m. 269**. Sometimes conductors will double the second phrase to address this imbalance. Dvořák is quite helpful at **reh. 7**, marking the strings *piano* and the woodwinds *forte*. Note that the high point is the triple *forte* at **m. 281** and not four bars earlier. Continue to make a crescendo to get the most powerful sound you can.

It is usually necessary to bring down the brass and timpani just after the downbeat at **m. 281**. You can only decide by how much at the rehearsals that take place in the hall where the performance will be. Treat the trumpets and violins equally in terms of balance during the long diminuendo that takes us to **m. 293**.

This is the spot that we all hate. Unless the orchestra has done the "New World" frequently, the violas truly have difficulty with the changes of rhythm in each successive bar. You should expect to rehearse this with them a few times.

Here is what I do: I eliminate the violas' last two sixteenths in the measure before the eighth notes start to ensure a clean attack in the next measure. This is usually enough time to get them to the middle of the bow, where they must stay until the end. The two bars of eighths are usually no problem, but the quintuplets always seem slow, and the next two bars slower yet.

One solution at rehearsal is to work the passage backwards, starting with the four quarter notes at the end. Then, go back one bar to the quadruplet and continue to the triplets, and so forth and so on, until everyone gets a feeling for how fast the notes are played in tempo. Then, as the icing on the cake, try it once without conducting, forcing the section to proceed by listening to each other. This sounds laborious, but it is worth it. In the meantime, don't ignore the first violins, cellos, and double basses.

The final note can be either long or short. If the latter, the middle strings will have to play divisi for the whole chord to sound. I opt for a broader note, kind of like a sigh of relief that the violas got through the passage. There is no need to go *attacca* into the Finale.

## Fourth Movement: Allegro con fuoco

Have any of you ever wondered if the opening of this movement was the inspiration for the shark motif in *Jaws*?

The tempo indication is spot on with *Allegro con fuoco*. However, with a metronome marking of ♩ = 152, we might be entering dangerous territory. Ferociousness does not have to mean fast and furious at the same time. I usually ask the strings to make a crescendo into the second note of the group, which can sound weak in comparison to the B. It is possible to conduct the opening in two, but you get a stronger syncopation on that second note if you beat in four.

Each string section has a different rhythm in the fourth bar, so it should almost sound like a continuous series of sixteenth notes. In reality, it never does, due to the slur in the first violins. Sometimes conductors decrease the dynamic a little to get a more forceful crescendo here. At **m. 8**, Dvořák gives us that opportunity himself, indicating a level of single *forte*. To heighten the effect of the crescendo in **m. 9**, the longer notes and trills should begin about *mezzo forte*, with the eighth notes accentuated.

Having already established the tempo, I usually go into two at **m. 10**, which does not present any problems with ensemble. All the quarter notes need to exude a degree of nobility, so I recommend sustaining them, especially on the third beat of **m. 21**. At the next double *forte* indication, I prefer marcato articulation rather than off-the-string bowing. While probably unintentional, Dvořák imbues **mm. 29–30** with a hint of his Cello Concerto.

Stay in two at **reh. 1**, where the brass play a noble *fortissimo*. In the seconds and violas, an implied diminuendo follows each crescendo, but in the third bar, each four-note group should have its own crescendo. The timpani's grace note is played just before the beat. Be aware that sometimes the two trumpet eighth notes in **m. 39** can overwhelm the quicker notes of the other instruments.

Two bars before **reh. 2**, I drop the brass and timpani dynamic to *subito forte* and only crescendo in the following bar. At **reh. 2**, you have the option of letting the violins play either on or off the string. My preference is for the former, as it lends more power to the notes and presents more phrasing options. Rehearsing the musicians who play just the eighth notes can be helpful to establish the three-against-two motion that occurs here.

Among the subjects I have not dealt with yet in this essay is doubling. Most orchestras today are larger than those from the Classical and Romantic eras. As the size of the ensembles as well as the halls increased, many passages in the woodwinds became obscured by the numbers of string players. Since many orchestras were offshoots of opera house bands, there were enough musicians who could be utilized to reinforce the sound.

These days, orchestras perform most of the standard repertoire with just one player per part. However, an additional member of a section commonly sits onstage to spell the principal occasionally and to play along during louder passages. In long works, this can be especially helpful. I remember being shocked when I attended Carlos Kleiber's debut with the Chicago Symphony Orchestra back in 1978. For Beethoven's Fifth Symphony, he had six horns and four trumpets, and he doubled all the woodwinds, including the piccolo. It did make a glorious sound, though.

I bring this up now because much of the first several pages of this last movement can benefit from discreet doubling. For example, look at the bassoon part at **reh. 2**. The audience never hears these longer notes, and perhaps they might if four instruments play them instead of just two. (At the end of this chapter, I will tell you about an option for the final note utilizing the doubling instruments.)

At **m. 50**, the first-violin note is a response to those who play the downbeat and should not sound isolated from the overall texture. Throughout the section that started at **reh. 2**, you must make a real distinction between the triplets and the dotted eighth followed by a sixteenth note. All too often, the whole passage can sound like a 12/8, an outcome you should avoid. As a general rule, when this rhythm occurs in conjunction with a dot on the sixteenth, you should separate that note from the previous one. This comes up a lot in Shostakovich's works.

You would think that the lone note for the cymbals would not warrant much discussion. It is usually played by the percussionist who did the honors with the triangle in the Scherzo. Yet this single note can be performed several ways. The indication *soli* implies a pair of cymbals, but some conductors opt for just one suspended cymbal played with a soft stick. Others use a triangle beater or a coin to brush the cymbal gently. My preference is to use two, but instead of clashing them, I ask the percussionist to scrape them at the edges.

Three bars before **reh. 3** is a good place to go into two if you went back into four at **reh. 2**, and tradition has it that we slow down a little for the clarinet solo. Feel free to introduce some rubato when shaping the long lines presented here. The cello interruptions often include a slight diminuendo on the last two eighth notes, but I like the effect of carrying the crescendo all the way through to the end. The tremolos should almost be inaudible.

Notice that the cello rhythms appear to change as this passage goes along. I don't understand the articulation at **m. 82**, as it seems totally out of place with the gestures that have been occurring. I treat this one the same as the previous examples and add slurs so that they all look and sound alike.

If you have slowed down a bit for the clarinet, clearly you must get back to the initial tempo by **reh. 4**. I start moving forward at **m. 84**. It is also a nice touch to have the cellos and basses play a long quarter note in the next bar. To emphasize that, I go back into four for the last two measures before **reh. 4**.

To hear the tune at **reh. 4** requires either reducing the dynamics significantly or taking drastic measures. I ask the orchestra librarian to put the first-violin line into the second-violin part for these eight bars, thereby doubling the number of musicians playing this passage. If your heart is set on having all the sixteenth notes present, you can shift the upper note from the second violins to the violas, creating a three-part divisi.

As a side note, I once heard a conductor change the trumpets' key from E to C. It was jarring, and the second bar of the phrase was simply incompatible. I do not recommend it.

A lot is going on at **m. 100**. I suggest rehearsing the trombones, cellos, and basses separately to secure the ensemble and give this an almost jazzlike feel. The upper strings have a nearly impossible articulation task at **m. 106** as written: marcato. Did Dvořák expect the notes without dots to be long? If not, how are they different from the marcato marking? Most conductors ask for this all to be played off the string.

The bassoon line that begins in **m. 114** needs to be audible and probably at *mezzo forte*. To achieve a lovely triple *piano* at **reh. 5**, I opt to alter the bowing two bars earlier. Try doing **m. 120** in two bows and then the following measure with a single bow to get the violins to the tip for the tremolo.

At this point, pay attention to the balance between the woodwinds and pizzicato strings. When the basses have their turn, you can start stronger and have everyone drop down even further with as much fadeout as possible. The length of the bassoon quarter notes is an open question in **mm. 122–23**. I play them as indicated, contrasting with the cellos' pizzicatos.

The trills in the flutes and oboes should connect to the next note. While it is possible to stop them, that choice feels abrupt to me. Throughout this section, the horns are best served by playing at single *forte* rather than forcing the sound. A very quick *forte-piano* happens at **reh. 6**, where the low strings grumble the tune. In the second measure, there almost always seems to be a problem coordinating the first note in the violins. Make sure they play the first one from the string and not off the string. Continue the staccato throughout.

The passage at **m. 152** often rushes at the end, and one possible solution is to ask the first violins to add a G on the second beat of **m. 153**. Starting in **m. 156**, the woodwinds should play the whole phrase in one breath. Although the violas are off the string, the first violins and lower strings should play on the string and lightheartedly. Try to achieve a *subito pianissimo* at **m. 160** with a *non espressivo* tone in the winds. Do the same at **m. 166**, with the woodwinds back at single *piano*, followed by *pianissimo*.

At **reh. 7**, the horns imitate what the trombones played back at **m. 100**, and these notes should be played at full length. The figures at **m. 170** are slightly different than those two bars later. I think this contrast is important, and the change of character must be honored. The violins sneak in with a scalelike passage and are followed by the brass playing vehemently.

Earlier editions of the symphony present different phrasing for the cellos and basses beginning at **m. 184**. We now know that this is not to be played marcato but almost legato, with a heavier presence. Dvořák reduces the woodwind dynamics at **m. 196** to single *forte*. We must be careful about the levels when the violins begin their descending scales. In the brass, an accent and then a slight decrescendo in each bar work well.

At **m. 208**, the trombones can take care of themselves. Start thinking about how to be as clear as possible for the upcoming rhythmic variation. When we arrive at **reh. 9**, the acoustics in the hall come into play. The music prior to that is quite loud, and this *Poco meno mosso* is soft. To hear the entrance clearly, you have to wait a moment before giving the downbeat here. Correspondingly, the fourth beat of the previous measure should not come all the way up so that you have room to give another upbeat.

The violas play the third bar of **m. 9** on the string. I start the second group of sixteenths *mezzo forte* to match the first one. The third set can be done the same way, but Dvořák specifies that this one is softer. The cellos and basses should also play on the string and clearly enough to be heard. Everyone continues to get softer and softer.

We have to get back to the *a tempo* at the double bar. While I suppose this can be done *subito*, it feels more natural to move forward during the two previous measures. Do, however, try to get very clearly delineated notes in the basses. I shift into two at **m. 226**.

The double basses' pizzicatos are very important and probably need to be marked up a dynamic. The cellos sing out, but the phrase starting at the pickup to **m. 235** should be less *espressivo*. Sometimes conductors will very slightly stretch out the A octaves at **m. 238**. Starting at **m. 243**, we have a reversal of sorts from what occurred at **m. 84**. The last note of the triplets is now short instead of long, and instead of a crescendo to a boisterous moment, the music relaxes and gets softer before **reh. 10**. To set up the next tempo, I return to beating in four before the *Un poco sostenuto* indication.

The violas should be a little more prominent than the cellos in the third bar here. Dvořák knew that the bassoon would be covered up if he wrote it as softly as the other instruments at **m. 259**, so he rightfully makes it *mezzo forte*. At **m. 263**, the line divides between the two bassoons, and we need to help them project by assigning them a stronger dynamic.

Some horn players fear this next section, which is both exposed and difficult. Every principal knows what to do here, so you do not need to give a cue, which can, in fact, be detrimental. The four-bar duet follows. At the first rehearsal, you should lead the two horns through the accelerando, but once they know what you want, there is little need to conduct these measures; just catch the end of their phrase.

Emphasize the triplet in the low instruments at **m. 278**, but do not let it drag. Stay in four for all this mayhem as many different rhythms occur. The mordents are on the beat. The third and fourth horns, as well as bassoons, have syncopations. The strings need to play their triplets on the string to cut through the texture, but there will always be something that you will not hear clearly here.

I go back into two at **m. 287**, simply because the complicated patterns have concluded. In the old days, some conductors would hold back the tempo for the trumpet entrance at the end of **m. 290**, but I think it takes away from the forward momentum. For the sake of the drama, I usually mark the trombones down to single *forte* at **m. 291** and then let them make a crescendo in the next bar.

Your choices at **reh. 12** will boil down to what you want to accomplish at this point. It certainly is a powerful moment, but I am interested in hearing what the violins are doing, not just the winds and timpani. I observe the accents in the brass and then drop them down a bit in each measure. Then, at **m. 303**, I start at single *forte* and make a crescendo a bar later. You will never hear the cellos and basses in **m. 305** as they frantically try to bring out their triplets.

Despite the six-bar diminuendo, many of my colleagues and I let the violins and violas make hairpins in **mm. 309–10** and then continue to get softer. Although it is tempting to slow down at **m. 313**, I think it is more effective to stay in tempo. The clarinets are legato, and you can even have them slur each bar. The dots in the strings on the duplets starting at **m. 316** can be difficult to get together. Because of the triple *piano*, I have them all play on the string at the tip. Make sure the rhythm of the final two notes of each phrase is not the same as the triplet.

The ritard leading to the *a tempo* passage is often interpreted as a *meno mosso* instead, but Dvořák's indication is worth considering. After many years, I have finally come around to doing it the composer's way. However, you do need to get back to beating in four at some point, and I find that this works well in the bar before the horn entry. On the downbeat of the *Meno mosso*, it seems odd, acoustically, to have the basses play a half note. Maybe someday I will change this to a quarter to match the timpani. The bowing here can be "as it comes," but you will need to have the strings change direction somewhere in the third bar to allow the Allegro to start on a down bow.

Now we arrive at a moment that marks a significant difference between what orchestras normally do and what the text says. Traditionally, the Allegro only takes hold for two bars, after which many conductors slow back to the *Meno mosso*. This is understandable, considering the inherent drama taking place and the desire to exaggerate the chordal difference between the third and fourth bars. When played as written, it sounds shocking, just because we are used to hearing it the other way. If you choose to hold back, do so after careful consideration of what the composer intended and why you might want to go against the score.

No matter which direction you choose, clearly **m. 337** must be in the quicker tempo. Do not fret over the triplet vs. the sixteenths but observe the *sforzando* markings on the offbeats. While Dvořák does not include dots on any of the final quarter notes in the string parts, we are used to playing them short, right through the last bar.

About that final diminuendo: Erich Leinsdorf kept the dynamic at *fortissimo*, but he is the exception, and it is hard to believe any conductors could get away with it today. Leaving the intonation aside, can we get down to triple *pianissimo*? The answer, at least for the winds, is no. If you have single winds, the best you can do is hang on to the note loudly before starting the diminuendo. In rehearsal, try to determine how softly you can get it so that everyone knows what it will sound like during the performance.

Doubling presents another option. In that scenario, all the winds play and hold the last note. Gradually, and not all at the same time, the extra musicians make the diminuendo and stop before the others. Then, those still playing continue to get softer. This creates a truly remarkable diminuendo and aside from the orchestra, no one will know how you did it.

\*\*\*

"The Americans expect great things of me . . . If the small Czech nation can have such musicians, they say, why could not they, too, when their country and people is so immense."

—Antonín Dvořák

## Notes

1. "Real Value of Negro Melodies," *New York Herald*, May 21, 1893. http://static.qobuz.com/info/IMG/pdf/NYHerald-1893-Mai-21-Recadre.pdf.

2. Antonín Dvořák, "Symphony No. 9 in E Minor, Op. 95: Critical Edition Based on the Composer's Manuscript." In *Souborné vydání díla*, series 3, vol. 9 , ed. Otakar Šourek (Prague: SNKLHU, 1955).

3. "Dvořák, Antonín / Symphony No. 9, E Minor, Op. 95 (From the New World) (ID 4211-101–114)," The New York Philharmonic Shelby White & Leon Levy Digital Archives, https://archives.nyphil.org.

4. Antonín Dvořák, *Symphony No. 9, "From the New World,"* ed. Jonathan Del Mar (Kassel, Germany: Bärenreiter-Verlag Urtext, 2019).

# Jean Sibelius: Symphony No. 2

"If we understood the world, we would realize that there is a logic of harmony underlying its manifold apparent dissonances."

—Jean Sibelius

Photographer: Daniel Nyblin,
CC BY 4.0

We are all products of our youth. For musicians, some of our most formative experiences come from a particular performance or inspirational musical moment. With music of virtually every genre surrounding me, I found myself drawn to large-scale works in which the sound of the orchestra itself is the most important element. Although this work was written during the first two years of the twentieth century, most of us consider it to be musically connected to the previous one, hence its inclusion in this volume.

The symphony we are about to discuss represents one of my earliest musical memories, and I have always idealized its sonic world. However, I am a product of the 1950s and '60s. When I hear this piece performed by a new generation of conductors, it seems a far cry from what I remember experiencing during my developmental years.

Before I ever saw the score, my listening experiences suggested that this should not be a particularly difficult piece to conduct. It sounded relatively straightforward, out of the mold of several late Romantic works. Then, I believe in 1956, my father led the piece with one of the suburban orchestras in the Los Angeles area. A few days afterward, I looked at the score he used, a miniature edition with a cover price of $3.00. It was published by Associated Music Publishers, Inc. and claimed to be "The sole American issue of the original Breitkopf edition."[1]

I had perused other works that my dad had conducted, and they usually contained a few markings better categorized as reminders than interpretive insights. When I opened the Sibelius to the first page, I was shocked to find scads of indications in black, blue, and red pencils. Each was like a code to unlock what Felix Slatkin must have believed were the secrets contained in this work. He marked virtually every bar, from which notes he wanted to sustain, to a ritard he wanted to add or the way he would accomplish the divisi.

My father died in 1963 at the age of forty-seven. His library remained with my mother, but by the next year, I was embarking on my own conducting journey and had access to all of my dad's scores. I kept coming back to this symphony. I wish I could remember how his performance went, but every time I heard another conductor do the work, my mind would always flash back to all the scribblings my father put in the score.

This may seem like just a memory, and you might well be asking, "What does this have to do with how we study the piece?" That will become clear as we tackle the intricacies and how the interpretation of this symphony, as well as how to conduct it, has changed over the past sixty-five years—at least for me.

Sibelius is a composer who seems to fall in and out of favor with each generation of conductors. The Second Symphony has always been played on a regular basis, with the First not too far behind, followed by the Fifth. The others never seemed to enter the standard repertoire, although the Seventh had its early proponents. The Violin Concerto never went out of favor with performers or the public.

I can understand why this back and forth with the music exists, considering the enigmatic quality of Sibelius's prolific and often profound output. Much of his work could also be considered lightweight and more appropriate to the world of Grieg. His music could be abstract, nationalistic, programmatic, and sometimes very ordinary.

At the age of thirty-five, after the successes of his early orchestral ventures inspired by Finnish legends, Sibelius embarked on the first of his abstract voyages with the First Symphony. Patterning some of his sonic palette after Bruckner—the composer he idolized most—he found new ways of integrating the brass section into the symphonic fabric and consolidated the music of his homeland into his symphonies, much as Tchaikovsky did with his final three works in the form.

National pride was running high at the turn of the twentieth century. At the time, Finland was fighting to gain independence from Russia, which had imposed sanctions on its language and culture. To counter this censorship, Sibelius wrote his more-than-patriotic work *Finlandia*, and this alone would secure his popularity, not only in his homeland but worldwide.

Written a year and a half after the First Symphony, the Second Symphony premiered in 1902. The composer called it "a confession of the soul."[2] To say that it continues in the Romantic tradition of the Austro-Germanic school of the nineteenth century would be an understatement. After all, it was a dilemma for any turn-of-the-century composer to find a balance between what music was and what it would become.

Although the public adored the new symphony, critics were divided. Again, the problem stemmed from those who were looking for pieces that moved the musical dial forward into the new century; this work did not satisfy the progressives. Still, conductors loved to lead the piece, musicians loved playing it, and audiences loved listening to it.

In the first part of the twenty-first century, a new generation of conductors from Finland has emerged, each of whom wants to present the works of the country's first important composer. Several others who are not Finnish have recorded complete cycles. While my impression is that their hearts were not invested equally in all the pieces, each conductor I have listened to seemed to enjoy the pleasures of darkness and light that accompany this Second Symphony.

The edition we will use exists in most orchestra libraries and is likely the score most of you already own, published by Breitkopf & Härtel. In 2000, they issued a newly edited Urtext version.³ Most of the differences are minimal but, as opposed to the earlier score, the revised edition contains measure numbers. I will nevertheless frame my remarks in terms of the rehearsal letters you would use in conveying starting points to the orchestra.

When the score contains numerous bars between rehearsal letters, you might consider adding a few extra indications in between and having those put in the parts. Of course, it is also possible to add the bar numbers to your score, and in the case of this symphony, measure numbers exist in the parts that can be found on IMSLP.⁴

A good example occurs in the first movement, between **reh. D** and **reh. E**. The trumpets do not come in until the thirteenth measure; this is a logical starting point if something has gone wrong that you need to fix. By adding **reh. D1**, you can save a lot of time.

The orchestration is the same as you find in Brahms, Tchaikovsky, and most of Bruckner, with a couple of notable exceptions. Other than the tuba, you will not find instruments that represent the extreme ends of the wind section: no piccolo, English horn, or contrabassoon, for example. He also omits the harp. In his First and Fourth symphonies, Sibelius includes a smattering of percussion, but for the most part, the music is sparsely orchestrated.

The instrumentation is for two flutes, two oboes, two clarinets in A (they will play in B♭ for most of the third movement), two bassoons, four horns in F, three trumpets in F, three trombones, one tuba, timpani (two drums are required, but usually three or more are used), and strings.

A few orchestras double the woodwinds. These days, we tend to only use the extra players to spell those who are already playing, but they can also add reinforcement in louder passages.

Before we get into the details of the work, it is important to understand that performances of this piece vary dramatically in timing. You can find recorded versions that take a brisk forty-one minutes and others that range into fifty-minute territory. Part of this stems from the lack of metronome marks in the score; however, Sibelius did write about them in a Finnish music journal, indicating the following:

Allegretto: $\dotted{\quarter} = 76$
Tempo Andante: $\quarter = 58$
Vivacissimo: $\dotted{\quarter} = 92$
Lento: $\dotted{\quarter} = 58$
Finale. Allegro Moderato: $\half = 88$.⁵

The other reason has to do with Robert Kajanus, founder of the first professional orchestra in Finland. Kajanus became the principal champion of Sibelius's music, performing it frequently and committing the works to discs. His recorded legacy of the symphonies did not begin until 1930, quite a long time after the premiere of the Second Symphony. Listening to that recording today, one that was considered definitive, I have difficulty believing that the composer thought the piece should be played that way, especially in light of other conductors' interpretations of this symphony. Sibelius did not seem to have harsh words for anyone who performed his works, and therefore we might never know what he really intended. Nonetheless, we can at least try to understand and utilize the tools needed to lead this work with the authority it deserves.

## First Movement: Allegretto

Any piece that does not start on a downbeat already presents problems for the conductor. You must give a clear indication to those that enter in the first measure while also conveying the 6/4 meter to those who are not playing. Unless the work is new to the orchestra, it is not necessary to say that you will be in two. If the work is unfamiliar, simply tell everyone that you will give just the first beat and that the strings enter after the second. Start with your arms up so that the downbeat becomes the preparatory beat.

As with any piece of music, you should firmly establish in your mind and body how fast or slow you want to be. I find it useful to mouth the triplet on the first beat and then give just a little flick of the wrist to indicate the quarter-note rest.

The difficulty lies in the tempo indication of Allegretto; every conductor seems to have a different idea of what it means in this movement. Since we have no other tempo marks, how can we figure out the speed? In my experience, it is best to find the most active place in the movement and then consider how that fits into the overall arc of the piece. The motion before **reh. H** is an appropriate reference point because continuous eighth notes can only go so fast before they become blurry.

Still, in keeping with the Romantic ethic, the movement will be characterized by plenty of freedom and rubato, including the opening measures. Defining Allegretto is therefore more complicated. It is used for the second movement of Beethoven's Seventh Symphony and the third movement of Brahms's First Symphony, but in very different ways. We usually think of it as quicker than Andante but not as fast as Allegro; then again, this definition is vague at best. The music itself should inform your decision. My preferred tempo is in line with ♩. = 84, or maybe a little less, depending on the acoustics.

Most of the essays in this series focus on the technical and editorial role of the conductor. Thus, I tend not to comment on or criticize any previous performances other than my own. However, this symphony is different, primarily because of the recorded documentation of Kajanus. Supposedly, it was the touchstone for performances by others, but that turns out not to be true.

Kajanus takes the opening at such a rapid clip that no one else dared to match it after the release of his recording. The timing of the first movement is a more-than-brisk 8:15, according to my stopwatch. Serge Koussevitzky made a much-praised recording five years later, but his timing was 9:30. Toscanini soon followed, coming a bit closer at 8:48. No other conductors seemed to break the nine-minute barrier. In contrast, Bernstein, a strong advocate for the composer, managed to stretch it out to 10:54.

One indisputable point is that the strings should play their first notes *mezzo forte* with a little separation. In the early score edition, the crescendo appears to end after the last note of the second bar, but the Urtext version extends it to the last note of the phrase. Sibelius does not indicate how loud it gets. We can assume that the *mezzo forte* dynamic returns in the middle of the third bar. The music gets softer but usually does not slow down.

The lower strings continue to play legato, and I can understand why Sibelius marked them this way. The lighter feeling associated with an Allegretto tempo appears in the playful nature of the oboe and clarinet entrance. Some conductors increase the speed slightly each time this phrase occurs, but in my opinion, that takes away from the steady pulse in the lower instruments. Others have the woodwinds make a slight ritardando at the end of their phrases.

When the horns begin the *espressivo* passage, renditions have varied. Recent conductors favor staying in tempo; after all, nothing tells us otherwise. In past decades, the order of the day was to hold back, sometimes to a fault. In some ways, the slower tempo is already written in, so if you wish to pull back, I recommend keeping it discreet. The tempo returns with the next woodwind entrance, and then you have the same decision to make before **reh. A**.

In the third bar of **reh. A**, Sibelius switches from lines to dots in the strings, but this does not really make much sense. I think most of us continue to play these notes as we did from the start. If you slow down slightly before the fermata, those quarter notes in the strings can be played a little longer. I also prefer to hold the final clarinet note longer than any of the previous quarters; this prevents an abrupt ending to the phrase. The same applies to the last flute notes that follow.

At the cut-time indication, a discrepancy having to do with the slur appears in all the editions. The bassoons' downbeat could serve one of two purposes: the end of the previous phrase or the beginning of the next one. I typically separate the first note and commence a new idea from the second, even playing it a bit *pesante*. However, if you look ahead to three bars before **reh. N**, where there is no introductory material, you will see that Sibelius is clear about how to interpret this group of notes. (Perhaps in future performances, I will see if connecting the sections feels right.) When the eighth-note figure comes in, some conductors will allow a bit of time so that it does not seem hurried.

Breath is another consideration in the bassoon passage. The phrase is quite long and increases to single *forte*, so whether they can play it in one breath might determine if you can interpret it as a single phrase.

The flute trill must be strong, maybe even *fortissimo* at first. A passionate moment for the violins follows, played with full bows but not aggressively. They can best accomplish the *subito piano* by playing the two previous notes on a down bow. I like to allow a slight portamento on the G string three bars before the fermata. Sibelius leaves us with the usual question about the diminuendo: How soft does it get?

Does the F♯ return to single *forte* eight bars before **reh. B**, or is it part of the diminuendo from the previous bar? Almost every conductor will reattack it quite vigorously, possibly retaking the down bow. No matter what you do, maintain a long line for this entire passage, even when there are rests. My solution is to ask the violins to take the bows as they come starting nine bars before **reh. B**. The next bar is on an up bow but with the same intensity as the previous measure. One measure before the fermata is down bow with the written diminuendo going to *piano*.

Even though the rest after the fermata six bars before **reh. B** is only an eighth, use your second beat as a cutoff, go into tempo, and begin the next measure with an introductory rest. Another possibility is to sustain the fermata until the end of the bar and then cut off on the downbeat, using it as the preparation for the next phrase. Either way, it is almost impossible to observe that eighth-note rest, from the conductor's technical point of view. Do not shortchange the last note of the next two phrases.

A *forte-piano*, such as the one before **reh. B**, can be thought of in two ways: gradual and *dolce* or sudden and very surprising. I prefer the latter, with the strings starting near the frog of the bow and pulling quickly to the tip. Sibelius is a composer of contrasts, as he demonstrates in the early stages of this movement. Why not give the listeners a little shock?

After **reh. B**, the flute trills should dominate, and the two grace notes should project clearly. Five bars after **reh. B**, notice that the last six notes of the first oboe are divided into groups of two. I find it appropriate to emphasize the first note of each group, especially in light of the next bar, where the second oboe takes over and Sibelius marks diminuendos that can also be construed as accents. However, these indications only apply to each group of two notes and do not mean the entire bar gets softer.

It is easy to forget about the double basses' pizzicato prior to the 6/4. Catch their eyes and give them an encouraging beat. Again, sustain all the last notes of even the shortest phrases; otherwise, this section will sound like a series of two-bar segments. The diminuendo in the winds before the strings' pizzicato passage can fade to *pianissimo*. However, do not make a ritard in the bar before the 6/4, as the rhythmic deviation in the woodwinds gets ruined if you slow down.

Many conductors, Kajanus included, speed up at this point; this is neither necessary nor even remotely indicated. Instead, this pizzicato line should stay in the same tempo. Its *mezzo piano* marking is just right. Sometimes, the first couple of notes seem too soft, and I can understand why conductors choose to make a bigger crescendo out of this passage, but they sacrifice the wonderful harmonic changes on virtually every one of the six beats in the measure. I like to bring out those changes that occur in the instruments other than the first violins.

The tempo marking at **reh. C** is simply *Poco allegro*, again somewhat vague. But Sibelius is smart, knowing that if this goes too fast, the eighth notes in the fifth bar will be smudgy. I think those eighth notes should start at *mezzo forte* and be played on the string, but I realize that some conductors like them off. We certainly do not play the *forte* seven bars after **reh. C** as a *subito* dynamic. Sustain that C♯ as long as possible, with the first violins hanging on a bit longer than their colleagues.

The articulation two measures before **reh. D** is really a matter of taste. I prefer these notes on the string, but many conductors like them staccato. I feel that the various crescendos are more controlled—and the quarter notes near the end of each phrase are more cohesive—when played on the string. This spot is up for grabs depending on your personal preference; of course, if you have chosen a very quick tempo, it may not be feasible to play the notes on the string.

Most of the older generation of conductors made a rallentando at the end of the seventh bar of **reh. D**, slightly expanding the tempo for the C-major climax. They moved ahead when the eighth notes appeared in the next measure. Although he does not include markings, it would be hard to imagine

Sibelius wanting the woodwinds to sustain the quarter notes thirteen bars after **reh. D**. Bringing out the trumpets' crescendo by increasing the dynamic to *mezzo forte* adds a nice touch.

The timpani has a fundamental role on the downbeats that begin seven measures before **reh. E**; the string section needs to hear the accent. Two bars later, the timpani has a dynamic of *pianissimo*, followed by *piano possibile*. These last four bars are marked *Poco tranquillo*, but this is not a ritard and might simply be thought of as a relaxation.

The beginning of the development is announced by the oboe, whose crescendo can increase to *forte*, if you wish. I prefer the underlying eighth notes in the violas to be played on the string, enabling the listener to hear both the rhythm and the harmonies clearly. Sometimes, the bassoonist can be a little too expressive during the solo and get behind. When the clarinets enter, it makes sense for them to play their quarter notes short, the same length as those before **reh. E**.

The violins enter and play in the same manner as the violas, keeping very steady. When the cellos come in, one edition includes a crescendo starting on the C. This is worth considering, as most conductors do it instinctually. This creates a striking moment, so I have them continue to build until the eighth rest, arriving almost at *fortissimo*. A somewhat violent set of sixteenth triplets precede an E♭ that is printed as a quarter note with a tenuto line. However, many conductors, including me, think of this note as supplementing the *forte-piano* in the bassoon and shorten it.

Sibelius is an organic composer; when he chooses to have something occur suddenly, we can usually figure out why he has done so. This is why I have a problem with the passage that begins five bars after **reh. F**. Nowhere else in this movement do the eighth and sixteenth notes have a crescendo and then a *subito* dynamic that matches the one that began the phrase.

The editor's commentary to the latest edition mentions nothing about this, but I have noticed that conductors alter this spot in their recordings. I prefer to have the cellos play the first two notes (B♮) at the indicated *mezzo forte*. After that, I ask them—along with the rest of the strings—to drop to *mezzo piano*. Meanwhile, the woodwinds' interjections are *forte*. With this alteration, the phrase makes much more sense and connects more fluidly to similar passages that are on the immediate horizon.

Six measures before **reh. G**, we can safely assume that the dynamic at the start of the bar goes back up to the *piano* of the previous measure. The same applies a couple of bars later. To avoid repeating myself, I will refrain from saying this almost every time a similar moment occurs in this symphony; there are simply a lot of unclear or contradictory dynamics.

In the fifth bar of **reh. G**, it is tempting to play the two notes in the brass and timpani very aggressively. However, it appears that these are part of the previous four-bar phrase. To make this sound like less of an intrusion and make the lead-in to the fifth bar feel more cohesive, I suggest that the first violins add strong accents to the G♮ and C♮ at **reh. G**; the woodwinds and horns can do the same when they have those notes three bars after **reh. G**.

At **reh. H**, Sibelius writes the ungainly instruction, *Tranquillo, ma poco a poco ravivando il tempo al allegro*. Basically, we relax and gradually get back to the Allegro tempo, but where? Musical logic tells us that the target is twelve bars after **reh. H**. So, we start somewhat calm, and then very slightly move forward, reaching the opening tempo twelve bars later.

Starting seven measures after **reh. H**, all the quarter notes, as well as the eighths that are not slurred, are played somewhat marcato, with the cellos imitating the timpani strokes. I would caution against rushing here. Stay very steady, making sure that the various rhythms are clear.

The legato line at **reh. I** can become lugubrious if the basses and bassoons do not keep the tempo. This bass melody, unusual for the time at which the symphony was written because the cellos do not double it, must take precedence over the trills in the woodwinds, which can sometimes dominate. To keep the tension for this buildup, the violins and horns need to stay at single *forte*.

At **reh. K**, start a little softer and build up more slowly. Many conductors will take time going into the *Poco largamente*, but you need to hold the tempo when you arrive there; otherwise, the syncopations in the horns will lose their impact. Two bars before the *Poco largamente*, the timpani's quarter notes are reattacked and played with the roll, resulting in an unavoidable accent.

With a long way to go before the dynamic high point at **reh. M**, you must decide where the climax is for this entire section so as not to give away where you are going too early. The quarter notes in the basses and cellos are marked with both slurs and lines; if the dynamic rises above *mezzo piano*, consider asking them to use separate bows.

Sibelius provides the instruction *largamente* for the oboes and three trumpets in the bar before **reh. M**. While in some instances musicians can diverge slightly from the tempo and then catch up later, here they must arrive at the next downbeat with everyone else. I usually solve this problem by holding back very slightly to establish a *pesante* feeling. You might try subdividing the second half of the measure, but only at rehearsal, just so the orchestra feels the rubato as part of the triple rhythm and not as if it were a triplet at the end of a 4/4 bar.

Get right back into tempo at **reh. M**. The eighth notes in the woodwinds need to stay steady. For reasons that I do not quite understand, some conductors slow down the first quarter note five measures before **reh. N**, taking it out of the previous rhythm. However, I agree with taking some time for the final notes in the brass one bar before **reh. N**. The *poco forte* five bars after **reh. N** should match the double basses' *mezzo forte*. Meanwhile, the violins and cellos should play their trills on the quick side. This passage includes lots of little dynamic shadings to observe, and you can either exaggerate them or just make them slightly expressive. The strings should drop down rather quickly on the *dim. molto* to allow the first flute and bassoon to project easily.

Since the first trumpet enters on a relatively high note, that musician needs to see a breath from you four bars before the *Tempo I* mark. The entrance is particularly difficult because it is soft and comes after several measures of playing *forte*. To coordinate the eighth note two measures before the double bar, I subdivide the second beat. Perhaps not too much diminuendo is needed prior to the fermata. When you cut off the brass section, make sure that your arms are not too high, as you still need room to give the preparation for the next downbeat.

Everything from here to the end of the movement is a variation on what occurred during the exposition. Still, some alterations are worth bringing out, such as the basses' pizzicato two before **reh. O**. So far, we have not had any divisi decisions to make, but this changes at **reh. O**, where the first violins are in three parts. I suggest that the first four stands play the upper staff, perhaps with the first two stands on the top notes; the pizzicato line can be played by the last few stands. The main consideration is to keep those playing the tune near each other, and this applies to the cellos as well.

Another fermata appears on the bar line just before **reh. O** but not at the end of the eighth measure. The fermata four bars before **reh. P** does not need to be held too long; when you resume, stay in tempo without speeding up, similar to what occurred before **reh. C**. The phrasings are slightly different, but for the most part, the music is as it was earlier. One interesting change includes the addition of grace notes in the woodwind parts after **reh. R**.

Sibelius introduces a significant deviation at **reh. S**, the high-point equivalent of the eighth bar of **reh. D**. This time, the composer marks the measure tenuto, with *a tempo* in the fourth bar. For the sake of consistency, I think these bars should be played that way the first time as well.

The final eight measures have the pizzicato double basses taking on the role previously played by the timpani. You can certainly consider going into six for the final two bars. Keep in mind that the composer did not put a fermata on the last note, so it should not be held very long.

## Second Movement: Tempo Andante, ma rubato

Many conductors transition directly from the end of the first movement into this one. It makes sense, given that the timpani begins on the note corresponding with the key of the whole symphony. Another possible reason is that this also creates a symmetry within the piece, making it appear to be in two movements, each consisting of two parts.

As with the first movement, Kajanus's recording of the second movement leaves us a bit confused. His interpretation is at least two minutes faster than almost any other performance, including those made around the same time. This big of a discrepancy cannot be ignored and at least deserves some consideration when thinking about the basic tempos you choose. For now, I will just deal with the text as presented.

The opening timpani roll is only *mezzo forte* and without an accent; it represents a somewhat gentle beginning to the movement that will turn out to be the emotional heart of this symphony. We are told that ♩ = ♩. at the second bar, so during the first measure, you must have the upcoming tempo firmly in your head. That speed is best determined by thinking about the bassoon duet that begins at **reh. A**. Determine how much time these two musicians need for each of the four phrases they will play, particularly the last and longest one.

A walking bass line, played pizzicato, sets the rather dark mood before getting picked up by the cellos. Keep in mind that the last bass note is played on an open string, meaning that it will resonate and possibly seem too loud relative to the cellos. In turn, the cellos might need to start a bit louder because no matter how hard you try, their timbre will simply not match their deeper-voiced counterparts.

The two crescendos that commence after the basses reenter increase to *mezzo forte*. Make sure you sustain the first one for six bars before the diminuendo. The last ritenuto bar can be conducted in three and the diminuendo taken down to *piano*. The twelve bars before **reh. A** have several hairpins, so they are usually played more expressively than the previous ones.

At **reh. A**, you must keep the cellos audible, so do not let the diminuendos get too soft. When the bassoons enter, tradition dictates that you can slightly separate the two groups of two eighth notes at the end of the second bar as well as at similar moments throughout the movement. The timpani takes the place of what would normally be a pedal point in the double basses, so I recommend a somewhat soft stick be used right from the start.

When the horns make their first entrance, they approximate a hunter's call in the wild. The sixteenth note must be precise so that it does not fall under the spell of the triplets underneath. The third and fourth horns imitate the first two, but they have an accent, telling us that they are not meant to just take over. However—and this is not easy—all four need to either have a matching set of instruments or be so in sync that the listener cannot distinguish between them. Throughout this passage, the basic cello dynamic is *mezzo forte*. Five bars before **reh. B**, they have one more expressive moment, guided by a hairpin parallel to the one just after **reh. A**. Both crescendos should come up to about *mezzo forte*. Those for the timpani are smaller, evoking distant thunder.

Two measures before **reh. B**, the entrance of the oboes and clarinets should have a dark sonority but not be played too loudly. Pay particular attention to the grace notes, as they are plaintive and not throwaways. It might be necessary to bring the cellos' pizzicatos up a little here. There is a small discrepancy between editions in the second bar of **reh. B**. The earlier edition includes two distinct diminuendos on the notes in the bassoons and horns, whereas the revised has only one, on the second note; musically, the latter makes more sense.

When the double basses enter on repeated D♯s, they must articulate them to sound as if the cellos were continuing their pizzicatos. The stringendo is slight, only lasting eight bars. The tempo of the subsequent *Poco Allegro* depends on how fast you think the sixteenth notes should be played; they are clearly on the string but only single *forte*.

The cellos have an important role eight bars before **reh. C**. If you separated the groups of two eighth notes in the bassoon duet back at **reh. A**, most likely you will do the same here and every time that phrasing occurs in the movement. Alternatively, the cellos could play them legato with perhaps a slight emphasis on the first note of each group.

The *meno forte* seven measures before **reh. C** only drops down a little, to *mezzo forte*. Even though the crescendo is leading to a *fortissimo* woodwind passage, the strings and horns should only take it to single *forte*. Then, a remarkable moment occurs one bar before **reh. C**. Both bassoons have a very resonant *fortissimo*, and you should encourage them to play this as forcefully as possible. The diminuendo that follows the B♭ is minimal, but the F at **reh. C** is once again a solitary, short note for the two musicians.

The bassoons should continue to play as loudly as possible so that their triplets really come through clearly. The strings interrupt, playing near the frog to impart a rough edge to the sound. Returning to single *forte* three measures after **reh. C**, the violins need to articulate the sixteenth note; a quick flick of your wrist will help emphasize this. Underneath, the pizzicatos in the violas and cellos are not divisi and are played quickly, on the beat. We now see the true reason that the opening tempo cannot be too fast.

Starting on a down bow and changing at the bar line, the violins play the thirty-second notes forcefully but cleanly so as not to muddy the waters. When they arrive at the *sforzando*, make sure that this note and its release are sustained. The A at the end can be either long or short, but you will have to be consistent, as this reoccurs several times.

At this *Poco largamente*, the horns and cellos, as well as the violas, have a phrase marked at just single *forte*. Depending on the density of the violins' sound, you might need to mark this up a bit. The timpani intrusion, with a somewhat exaggerated hairpin, sets up what happens at **reh. D**.

For some composers—Elgar, for example—the indication *Molto largamente* does not usually signify a tempo but rather a mood. Here, because of the length of the long notes in the brass, we must consider how long they can sustain the note. Yes, they have a diminuendo, but a large crescendo follows it, with a quarter note at the end. I envision this tempo around ♩ = 64.

Without a way to really set up this speed for the strings' ascending run, you just have to rehearse it a couple of times so that they feel how it is different from similar passages a few bars earlier. I suggest that they start on a down bow and change direction for the last note, regardless of whether you prefer it to be long or short.

Returning to the brass, their concluding note after the crescendo has a rarely seen dynamic mark: *fortissimo forzando*. The two trumpets with the preceding eighth note need to be strong but still save something for this extreme accent. In the old days, some conductors would move through the rests a bit more quickly, possibly because they thought the silence would confuse the audience, but contemporary maestros do not.

Observe the various dynamic changes and expression marks that occur leading into the *Andante sostenuto*. The low strings help underpin the tuba part—not that this player usually needs support—but the color is very Sibelian. Whatever tempo you choose for this passage, do not rush the sixteenth notes; in fact, they can be almost *pesante*. Direct the eighth-note upbeats in the brass separately.

Four bars before *Andante sostenuto*, tradition dictates waiting a moment before commencing the horns' upbeat, and even then, you might also hold back on that note. The three-bar diminuendo that follows is not easy to accomplish, as often the music gets too soft, too soon. Perhaps telling those involved that the downbeat three bars before the fermata is single *forte* will give everyone the idea to save breath and bow.

While some are tempted to take the *Andante sostenuto* at a very slow pace, from my perspective, it is the same speed as the music at **reh. A**. This is a superbly structured movement, and to take away some of the symmetry gives it too much of the quality of fantasy, at least in my opinion. We must also consider the sixteenth notes that are coming up; if they are too slow, the whole passage takes on a melancholy feeling and much of the tension is lost.

We must also consider the triple *piano* marking as well as the *espressivo* indication. They seem at odds with each other; don't they? These conundrums come up often in music by Sibelius, and we must use our sense of musical logic to work out the solutions. This usually means looking ahead. The next actual dynamic change comes in the fifth bar of **reh. E**. However, this *mezzo piano* also has its problems, as the strings will have to stay under the woodwinds. We do have a *forzando* right at **reh. E**, but this is just an accent within the very soft dynamic.

My preferred way to shape this passage is to ask the strings to begin the Andante *sul tasto*, with the bow almost on the lower part of the fingerboard. But certainly, vibrato is also necessary to achieve the *espressivo*. Since the flute and bassoon lines ascend, a crescendo will occur automatically.

To my ear, *mezzo piano* is just a tad too loud and abrupt after the seven very soft measures, so I only raise the dynamic to single *piano*. When most musicians see the sixteenth notes without slurs—as in the flutes and bassoons five bars after **reh. E**—they tend to play these notes with a bit of separation; however, I personally prefer legato phrasing here. Observe the little accent in the basses as well as the *mezzo forte* marking.

You might remember that I spoke of consistency when it comes to certain phrases; I have to amend that rule for the sixth bar of **reh. E**. It doesn't make sense to separate the two groups of eighth notes in the oboes and clarinets; maybe some conductors have done it, but I have not heard it played that way.

The accented quarter notes in the 3/2 bar are usually performed quite legato, with a rich sound. However, you might ask the horns and low strings that continue with the quarters to add a little lift before the half note two measures before **reh. F**; this gives some heft to the *sforzando* on the second beat.

Do not make an accelerando when the violins begin their lead-in to **reh. F**. The change of tempo, which is not by much, must feel like an explosion of sound. Despite the lines over the eighth notes, most conductors perform them legato.

Now we come to a hotly debated moment, at least among tubists. Why didn't Sibelius let them play the first of the three notes that occur at this point? (They also do not understand why this composer abandoned the instrument for his remaining five symphonies.) I asked some of my tuba friends. Here is what the Chicago Symphony's Gene Pokorny has to say:

This famous passage has the tuba doubling the double basses for the first two bars, except for the pickup notes (F♯). However, in the next two bars, the sequence occurring a ½ step higher does not eliminate the pickup notes (G). Usually, the tuba adds those F♯ pickups in the first two bars of **reh. F**.[6]

He goes on to speak about a similar spot later in the movement:

The pickup notes are eliminated completely in these four bars (**mm. 214–17, reh. N**). It is better to add them, but I have no reason to know why Sibelius left them out in the first place. There was not an issue with early tubas having mechanical issues with those notes ... any more than the earlier ones at **reh. F**.

I received a similar response from virtually all the people I asked. If you listen carefully to a few of the new recordings, it is possible to hear the conductor sticking to what is on the page. But for the most part, you will find the notes added.

Seven measures after **reh. F**, before the double bar, there is a discrepancy between the two editions that can make a big difference. In the earlier edition, the timpani crescendo lands on the downbeat of the fermata bar. In contrast, the revised edition places the *mezzo forte* in the middle of the bar. I rather like the almost Mahlerian shift to the third beat.

At the key change, the upper strings have a somewhat dry and *non espressivo* accompaniment figure. Although today we rarely hear an actual trumpet in F, the sound here is dark and quite expressive, like that of the larger, deeper instrument. Underneath that solo, the cellos are told to play spiccato. Some conductors have changed this passage to pizzicato, but I think that is outright wrong. However, it can be played at the tip of the bow, on the string, *pianissimo* and marcato; a true spiccato seems out of place if it is too short.

The flute has to embody the same character as the trumpet and should be encouraged to imitate the sound rather than echo it. There follows a *Poco stringendo* that takes place over five bars. The violin triplets are played on the string and with some weight.

The problem with this recapitulation of material heard after **reh. B** is that this time around, Sibelius's tempo indication is simply Allegro, minus the *Poco* that appeared earlier. Certainly, this is either a mistake or an oversight; the tempo should be the same both times.

While the composer incorporates slight variations in the material heard previously, the idea is basically the same. The change occurs five bars after **reh. H**, where he writes a much lengthier buildup, starting at *mezzo forte* and including a stringendo.

However, you will have to deal with several discrepancies here as well. Most of them concern dynamics, or rather, the lack of them. The first time around (beginning four bars after **reh. C**), Sibelius did not write in diminuendos at the end of various phrases; now they are all over the place without any indications of how soft they become. A few conductors have eliminated them altogether, and this can work well. Yet, I also find something appealing about the releasing of tension, almost as if Sibelius were telling us that some of the instrumental groups are giving up.

My good friend Mr. Pokorny weighed in on another troubling aspect of this section, explaining, "The two sixteenth notes found in the bassoon and double basses at **m. 151** and **m. 153** (six and eight bars after **reh. H**) are many times added to the tuba part."

It makes sense, but perhaps this change takes away from the bizarre nature of Sibelius's unique orchestral language. This passage, from the *Poco largamente* to the *Più moderato* seven measures after **reh. I**, is the closest we get to the style that will become this composer's hallmark. Harmonically vague cross-rhythms and delayed climaxes abound. For me, the priority is to sustain the long notes while maintaining the tension. Even when you get to **reh. I**, do not let it slacken. If you wish to fuss about the syncopations that begin in the horns seven measures before **reh. I**, make sure you have enough rehearsal time to really get it right. Otherwise, your main goal should simply be keeping the ensemble together.

All editions contain a puzzling marking for the timpani at the *Più moderato*. It says *fortissimo*, but that is the same dynamic as the downbeat. What is the point of reiterating it? Perhaps a slight accent on the downbeat is appropriate. This passage is an expansion of the one back at **reh. D**. The opening few bars add the woodwinds with sustained notes, and the time between the phrases is halved. The timpani holds on to the last note longer than the others, as opposed to the first time when everyone cuts off simultaneously.

One of the most beautiful passages in all of Sibelius's writing commences at **reh. K**. Although totally connected to the material preceding it, it signifies a definite break from the sometimes-bleak nature of all that has come before. Despite a dark beginning featuring lower woodwinds and strings, it exudes a warmth that has not been present for the first ten minutes or so of this movement.

The dynamic is *mezzo forte*, with the brass and timpani interjecting *fortissimo* in the fourth bar. I prefer that the violins use two bows for the flourish, starting on a down bow and then playing a long eighth note on an up bow. This creates a stark contrast for the return of the opening material. A slight pause can help to achieve the *subito pianissimo* in the seventh bar. You might even subdivide the first two eighths to emphasize the separation. One additional subdivision can be helpful to synchronize the sixteenth note at the end.

Now we enter a Tchaikovsky-like world sitting mostly in D major. The basses and cellos play a variation on their opening pizzicato passage. Be careful not to start too loudly with the tune, as there is a long way to go before reaching the climax. The woodwinds have a gentle crescendo, and I find that bringing out the oboe four bars before **reh. L** creates a wonderful dissonance between that A♮ and the B♭ in the first bar of the melody.

Your next decision has to do with whether you want to take breaths or create longer lines starting three measures before **reh. L**. Conductors seem to be equally divided about adding a slight lift in the first violins just before the seconds enter. The woodwinds might hold part of the answer, as they probably need time to breathe. Another tip is one that works for many such passages in other works: sing it and see what your own instinct tells you.

The lift is necessary before the fourth beat in the bar before **reh. L**. Be careful not to overthink this section. Really listen to what the orchestra's tendency is when reading through the symphony and pay attention to what they do. It might be different than what you had in mind, but it might also be better.

I can point out a couple of things here: The basses' eighth notes on the repeated Ds should sound like a continuation of the cellos' pizzicato. Beginning four bars after **reh. L**, the divisi in the violas and cellos should be based on where they are positioned on the stage. If the cellos are on the outside, the division should be by the stand to allow the audience to hear both lines evenly. The same holds true if the violas are placed there. You can figure out the rest, but keep in mind that what matters is not always what you hear at the podium but rather what is projecting to the hall.

When the second violins enter two measures before **reh. M**, they should do so gently, taking care not to cover the last few notes of the first violins. One bar later, the firsts come back in with a more direct sound, with no crescendo needed. All usually proceeds without incident for a few bars, but sometimes the *subito mezzo forte* in the fifth bar of **reh. M** is played too softly. You might want to bring up the trombones a bit, as they are providing the only steady harmony here. This is especially true on the fourth beat of the seventh bar, as their sustained E♮ creates an almost out-of-context dissonance.

Sibelius writes *senza stentando*, letting us know not to slow down or drag; it is somewhat tempting to do so, but he knows what he is talking about. The whole thrust of this section depends on steady rhythm, even when nothing seems particularly rhythmic about it. For the final time here, a brief lift between notes in the low instruments is possible two before **reh. N**, prior to what needs to be a very strong *sforzando*.

All is the same as earlier when it comes to the Andante, with Mr. Pokorny's suggestion applying, this time for two more bars.

Four before **reh. O**, Sibelius starts to venture into territory he will explore in his later symphonies, with a lot of stop/start passages. These begin with the cellos' separated figure, this time with a crescendo, which should carry through to the next bar. A rather unusual stroke of orchestration has the flutes playing the tune with low woodwinds, trumpets, and timpani as the harmony. Notice that the second trumpet has a low—but not impossible—note to play; hopefully, your musician will not sound growly here. In my experience, having the flutes hold on one eighth note longer just sounds like they failed to cut off with the others.

I could devote a whole essay to the many alternative interpretations of the section between **reh. O** and **reh. P**. Right at the start, many conductors add a very slight accelerando to the proceedings, probably to set up the flurry of notes coming up in the woodwinds. This used to be common practice but has mostly disappeared these days. Either way, it is important that the preceding Andante not be too slow.

Let's assume we are staying in that tempo. When played on the quick side, the thirty-second notes sound like a group of birds noisily chattering away. The final note is an eighth, which can be either long or short. I prefer the latter to preserve the character of what has come before it.

Again, the tradition was to play the three string notes marked *con forza* with a *pesante* quality as well, with particular emphasis on the accents. These days, some conductors stay right in tempo. That is certainly a valid choice, but I wondered what Maestro Kajanus did with this Coda.

At the Andante, his tempo is a little slower than I expected, but it works. Then, he picks up the speed at **reh. O**, as many other conductors used to do. The big surprise is that not only do the woodwinds under Kajanus's baton play the thirty-second notes very fast, but they also add notes, almost making it a trill! The three eighths that follow are very slow and lead to a furious outburst in the fifth bar. The result is quite effective but certainly not what is in the score.

Conductors typically hold back the tempo at **reh. P** and have the pizzicatos played forcefully. The same issue of a misaligned cutoff in the flutes recurs in the third bar, but thanks to the sustained horns, we are not aware of the discrepancy.

Try to sustain a slow tempo starting four bars before the end, as even a slight acceleration takes away some of the drama. With a sixteenth rest and a slur, we should assume Sibelius wants to sustain this ending with very little, if any, break. Three measures before the end, consider subdividing the second half of the bar, especially if you are going to conduct a very heavy last sixteenth.

Look carefully at what occurs next. Almost every conductor adjusts the dynamics. Some equate this ending to the final bars of the composer's First Symphony, which ends softly, although a few conductors change that ending as well.

What does Sibelius write here, and does it work? The instruments with a diminuendo in the older edition are the trumpets, trombones, and timpani, but not the tuba. In the newer edition, only the trumpets back away, and the score does not specify their final dynamic; the timpani is marked *piano* in both editions.

Following the latest thinking, the movement ends *fortissimo*. Importantly, however, the music does not conclude at the downbeat of the final measure. Rather, the cutoff is on beat two. I conduct a very slight crescendo on this final note to maximize the tension. Then, I do not move a muscle for several seconds to allow for some needed silence. This is an exhausting movement, both physically and emotionally, so take plenty of time before you continue.

## Third Movement: Vivacissimo

The Scherzo is certainly the least complicated in terms of gestures to give to the orchestra. During the fast music, the musicians are too busy reading their parts to pay attention to what you are doing, so they need you most in the slower sections.

With no metronome marking in the score, Sibelius at least gives us a hint by putting in ♩., indicating that he expects one beat per bar. Your tempo decision is probably dictated by four notes in the brass that can only be played so quickly, even with double tonguing. When the brisk music returns at **reh. F**, some of the brass play a four-note group instead of the steady three-note groupings that have comprised the bulk of the fast passages. I find that if you stay around ♩. = 80, it will come out clearly.

Do not take chances with the opening. Give a very strong two-bar preparatory beat, especially if the violins are divided across the stage. All the eighth notes are on the string, with the louder ones played near the frog. The divisi here is mostly done on the stand, but I recommend checking the parts for any awkward page turns; you do not want half the section dropping out.

The contrasts in dynamics cannot be so extreme that notes following *forte* passages get lost. Sometimes we must start a *pianissimo* just a little louder or drop the top dynamics down a bit. It helps immensely if you can get everyone to play as clearly as possible.

Sibelius does not indicate the ending dynamic of the little crescendos he places on phrases that move upward. In a way, the slight increase in volume takes care of itself. The three B♭s before **reh. A** are almost always played with consecutive down bows. Whenever the strings' flurries of eighth notes occur at the same time as a slower phrase (at **reh. A**, for instance), the woodwinds tend to drag; make sure they keep moving through their short intrusions.

Make eye contact with the second violins at **reh. B** when they enter in the second bar; sometimes they are late, causing the firsts to also come in late in the next bar. Note the difference in dynamic for the clarinets and bassoons before **reh. C**, a contrast which creates an echo effect.

With all deference to Mr. Pokorny, the tuba is usually too loud relative to the horns five measures after **reh. C** and in other similar places. Aside from that, most of the balances work out quite well.

Despite the score's heretofore logical and well-thought-out set of rehearsal letters, an awful lot of time passes between **reh. C** and **reh. D**. I would suggest, if the library can do it, adding **reh. C1** twelve bars after **reh. C** and **reh. C2** twelve measures before **reh. D**. Balance the basses' pizzicato line with the flutes eight bars before **reh. D** to reveal a wonderful color. Five bars after **reh. D**, pay attention to the *sforzando* markings, reiterated *forte* dynamics in the woodwinds, and the against-the-grain *piano* indications for a few instruments.

Adding a **reh. D1** at the thirteenth bar can help as you address an important issue. Toward the end of the sustained horn note, Sibelius indicates a crescendo, then a diminuendo, and a final note with a *forte-piano*. The same is true for the woodwinds and the strings. For the latter two groups, the *forte-piano* instruction is clear, but the horns have a tied note. How do they achieve this effect?

A few—but not many—conductors will try to accomplish the horns' *forte-piano* as a part of the release. However, I find it more effective to ask them to separate the last note and to blend with the woodwinds to make it less intrusive. While you do not need to beat during the solo timpani notes, a slight indication as to the length of the rests can be helpful.

The tempo of the Trio at **reh. E** is somewhat free. Normally, I wait to see what the oboist will do, especially with the tenuto marking. *Lento e suave* tells us that the solo is slow and smooth but does not connote melancholy.

The latest edition adds something a bit strange in the second bar for the oboe: The third note of the triplet and the quarter note have both lines and dots over them, whereas the earlier version included just lines. The new articulation did not really work for me when I tried to sing it. In the old days, when portamento was more in fashion, cellists would put a discreet one in between the last G♭ and F of their solo. I still enjoy this, but only one time and not on the repeat.

Conductors have often held back the tempo five bars before **reh. F**, with some choosing to beat in twelve. If you ask the strings, oboes, and clarinets to listen to each other, their instincts usually lead to the appropriate rubato; you can certainly subdivide the last three notes. Note that the clarinets in the next measure are to play louder than they did the first time they performed this passage.

In contrast to how you began the movement, the two-beat preparation at **reh. F** does not need to be too obvious, but you must pay attention to the trumpets and first trombone to ensure that they articulate the first four notes clearly. Most of what follows, at least for a while, is analogous to the first time around. This time, however, roles are reversed, with violins playing what the cellos had before and vice versa.

A variation on the material begins at **reh. G**. The difficulty here is achieving clarity in the double basses; it really doesn't work to have them start *pianissimo*. The bassoons will have no problem projecting.

A hint of what is to come appears in the horns six bars before **reh. H**, commanding the attention of the listener. You have a small decision to make about whether to drop down after four bars of crescendo or continue to increase the sound over seven bars. I am inclined to bring up the horns along with the timpani, but this is purely a matter of taste.

Everything is parallel to the first time, including the *forte-piano* in the horns one bar before **reh. J**. The last note for the first violins directly at **reh. I** should be a D, not a B♭ as misprinted in the older edition. Instead of the timpani filling in, we proceed directly to the Lento. The principal difference is in the flute part, where Sibelius presents a slightly different rhythmic pattern in the fifth bar.

Achieving a sense of ensemble between the section cellos and the oboe in the sixth bar can be difficult, so I recommend rehearsing them separately and pointing out what to listen for in this spot. The same advice holds true when the violas enter.

Eight bars before the start of the last movement is one of the most difficult passages to execute, with a major decision to make in each measure. For example, the indication *Poco accelerando*, on the face of it, seems clear. However, the next instruction, four bars later, is *Largamente*. I have discussed the idea that this may not be a tempo but rather a mood. Correspondingly, I do not believe I have ever heard an abrupt change of tempo at this point—perhaps a slight adjustment, but not exaggerated.

Aside from the occasional chord, two elements are going on simultaneously: the moving eighth-note figure in the strings and the melodic line that bounces around the rest of the orchestra. The first has no crescendo and is only marked *poco forte*. Therefore, we can surmise that this is background material.

The problem occurs in trying to balance the melodic element. When it first appears, two horns and the cellos play, which works well. The next iteration is in the bassoons and the lower two horns, but with double basses playing pizzicato instead of cellos playing arco. Did Sibelius intend for these to sound equal? Absent the body and depth of the cellos, the line feels just a bit weak.

Notice that the composer plays around with the use of the clarinets and bassoons, putting them both together in the bar before **reh. L**. Consequently, when the melody is in the horns and cellos, no adjustment is needed, but in the other phrases, the balance is slightly thrown off.

Here is a possible solution if you desire equality: always have the clarinets and bassoons play together. This provides symmetry, but as we have seen before, that may not be Sibelius's aim. Nevertheless, this method may work if you do it discreetly.

As mentioned, the *Largamente* does not necessarily mean that you should slow down, although the music is clearly transitional and relatively heavy. Aside from the occasional diminuendo in some of the parts, the remaining four bars represent a crescendo to the Finale. However, keep in mind that the horns' rhythmic figure must be heard clearly, as it sets up the trombones at the start of the next movement. Nothing should be *fortissimo* until the final bar, at which point you should go into twelve.

The last measure offers a couple of interpretive options. Does the allargando take us into the new tempo, with the quarters leading into it? Or is it a gigantic slowdown, with the fourth movement suddenly in a new tempo? The surprising diminuendo in the trumpets and trombones at the end of the bar also presents choices, mostly based on what you want to do when you arrive at the last movement.

## Fourth Movement: Finale. Allegro moderato

The *Allegro moderato* starts with somewhat of a twist. After such a lengthy buildup, you would think that the culmination would be the resolution to D major. The key is right, but instead of leading to a monumental sound, as

Bruckner might have done, we suddenly start a bit gentler at single *forte*. The only disruptions are the upbeats in the tuba and double bass, amplified by the timpani and an accompanying rhythmic motif in the trombones. In my opinion, ♩ = 84 or perhaps a little faster feels right.

This opening needs some weight, so do not overdo the reduced dynamics. Even though the basses have a slur, this line is usually played with the Ds on an up bow and the accented C♯s on a down bow. The basic nature of this opening is majestic and noble, not bombastic.

Three bars before **reh. A**, be mindful of the slur at the end of the bar. Similar to previous spots earlier, Sibelius wants this almost totally legato, and here, the slur basically covers the string crossing. At **reh. A**, the cellos and basses have the same crescendo as the timpani but with different dynamics. To honor the way it is written, the strings are more aggressive, and this is best accomplished with a series of up bows.

Some conductors will move ahead slightly in the fifth and sixth bars of **reh. A**, pulling back to the original tempo after the *forte*. Here we have a crescendo and no indication that the sonority drops down as it did when the movement started. The sound will continue to get fuller over the next several measures.

Even though the timpani is only marked *mezzo forte* for the three eighth notes five bars after **reh. A**, the dense texture around this figure justifies bringing it out. To achieve the lower dynamic seven measures before **reh. B**, allow a little time for the rich sound to clear. Often you will hear a conductor do a *poco più mosso* rather than the indicated stringendo. Traditions have a way of enduring.

In the bar before **reh. B**, you can either play all the notes equally or take another down bow on the second note to emphasize the three-note phrase of the opening. At **reh. B**, the fourth horn takes over the role of the tuba, and the accent must be clear and distinct in each measure.

From the sixth bar of **reh. B**, the familiar two-note grouping should once again include a hint of separation in the oboes and clarinets. The scales two bars later look more difficult than they are; finishing together at the end of the bar does not present any problems. (This will be quite different when it occurs in the recapitulation.) Simply continue right in tempo.

A tradition that seems to be disappearing is slightly holding back the three quarter notes before the *Un poco con moto* marking. Many conductors used to stretch this out, but moving forward also has its merits. The bassoons and basses must play their entrance quite aggressively; otherwise, it sounds weak.

One measure before **reh. C** is yet another contradictory place requiring a decision from the conductor. You can see that the second violins and double basses have a crescendo, but the firsts and violas head in the opposite direction. If you jump to the bar before **reh. O**, which contains the same material, everyone is getting louder. Generally, it seems that when Sibelius does something once, he probably wants it that way again. But as I have suggested during the course of this discussion, this is not always the case.

So, we have three options: play it both times as written, change the dynamics the second time to match the first time, or have all the strings make the crescendo the first time. We have become a more literal musical society. The question we must ask ourselves time and again is whether we can justify changing what the composer presents. Perhaps the composer is not always right—that is why we have scholars, editors, publishers, and interpreters.

Still, you cannot alter something unless you can back up your decision with musical logic. I do not mean musicology, although that can enter into your thinking. Should you be asked why you made a certain choice, you should not say, "I felt it that way." That response is meaningless, other than signaling that you really did not think it through. You can play the bars in question several different ways. Whatever you decide to do—and who knows, you might find yet another option—always back it up with well-considered reasoning.

Enough preaching for now. Let's return to the first of the Rossini-like moments where layers accumulate and get louder and louder. The ostinato figure in the violas and cellos provides rhythmic stability, and everything else must fit in accordingly. Take note of the dynamics, including hairpins. When the violas join in, avoid accenting their first note to prevent any feeling of intrusion and ensure a continuous flow.

The oboe gets the first word with the melodic figure that sets up the next minute and a half of music. The final note of the oboe's second bar is clearly the end of the phrase; this distinction will matter when you come to the four-bar phrases that begin fourteen measures after **reh. C**. Most conductors and musicians understand this, although it helps to remind the strings. In the past, however, some interpreters considered that final note an upbeat. Conduct a very slight diminuendo at the end of the measure, followed by a breath, to clarify that the next phrase starts on the downbeat. Keep this phrasing consistent no matter which instrument or group plays it.

Adding a crescendo in the strings six measures before **reh. D** ensures that their *mezzo forte*—and also the *forte* in the horns—does not seem too abrupt. The brass entering four bars before **reh. D** stay at single *forte* and can either perform this phrase marcato or with more weight on the quarters.

With an allargando approaching, I recommend that you do not slow down too much at **reh. D**. The quarter note in the first two horns eleven bars after the Moderato is most effective when played on the short side. The first clarinet's last note in the bar before **reh. E** seems wrong, but do not change it.

Observe the different dynamics in the three string phrases beginning six bars after **reh. D** through **reh. F**. The first phrase is slightly rich in tone, the second serves as an echo, and the third returns to *mezzo piano*, perhaps louder than the first. It is certainly permissible to conclude the bar before **reh. F** with a diminuendo and even a ritard.

From **reh. F** all the way to **reh. K**, Sibelius presents an extended accelerando, one of the longest he would write until the one in the first movement of his Fifth Symphony. As with any lengthy passage that moves forward slowly, I suggest adding a few metronome marks along the way as signposts to remind you where you are in the proceedings.

I usually begin around ♩ = 72, somewhat slower than the tempo that began the movement. The cellos can phrase in two-bar groups starting in the fifth measure, playing two bars legato and then the next two bars separated into groups of two notes. Thereafter, the quarter notes are separate, as are the eighths, of course.

Resist the urge to move the bassoons along when they come in at **reh. G** and maintain a heavy feeling instead. All the strings' eighth notes should be played on the string. Obviously, both oboes should sound equal in all respects, five measures after **reh. G**. Once in a while, a conductor will ask the first oboe to play all five bars of this phrase.

At **reh. H**, try to get the upper line of basses to articulate their notes so that the pitches are clear. One possible solution is to have just the last stand play the sustained B♮, as that note is covered well by the second bassoon. At this point, I suggest a speed of ♩ = 84 at the most. Increase to ♩ = 104 by **reh. I** and then to ♩ = 120 at **reh. J**. Seven bars after **reh. I**, when the two trombones get their turn at the tune, it will feel like they come in a bar too early; bring them out to clarify that this entrance is not a mistake.

The accelerando continues, and you can go as fast as you like, but soon it is time to slow down. I usually start the allargando two bars before indicated, but I only use it to return to the starting tempo. I know that other conductors take a lot of time, but I feel strongly that **reh. K** should not sound like a *subito più mosso*.

Everything is as it was until the key change at **reh. M**. The run before **reh. N** ends on the downbeat, but we know from the earlier passage that the phrase begins on the second note. Therefore, I advise adding a slight separation and a smidgen of time between the first and second quarters. You can show this through a slight expansion of the first beat, but you should also explain it, especially to the cellos.

Beginning at **reh. O**, Sibelius essentially repeats the earlier long crescendo, this time preceded by a crescendo for everyone in the previous bar. If you follow the composer's instructions regarding the dynamics, most of this next passage works out fine. Notice that the four-bar phrase is sometimes divided between strings and winds, as at sixteen bars after **reh. O**. This is a good place to write in an additional rehearsal figure, perhaps **reh. O1**.

The softest of the phrases occurs four measures before **reh. P**. The basses join the ostinato one bar prior to **reh. P**; be careful not to raise the dynamic level too much, as the buildup must continue. You might choose to bring out the triplet in the trumpet and timpani as part of the melodic line; take care not to overemphasize it, however.

In the passage at **reh. Q**, the timpani accent on the third beat is a new idea that deserves to be heard. Sibelius introduces another idea in the trombones, tuba, and double basses eight bars before **reh. R**. I follow the composer's dynamic markings and bring out the quarter notes, in balance with the timpani. Then, at **reh. R**, I bring up the trombones so that the line now sounds complete. This is purely my preference, but I encourage you to consider it.

Conductors appear to be equally split regarding one note that appears seven bars after **reh. R**, although this is not even mentioned in the supplemental material accompanying the latest score edition. The scale passage in the woodwinds, second violins, and violas is printed as a continuation of the B♭ that has been going on for almost two minutes. But this bar also has an F♯ in the tune, modulating into the major key. I listened to twenty recordings and found that half of the conductors changed the B♭ to B♮.

As I was writing this essay, I was also conducting the piece. My practice has been to change that note to B♮, but the first oboist, an extremely experienced professional, proclaimed that he had never done this and made a strong argument that the D-major climax occurred in the next measure.

With ample rehearsal time, I had an opportunity to try both options. In very different ways, they both worked. But to really be convincing with the B♭, I broadened the end of the measure and asked those with the moving line to make a crescendo into the B♭. You will have to decide for yourself. Considering that this transpires at a high point in the movement, it is of great significance.

Four bars before the *Poco largamente*, you can already be a little slower. However, when you arrive at the triple *forte*, strive for a truly heavy, almost ponderous effect. The strings should play a slow tremolo rather than sixteenth notes to give thickness to the passage. Traditionally, conductors place a substantial ritenuto before the *a tempo* at **reh. S**, which is usually played a little slower. At this point, the strings can return to playing sixteenth notes because the rhythm is steady.

According to Gene Pokorny, at **reh. S**, "The long D pedal point is occasionally eliminated in favor of doubling the cello line for four measures." I think this depends on the ability of your orchestra. From my point of view, the tuba could sound out of balance with the low strings.

The *subito mezzo piano* in the upper strings five bars after **reh. S** creates a lovely effect. I return to a slow tremolo, as the ritard is again in place. This next spot is an example of a composer requesting too much of a good thing. Triple *forte* in Sibelius is not the same as it is in Rimsky-Korsakov, for example. It always needs to have great nobility, and reaching it twice seems like overkill. I reduce the dynamic in the brass to a rich single *forte* the first time and then let them truly come to the fore at **reh. T**.

Even though the tempo is steady at the *molto largamente*, I prefer for the strings to continue the slower tremolo because I find that the sixteenth notes rob their sound of some richness. Having reduced the dynamic of the brass, I ask the timpani to make a crescendo going into **reh. T** and direct the other instruments to follow suit.

Take a little time with the upbeat to the last four bars, subdividing for the benefit of the brass, in particular. The clarinets have a curious and likely overlooked rhythmic indication during these last four bars. For reasons unclear, they are the only musicians with a whole note followed by a rest. I think it makes sense for them to play in the same manner as everyone else.

Customarily, all instruments take a breath before the three D-major chords at the end, although I have heard some conductors continue the timpani roll without a separation. As with the second movement, the last bar continues for one full beat. Make the fermata as long as necessary, give the downbeat for the final bar, and cut off on the second beat. I am not sure if a crescendo is needed here, but perhaps a little one can be effective. While certainly complicated, Sibelius's Second Symphony is always one of the most intoxicating pieces to conduct, and you will undoubtably feel a sense of exhilaration when it concludes.

## Conductor's Etiquette

This symphony features surprisingly few extended solos. I usually ask the two bassoonists, and then the oboist, to take bows, followed by the timpani, brass, woodwinds, and strings. It is not necessary to have the principal cellist stand.

*\*\*\**

> "The framework of a symphony must be so strong that it forces you to follow it, regardless of the environment and circumstances."
>
> —Jean Sibelius

## Notes

1. Jean Sibelius, *Symphony No. 2* (New York: Associated Music Publishers, Inc., 1933).
2. Kari Kipeläinen, "Afterword," *Sibelius Symphony No. 2 in D Major, Op. 43*, ed. Kari Kipeläinen (Wiesbaden: Breitkopf & Härtel, 2004) p. 211, https://www.breitkopf.com/assets/pdf/6293_PDF_PB5376_NW.pdf.
3. Jean Sibelius, *Symphony No. 2 in D Major, Op. 43*, ed. Kari Kipeläinen, Urtext Based on the Complete Edition "Jean Sibelius Works" (Wiesbaden: Breitkopf & Härtel, 2004).
4. "Symphony No. 2, Op. 43 (Sibelius, Jean)," International Music Score Library Project (IMSLP)/Petrucci Music Library, https://imslp.org/wiki/Symphony_No.2%2C_Op.43_(Sibelius%2C_Jean).
5. David Cherniavsky, "Sibelius's Tempo Corrections," *Music & Letters* 31, no. 1 (1950): 54, http://www.jstor.org/stable/729017.
6. Gene Pokorny, email message to author, December 13, 2022.

# Nikolai Rimsky-Korsakov: *Scheherazade*

"I had no idea of the historical evolution of the civilized world's music and had not realized that all modern music owes everything to Bach."

—Nikolai Rimsky-Korsakov

No known restrictions on publication. Library of Congress, Prints & Photographs Division, photograph by Harris & Ewing [reproduction number, e.g., LC-USZ62-123456] Rimsky-Korsakoff, ca. 1937. Photograph. https://www.loc.gov/item/2016872663/

During the nineteenth century, most composers hailing from Russia were primarily concerned with producing works that spoke to the country's rich history and folklore traditions. A collective of composers known as "The Five" came together in the 1860s to create a national school of classical composition. At this point, Russia did not yet have a symphonic tradition, and it would be up to Peter Ilyich Tchaikovsky to move the needle and point it toward Europe. "The Five" comprised César Cui, Mily Balakirev, Alexander Borodin, Modest Mussorgsky, and Nikolai Rimsky-Korsakov.

Rimsky-Korsakov expressed an underlying interest in the exotic, and it was here that he would separate himself dramatically from his colleagues. By 1887, he had already written Symphony No. 2, "Antar," based on an Arabic legend, as well as the equally exotic *Capriccio espagnol*. As far as we know, *Scheherazade* was not composed on commission; rather, the composer was apparently fascinated with pictures he had seen depicting various episodes from *The Arabian Nights*.

Instead of going the route Mussorgsky had taken in his *Pictures at an Exhibition*, Rimsky-Korsakov felt strongly that the general mood was more important than the actual stories themselves. Originally, he planned to use a specific musical term to distinguish each movement—Prelude, Ballade, Adagio, and Finale—before being persuaded to assign them thematic titles. In a revised edition of the score, he eliminated the movement labels, explaining, "All I desired was that the hearer, if he liked my piece as symphonic music, should carry away the impression that it is beyond a doubt an Oriental narrative of some numerous and varied fairy-tale wonders and not merely four pieces played one after the other and composed on the basis of themes common to all the four movements."[1]

The composer conducted the premiere in Saint Petersburg in October 1888. It was an immediate success and has never left the standard repertoire. The score was originally published by M. P. Belaieff, printed in Leipzig. For our purposes, we will use the Dover edition reprint.[2] Sadly, measure numbers are not included. The cover boasts a "Lay Flat Sewn-Binding," but that turns out not to be true, at least the "lay flat" part. You may have to get creative to keep the pages from flipping over by themselves.

The orchestration is typical of late nineteenth-century Russian works, especially those dealing with exotic material: two flutes, piccolo (second flute doubling second piccolo for a few bars), two oboes (second oboe doubling English horn), two clarinets in A and B♭, two bassoons, four horns in F, two trumpets in A and B♭, three trombones, tuba, timpani, bass drum, snare drum, cymbals, triangle, tambourine, tam-tam, harp, and strings.

To play all the parts as laid out, five percussionists are required, not including the timpanist. Some creative section leaders, who might also be efficiency experts, have reduced the number of percussion players to four; the distribution of these parts is best left to discuss movement by movement. The string count should be 12-10-8-8-6 at minimum.

Rehearsal letters are provided, but in some places, they are further apart than I would like. You can either put in additional letters, which would need to be passed along to the orchestra, or you can mark your score to indicate the number of measures between the letters. For example, in the first movement, the eleventh bar (out of twenty-four) between **reh. A** and **reh. B** is clearly a new phrase, and you can notate that in your score. Yes, the musicians will still have to count measures, but this can save you a bit of time in the long run.

Performance time is between forty-two and forty-six minutes, with a few interpretations approaching the fifty-minute mark.

## I: The Sea and Sinbad's Ship

A fundamental question confronts us before we even consider one note of the score. Will we try to tell the story and define the principal characters, or can we simply make the piece an evocative tone poem? Either way can work, but the music is filled with so many diverse elements that it is almost impossible not to convey them, even from the very opening.

The layout of the instruments on the page is traditional: woodwinds on top, followed by brass, with horns above trumpets. However, please note that the first two trombones are written in alto clef, not bass. Rimsky-Korsakov, as we will see in the second movement, had three different instruments in mind for the members of the section: alto, tenor, and bass. Next comes the tuba, timpani, harp, and strings. Percussion instruments do not contribute to this opening movement and therefore do not yet appear in the score.

The tempo indication is *Largo e maestoso*, ♩ = 48. This is quite slow but appropriate for the musical content. Giving the upbeat is challenging, as all the lower instruments are playing; to get everyone to play together requires taking a collective breath. While you could just give a broad upbeat, I have found that thinking about a triplet during the half note gives the musicians a better feeling for when to come in. As it is, a triplet appears in the second bar, anyway.

Make sure that the level at which you start your upbeat is exactly where the downbeat will land. Use both arms while conveying the ponderous nature of the phrase and orchestration with your whole body. How you open the work sets the tone for the entire piece, and if you do not have the sound firmly in your head, the result will be weak and phlegmatic.

When is a trill, such as the one in the third bar, supposed to stop? It seems clear that this ends on the fourth quarter of the bar, but does this mean the note stops, or does the C continue without the trill? It is certainly possible to interpret it either way, and as we will see later, this trill does not always end in the same place.

Whichever you choose, coordinating the sixteenth note can be tricky; I usually subdivide the second half of the bar. The fourth measure presents another dilemma: The violins do not have a low F♯, so they cannot play the conclusion of the phrase, yet the sound must remain rich and full, even with up to forty musicians dropping out.

Here we can rely on a visual element to convey to the audience the ominous character of the evil Sultan. As you get to the midpoint of the third bar, turn your body toward the lower strings, almost as if these were the only instruments playing all along. A similar moment occurs in the second bar of the last movement of Tchaikovsky's Fifth Symphony.

With dots over the two half notes, plus accents, you must decide the degree of emphasis and how long both notes last. I prefer two down bows and ask the strings to retake at the last moment. There is no need to move during the grand pause.

The woodwinds play a series of chords reminiscent of Mendelssohn's *A Midsummer Night's Dream* Overture. Even though only four instruments are involved, getting them to play together can be a problem. In the context of four consecutive fermatas, to a certain degree, there is no tempo. I usually give a slightly quicker three/four for preparation, and this seems to work.

These chords can be an intonation nightmare. If this occurs when you sightread the piece with the orchestra, do not wince. If the same trouble recurs when you rehearse, here is a piece of advice that will serve you well in this and all similar situations, assuming that the chords are triads or some variant of them.

For the first chord, ask the two clarinets to play their notes. Once the tonic is established and in tune, add the fifth of the chord in the first flute. When that is secure, drop in the second flute; that player then knows how to adjust to the other three musicians. You can use this strategy for each chord here as well as in other works, such as the aforementioned Mendelssohn overture.

How long to hold the fermatas is a matter of taste, and deciding how much time to take between each bar is not easy. Each of you will have your own idea, which must be firmly in your head and related to your gesture. I use the same three/four that started the first fermata bar, with the cutoff being that third beat. Some conductors take a lot of time here, which is okay, as long as it does not detract from the overall musical scheme. Keep in mind that you will have to repeat this passage in the last movement.

Although the grace note two bars before the 4/4 can be played before the beat, very few conductors try it this way, opting instead to do it as a quick downbeat, almost equivalent to a sixteenth note. Keep in mind that the previous three measures are *pianissimo*, and this one increases to *piano*, with a diminuendo on the final fermata.

Much of the decision to program *Scheherazade* depends on the ability of the concertmaster to play the solos that occur in each movement. They are not particularly difficult and were likely part of that musician's audition. Of course, if you feel your concertmaster is not up to the task, this also means other works in the repertoire are out of reach, including *Ein Heldenleben* and *Also sprach Zarathustra*. More than likely, if your leader is mostly able to negotiate this piece, you should go ahead and schedule it.

Legend has it that Scheherazade told 1,001 captivating tales, so the first one sets the tone for our heroine to stay alive. The bloodthirsty Sultan has a habit of dispatching his wives after the first night of marriage to guarantee their fidelity. Wishing to avoid that fate, Scheherazade leaves cliffhangers at the end of each story that forestall the execution order for another day.

Rimsky-Korsakov does not specify a dynamic for the initial entrance, offering only the word *espressivo*. The solo should start sweetly but not timidly. The tempo is Lento, ♩ = ♩, and to further complicate matters, the word "Recit." also appears. Very few conductors or violinists follow these measures precisely as written. If we did, the time between the violin entrance and the first arpeggio of the harp would be quite long indeed.

We can surmise that a little more time should transpire before this first harp chord, as opposed to the next two, where only one beat separates the violin's E from the harp's entrance. The different dynamics for the harp can create a nice set of colors, helping to convey the gentle mood in which the story will be told. One way of accomplishing this is to ask the harpist to play the first arpeggio relatively quickly and then spread out the notes to last longer as each arpeggio gets softer.

How much leeway does the concertmaster have with these solos? The answer is always "plenty." The violinist is the one telling the story, and you will find that most play it freely, in more or less the same manner.

In general, your role is to give the harpist a cue to play the chords. You should neither show when to cut off the resonating strings nor conduct these bars by beating time. Make eye contact with the concertmaster for the last F♯ and begin your upbeat to the Allegro when the E sounds.

Much can be resolved by spending a few minutes with the violinist before the rehearsal. The better the orchestra, the less necessary this is. This piece contains only a few spots where the two of you must agree upon a tempo, and they are mostly a matter of your watching and listening to what the concertmaster is doing.

The first movement is the most straightforward of the four. Except for an occasional subdivision, everything is conducted in two. The fifth bar of the Allegro contains an example of a trill that continues through the duration of the tied note, but this will not always be the case.

The dynamics are consistent, and if you observe them, they almost always work out, with only a few problems. One of them occurs in the seventh bar. Notice that the first flute and first oboe have a falling figure. The second note tends to get lost, so make sure that the two musicians involved play it a bit louder. The underlying pizzicato is *non divisi*, starting before the beat and played quickly. I have heard some conductors add the B to double the top note and make it similar to the next entrance five bars later.

Keep in mind that the first *tutti fortissimo* does not occur until **reh. E**, several minutes after the Allegro has started. Be patient with the climactic moments and do not allow them to appear early. This means that the single *forte* two bars before **reh. A** is still restrained, even though the accompanying figure in the second violins, violas, and cellos is briefly marked *fortissimo*.

Keeping a strict tempo can become wearisome as the movement progresses, so I encourage you to consider incorporating rubato. Many conductors move a few of the passages along a little and then return to the main tempo when appropriate. A good example starts at the *pianissimo* in the thirteenth bar of the Allegro, where a bit of forward motion is acceptable before getting back to tempo four bars before **reh. A**, perhaps guided by a small ritardando. You can do this with most of the phrases that follow this pattern.

The *Tranquillo* indication at **reh. B** refers not to a tempo but rather a mood. We can infer this because Rimsky-Korsakov gives no direction to go back to the Allegro tempo. Perhaps he thought it would be implied by the nature of the music. Certainly, it is possible to slow down slightly at the double bar, where a bit of relaxation seems natural.

It might not be a serious problem, but the cellos do not have much time to get to their pizzicato note at **reh. B**, and they must hop across two strings, as well. One solution is to have the outer half of the section play the three arco notes and the inner half play the C♮.

As you approach **reh. C**, consider increasing your speed so that the violin solo is in the Allegro tempo. As far as balance, the orchestration is not heavy, and the violin is always in a register that can be heard clearly. You should aim for the clarinet to sound equal in dynamics to the violin.

Limit the volume to single *forte* at **reh. D**. In general, the quarter notes that follow each group of six eighth-note triplets should include a lift before the next cascade. Note that the first and second horns have slurred notes in the second bar of the phrase, a detail that sometimes gets overlooked.

In the fifth bar of **reh. D**, Rimsky-Korsakov indicates *non legato*. At the same time, the woodwinds, playing the same figure as the violins, have slurs over each group of seven notes. Do we have a conflict here? I believe Rimsky-Korsakov intends for the violins to play marcato, but certainly not off the string. When coupled with the woodwinds, the line sounds both smooth and separated at the same time.

Balance the horns so that the third and fourth dominate five measures after **reh. D**, with the first horn taking over four bars later. The violin trill in the eighth bar expands to include the entire note, so you could argue that all the others are meant to stop after the end of the full first beat.

The ninth bar before **reh. E** contains an omission in the third trombone and tuba. For reasons unclear, Rimsky-Korsakov has left out the eighth notes for the phrase. Several conductors follow what he wrote exactly, but most others, including me, add them every time this pattern occurs.

Even though it is not indicated, I recommend adding a crescendo in the timpani leading into **reh. E**; otherwise, a *subito fortissimo* feels intrusive. Bring out the low B in the basses, second bassoon, and tuba in the bar before **reh. E** as well.

Five measures after **reh. E**, the trills in the violins finally appear as they should have all along. In the previous bar, the lines over the two quarters in the violins tell us that these notes are very slightly separated; a few conductors have done them with two bow strokes. Interestingly, the composer does not ask the trumpets to play *fortissimo* during their imitation of the two violin notes that end the phrase.

Thirteen bars after **reh. E** is one of those places where it might be helpful to add **E1** in case you need to start there. This is also a spot where a slight drop in dynamic can work well, perhaps even as far as *mezzo forte*, to allow for a buildup to the *fortissimo* five measures before **reh. F**. This will require a crescendo as you approach the stronger marking. Oddly, the composer does not have the second violins play the final two eighth notes three bars before **reh. F**. I think it makes sense to add them.

The musical material here at **reh. F** is much the same as at **reh. B**, but Rimsky-Korsakov does not specify *tranquillo*, saving that direction for **reh. L**. The six violins asked for can be divided by stand with two players per part. In the fifth bar, it can be helpful for the violas to play their pizzicatos a little louder than *piano*.

The double basses have an interesting line, independent from the cellos, at **reh. F**. Rimsky-Korsakov has just one bass play starting in the ninth bar. If you have slowed down a little, get back to the Allegro tempo by **reh. G**.

A few conductors have asked the first trumpet to double the first trombone at the double bar five measures after **reh. H**, but of course, an octave higher. In the next bar, I advise asking the first violins to separate the last two eighth notes. When this occurred earlier, the slur worked because the section was in an upper register, but here they are an octave below the flutes, and therefore the notes tend to get lost.

Everything goes forward as before, other than an interesting touch in the fifth bar after the key change where the composer uses only the timpani to make a crescendo at a few points in this buildup. The same two-note addition for the third trombone and tuba can be inserted four bars before **reh. K**. Some conductors hold back a bit in the second bar of **reh. K** before resuming the main tempo in the next measure.

The addition of hairpins in the trombones and tuba can be effective four bars before **reh. L**, complementing the sweep of the viola and cello figuration. If you choose to add this, take care to do so discreetly and do not include one in the bar before **reh. L**.

*Tranquillo* makes perfect sense here, and this time we can consider slowing down a bit without hesitation. As before, pay attention to the violas' pizzicato to ensure that the ensemble is secure. The sound should not be aggressive in any way.

Five bars before the end, try to achieve a *pianissimo* in the woodwinds; this is challenging because the flutes are in a high register. If your efforts are unsuccessful, ask the solo cello to play a little louder. A ritard at the end of this solo is not necessary.

Focus all your attention on getting the strings' pizzicatos together. They must all feel the triplet pulse, but this is interrupted just before the last measure. All the instruments cut off except the fourth horn, leaving the low note to sound alone. This requires us to go out of tempo. My solution is to give the second beat of the penultimate bar, hold, and then cut off everyone but the horn. The cutoff is an additional second beat but contains the same three-note pulse. Then, everyone plays the final chord.

## II: The Story of the Prince-Kalandar

The world of *Scheherazade* takes a different turn as we go from the sea to someplace mystical. Kalandar was once a prince but, through a series of misfortunes, is now a blind mystic who relies on charity as he wanders the land. *The Arabian Nights* includes three characters fitting that description, and we do not know which of the stories Rimsky-Korsakov is presenting, but the peacefulness of the first movement will now be disturbed.

The movement starts with Scheherazade spinning the tale, represented once again by the solo violin, accompanied by gentle harp arpeggios. The final bar of this cadenza is the most dramatic yet. At the end of it, make eye contact with the concertmaster to bring in the harp and double basses.

In Rimsky-Korsakov's day, it was still quite unusual for basses to play with mutes, so the sound of these underlying notes is mysterious. Should they use vibrato? The danger of eliminating it is that the intonation might not be as accurate as you hope. I find that just a hint of vibrato is enough.

Marked Andantino, ♪ = 112, the bassoon solo projects a sense of relative calm. At the same time, the *capriccioso* direction indicates a playful style. Each bassoonist comes up with different ideas, but many will have some fun around the sixth measure, incorporating a bit of rubato when it comes to the shorter notes. Make sure that everyone understands that this passage contains a series of five-bar phrases and not four.

The conductor needs to stay out of the way, only indicating to the basses where they change pitch. It is not necessary to shape these chords around whatever the bassoonist is doing. Rimsky-Korsakov writes one bar that is phrased differently than the 3/8. Six bars before **reh. A** is played as a 6/16, with two beats instead of three. You will get a chance to conduct it during the oboe solo, if you wish.

Balancing the basses becomes quite important when the four are each playing a different note, and this only happens one measure before **reh. A**. The written instruction is *rit. assai*, but there is usually a short fermata on the D. My suggestion is to begin beating time two bars before the conclusion of this solo and follow the lead of the bassoon.

The oboe is in the same tempo as the bassoon cadenza. On the third beat of the bar before **reh. B**, imagine a short fermata and then give the pickup to the next measure in the new, quicker tempo. The indication *grazioso* in the first violins is exactly right: graceful. Keep it simple, with little exaggeration. Pay attention to the accents, as they do not always appear where you might expect them.

Starting five measures before **reh. C**, the composer presents the first in a series of *pesante* eighth notes, followed by an acceleration of the triplets. At some point—and this differs depending on the phrasing—the music will slow down and transition to the next section, which is usually in a different tempo. For this first one, all you do is speed up and slow down your beat.

The ending of the bar before **reh. C**, however, can be a problem. There is a fermata on the second beat, followed by what appears to be an *a tempo* on the third. This seems abrupt, so I, like most conductors, place another fermata on the sixteenth note, playing it slightly longer than indicated, and then give the quick upbeat needed for **reh. C**.

Despite the lack of a metronome mark at **reh. C**, this passage is a bit faster than the previous one. However, it is still beaten in three. Note the *subito piano* in the fifth bar in the winds and timpani. We can assume that the composer meant the same to occur in similar bars that come a few measures later because the crescendo needs to start softer than the *sforzandos* that follow it.

You can add a little ritardando leading into the cello solo, but perhaps more effective is to do it in tempo and then wait a moment before commencing. Do not speed up when the oboe enters eight bars before **reh. D**, as the accelerando should not be exaggerated.

Even though it basically represents a bar of silence, you can give a slightly emphatic beat at **reh. D**, followed by an even stronger one in the second bar. Before discussing the trombone solo, I would like to address the diminuendo in the *Molto moderato*. The score seems to indicate that it starts right away, but many conductors delay it until the trombone has arrived at the final note of the solo. From my perspective, deferring it seems more dramatic and in keeping with the nature of the storyline.

So, why does Rimsky-Korsakov choose the second trombone and not the first for this important moment? Speculation has ranged from an ill-prepared principal to a trombonist who was having an affair with an acquaintance of the composer. The answer, however, is most likely a technical matter. In Rimsky-Korsakov's day, three different trombones were used: alto, tenor, and bass. Even though the same clef was used for the first two, they did not sound alike. He must have wanted the darker sonority of the tenor trombone.

The second measure of this recitative is interesting in that the composer waits two-and-a-half beats before having the muted trumpet respond to the trombone. This is an irreverent moment, with the second instrument usually playing about twice as fast as the first. Giving an entrance cue can be helpful, but neither of the solos needs to be conducted.

The flutes play a soft fifth and cut off on the downbeat of the third measure of the *Tempo giusto*. Everything repeats, albeit in a different key, and winds up in C minor, with a grand pause three bars after **reh. E**. We could debate the actual meaning of "grand pause" for hours. I think it must be longer than the bar in which it occurs; otherwise, the composer could have just written a measure of rest. He also could have put in another fermata. I shall let each of you decide how long this silence should be.

No matter your solution, you must give the second violins a strong downbeat for their entrance. They start a chain of musical events requiring rhythmic accuracy. The first note is a sixteenth, followed by a triplet. If Rimsky-Korsakov had wanted the upbeat to be the same length as those three notes, he could have composed the passage in 6/8 or just have written an eighth note instead. This quick note gets repeated not only in the first violins four bars later but by the brass as well. Do not let the musicians slip into an imprecise rhythm.

As the trumpets and trombones trade phrases, you might notice small circles over the trumpet notes. By this time, valved trumpets were in use, so this indication doesn't really make sense here, and Rimsky-Korsakov will not put it in again.

To set up the passage at **reh. F**, I go into one two bars before the *Moderato assai*. This shows the strings what the pulse will be during these *ad lib.* measures. With the tempo established, the role of the strings is similar to that of a guitar. The dynamic is *piano*, not *pianissimo*. Many conductors bring out what seems to be almost a melodic line when the sixteenths move upward in the first violin. However, if you play it as written, it can sound perfectly fine.

Should we care if the strings are together or not? A few of my colleagues beat during the clarinet solo to keep groups of four sixteenth notes in order. Some add a tremolo pizzicato during the fermata, and this is surprisingly effective, even though it appears that the composer did not want it to sound this way.

If you opt for groups of four notes, the transition to the second measure and subsequent bars can be awkward, and the clarinetist might feel constricted by a specific pulse. Your job here is just to listen to the soloist and make eye contact at the very end so that the start of the next bar is clear. Each successive ritard is more substantial than the previous one.

The music at **reh. G** returns us to the tempo established at **reh. E**. The beat slows down for the *Vivace scherzando*. The metronome says ♩. = 132, which might be a bit too quick to fit in all the sixteenth notes. Twenty-nine bars after the *Vivace scherzando*, where the second bassoon plays a delicious low C, is another good place to put in an extra rehearsal letter. I like to increase the bassoon dynamic to around *mezzo forte*.

Commence **reh. H** at the same pulse you established for the previous passage. This allows more than enough time to make the stringendo, which gets you back to *Tempo primo*. A speed of ♩ = 144 might be a shade too fast for the winds to play the rhythmic figure nine bars after **reh. I**. If this is the case when you read through the piece, then certainly don't make too much of the stringendo.

At **reh. K**, an unusual combination of dynamics occurs at the same time: *forte* for those playing the melodic line, *mezzo forte* for the pizzicato, but *piano* for the winds and brass doubling the strings. More than likely, Rimsky-Korsakov wanted the strings to stand out a bit.

The solo at **reh. L** is a variation on **reh. F**, this time in the bassoon, preceded by a figure in the upper woodwinds. Conduct the first bar of **reh. L** in straightforward four; then, the next measure is the same as it was after **reh. F**.

A *sforzando* without a dynamic, as at **reh. M**, is always tricky to interpret. The instruments that finish the phrase are playing softly, but the composer has chosen the horns, trombones, and timpani for this isolated chord. A sudden intrusion seems too much, so I prefer this at a dynamic level of *mezzo forte* with an accent. Pay particular attention to the double basses' pizzicatos, which should sound clear and distinct. This passage is marked slightly faster than any that have come before it in the movement.

Rimsky-Korsakov provides the instruction *con moto* at **reh. N**; I advise against speeding up here, as this direction is more of a mood than a tempo. Traditionally, conductors hold back the last two eighth notes that occur seven bars before **reh. O**. The fermatas are not held very long, and you do not have to give a preparatory beat to restart the triplets. Just give a strong gesture on beat three for the first and second fermatas, followed by the downbeat of the bar before **reh. O**. Then, conduct a long second beat and a quick sixteenth to end.

The pace picks up at **reh. O**. In the eleventh bar, *ben tenuto* applies not only to the tempo but also to the melodic line, which should be as sustained as possible. Nine bars before **reh. P**, the composer presents a lot of information. He instructs the strings to play spiccato, and the bowings indicate a separation after each fermata. As with the winds before **reh. O**, you only need to give a clear third beat for these first two fermatas. The best way to conduct the change that occurs five measures before **reh. P** is to think of that bar as being in four, with the fermata again on the second beat. Then, give the third and fourth beats and stay in tempo before increasing the speed slightly at **reh. P** itself.

Interestingly, Rimsky-Korsakov only instructs the first violins to play on the G string, but some editions specify this for both sections. The tempo slows down eight bars before **reh. Q**. To allow enough time for the strings to put their mutes on, you may need to stretch out the diminuendo in the horns.

Only the notes with fermatas are done as tremolos; the others are measured. The release of the note after the fermata is just that: a lift and not a rearticulated sixteenth. Sing it to yourself, and you will understand. Again, a simple gesture on beat three will set the phrase in motion. Let the harpist play freely three bars before **reh. Q**. Obviously, this cannot go on forever. Should you not care for what you hear, a short discussion with the musician, perhaps held privately, usually solves the problem.

The tempo fluctuates, so even if you do not follow the precise metronome marks, it is imperative to alter your speed where indicated. Seven bars before **reh. R**, some conductors choose to have the strings play *sul ponticello*. It works wells if done subtly to convey a slight color change.

At **reh. R**, we return to five-bar phrasings with a lot of activity. Most of the musical material encountered earlier returns. The composer writes one continuous accelerando to the end. If your orchestra can do it, ask the strings to play the arco notes spiccato. If this poses a problem, start the violas and second violins on the string, but move to an off-the-string bow stroke when the firsts enter.

I can suggest another tradition that you might want to consider: At the *Animato*, dropping down to *mezzo forte* can help create additional tension and build up the crescendo. A few of my colleagues put a trill in the first and third horns as well as the first trumpet three bars before the end; I am not so keen on that. Other conductors have the two trumpets play the written notes while continuing with the triplet figure, and I find this effective. Just for fun, it would be nice to hear the piccolo's grace notes, which are usually swamped by the other instruments.

Take plenty of time before beginning the next part of the journey.

## III: The Young Prince and the Princess

Our heroine makes an appearance in the middle of this movement, which follows no particular storyline. While its formal structure is straightforward, the various tempos can be tricky to align, as we shall see.

The opening is marked *Andantino quasi allegretto*. Sometimes, conductors do not pay enough attention to the last word and get bogged down. In my view, this movement is characterized by a tender simplicity that must prevail, so I usually follow the metronome mark, which is ♩ = 52. As with the start of Brahms's Fourth Symphony, a few conductors stretch out the upbeat; however, I feel that this should be saved for later in the movement.

We can conduct this opening in either two or six. I choose the former, which requires giving a long downbeat and then a gentle click on the second eighth. Keep in mind that the tune is *piano* and the lower instruments are *pianissimo*. You can incorporate various expressive elements, at your discretion, but again, I would minimize rubato during these starting phrases. The grace notes should be on the slow side. We must also observe the dot over the first note of the third complete bar.

Additionally, in the seventh measure, Rimsky-Korsakov places a dot over the final two notes, a marking that comes up often in Russian music. This indicates a separation between the dotted eighth and the sixteenth as well as a little lift at the end of the bar.

If you have decided to conduct in six, your clarinetist will be a bit pressed to figure out how you want to divide the twenty-six-note run; it might be best to be in two for these bars. One measure before **reh. A**, bring out the important B♭ in the second bassoon.

Even though the composer does not indicate any dynamic, the cellos should come up to at least *piano* for their melodic statement; this falls in line with the dynamic marked in the oboe part. The use of portamento was certainly part of the performing tradition many years ago. Today, conductors and orchestras shy away from this effect, but I believe it should be introduced occasionally.

A good example is in the fourth bar of **reh. A**, where a slide down from the F♯ to the B is lovely if it is not exaggerated; just do it at the last moment and make sure it is audible. A slightly more pronounced slide is printed seven measures before **reh. B** as the cellos ascend from the A to the G. Remember to check in with the second violins once in a while to help them place their pizzicato notes.

When the second violins get the tune at **reh. B**, the first violins are anxiously looking at the second bar. You can certainly go into six, preparing to do so at the end of the first bar. Keep the cellos in mind as well so that their figure at the start of the second measure is clear. The beginning of this bar is played *forte* by all the instruments.

The thirty-second notes in the flutes and clarinets can be conducted in two, depending on the tempo you have selected. Some conductors take a little time on the two eighth notes in the first violins just before **reh. D**. Meanwhile, a few seem to ignore the crescendo, which is a shame because it sets up the diminuendo over the next two bars.

The quickened pace at **reh. D** marks the beginning of a section comparable to the Trio of a symphony. The word *tamburo* can be confusing because it can refer to an instrument of almost any size. Here it means a snare drum, tightened so that the timbre is high. Percussionists always seem to know what to do, and rarely have I had to ask them to change the instrument. The clarinetist should impart a playfulness while staying strictly in tempo.

Notice that the second flute joins in at **reh. E**, leaving the first flute to imitate the drum, even though the figuration is slightly different. Although the violins are marked muted for the pizzicato, I don't think it makes a lot of difference to the sound, especially at *pianissimo*; however, we will soon see why Rimsky-Korsakov asks for mutes.

It is worth rehearsing the connection between the clarinet and flutes at **reh. F**. The former will more than likely have to play a little louder than *pianissimo*. The violins are muted here, but as you can see, the firsts really do not have the time to put theirs on, which is why the composer indicates this earlier. The lower strings remain unmuted.

The fifth bar of **reh. F** marks the first time all four percussionists play together. Meanwhile, the woodwinds have a nice accent worth bringing out. Keep the dynamic soft through this passage, as you will have ample opportunity to let fly a bit later.

Occasionally, conductors slow down a little four bars before **reh. G**. I respect that choice, as long as you don't go overboard. If you do hold back the tempo, you can be in six for the pickups to **reh. G**. Even if you are in two, I recommend subdividing unless you have decided to stay strictly in tempo.

We have not discussed doubling the harp because until now, it has not been necessary. However, if your budget can accommodate it, two harps are effective two bars after **reh. H**—as well as four bars later—to help bring out this line, which supports the clarinet. At this point, the first violins have six triplet-sixteenth notes with both dots and slurs. This is a bowing indication; the triplets are played down bow and the eighth note is on an up bow.

It is permissible to let the trumpet take a little time for the pickup notes five measures before **reh. I**. If you wish, you can also continue in the slightly slower tempo. You do have to get back to the opening speed at **reh. L**, however, and conducting the previous bar in six can help accomplish that. Most of this section will stay in two, but you might also want to go into six for the second bar of **reh. K**, depending on your chosen tempo. The *a piacere* gives the flute a lot of freedom to slow down significantly toward the end.

In a way, the basic tempo of this movement can be determined by looking at **reh. L**. This is a passage that the concertmaster cannot play if you are too slow; the ricochet bowing only works at a somewhat flowing speed. You will have to wait for the soloist to finish the flourishes and start the eighth notes four bars before **reh. M**. From this point on, being in six is a wise choice.

Rimsky-Korsakov brings this movement to a climax at **reh. M**. The timpani makes a strong crescendo, and usually, those playing the melody begin *forte*. The *Allargando assai* direction allows ample leeway to take as much time as you would like. Most conductors ask the first violins to take separate bows for the two eighth-note upbeats.

Eugene Ormandy was the first conductor I am aware of to have asked the first violins to shoot up an octave and play full throttle from the middle of the second measure after **reh. M**. I assume that the second violins divided the top line, with half of the section taking over the original first-violin line. What a magnificent effect! Still, it goes against pretty much everything that is written.

If you want to try it, be my guest, but you must totally believe in this alteration and not decide to change it just to be different. In any event, you still have to deal with the fermata, which is easily dispatched by using the right arm to gesture to the right on the fifth beat and then holding that position. When you are ready to proceed, simply continue, as if you had pressed the pause button in the middle of your gesture; effectively, you are adding an extra beat five.

Go back into two for the *a tempo*. If your concertmaster plays the bounced-bow parts a little quicker than the main tempo, then start the violin solo a little later than written. This helps coordinate the orchestra on the downbeat.

Several conductors of an older generation used to make a cut here, from the last two eighth notes of the *a tempo* bar to the two eighth notes immediately preceding **reh. P**. These days, this excision is rare. Nevertheless, I can see the reasoning, as the music duplicates and expands on what has already occurred, and the climax has already taken place.

Assuming you are not making this cut, the usual practice is to let the horn play the two eighth notes before **reh. O** quite broadly and then keep relaxing the tempo. Return to the Trio section tempo, or perhaps a little faster, at **reh. O**. Never let this section become lax; it needs forward momentum. In the bar before **reh. P**, you can introduce a ritard, and I suggest conducting in six from this point.

You have one last problem to solve in this movement, five bars before the end, where you must return to the quicker tempo for the two eighth notes in the flute. A few conductors have allowed these notes to be played slowly, returning to the faster tempo on the next downbeat, but that is cheating. Start off in six, and when you get to the fourth beat, give a single upbeat for the second half of the measure. Since just one instrument is playing, the flutist can fit in easily. Be sure to rehearse this, especially if you want the resolution on that fourth beat to sit for a while before the flute commences.

The movement ends with the rarely seen indication of *dolce* for the pizzicato chord. It starts before the beat and can be played in a guitar-like fashion but without the string section putting their instruments on their laps.

## IV: Festival in Baghdad. The Sea. The Ship Breaks Up against a Cliff Surmounted by a Bronze Horseman. Conclusion

The last time I looked at a map, Baghdad was not really near the sea. Clearly, this final tale traverses all the lands of Arabia. What a thrilling ride it is, offering musical glimpses backwards as the themes of our protagonists are tossed about. Plus, new material is introduced as well as one extraordinary stroke on the tam-tam.

It all begins with the Sultan's motif that was introduced at the start of the piece, here played as heard in the second movement. In that section, the speed was ♩ = 144, whereas now the metronome mark is ♩. = 152. This pulsating passage can be done in one, but most conductors usually lead it in two. Take plenty of time with the silent fermatas.

A very soft B leads into the violin solo and does not require any particular tempo indication. The next Allegro is the same as the opening but slightly extended.

Stokowski introduced an interesting idea in his renditions. Instead of the cellos and basses playing a *pianissimo* E under the second solo, he changed it to *forte*, and in another recording to *forte-piano*. I tried the loud version once and really liked it. The violin still cuts through, and it adds a layer of tension. This goes against my usual reasoning about how to justify changing what is written. But sometimes, not often, I go with my gut, which tells me this alteration is worthwhile.

The Vivo is conducted in one, but Rimsky-Korsakov includes something very interesting in the time signature, considering the time when the work was composed. He sets it at 2/8 but also lets us know that sometimes the rhythm will be duplets (6/16) and other times triplets (3/8). The metronome marking is for both, ♩ = ♩. = 88, which is a little faster than the tempo of the opening passage.

The new instrument here is the tambourino. This can mean a small medieval drum or, in this case, a tambourine. Some conductors have had only one flute play the line that begins in the ninth bar, but the color of the two together is remarkable and should not be changed.

At **reh. A**, the violins play very lightly and somewhat playfully. The offbeat accents are nice if brought out a bit. Obviously, the connection between the basses' and cellos' pizzicatos is important. While not marked as such, the melody at **reh. B** is usually played staccato. The brass figure at **reh. C** becomes more complex with each successive appearance. Interestingly, Gustav Mahler cut the bar before **reh. D**, presumably to give symmetry to the phrasing. However, because that odd extra bar makes this place so unusual, my advice is to leave it alone.

Stay in tempo for the first three bars of **reh. D**, but then—while still conducting in one—hold back during the four bars of the *Un poco pesante*. Notice that the dotted line following that indication ends after four bars. Although not stated in the score, the usual practice is to go back to the quicker tempo and then slow down again five bars before **reh. E**. If your musicians are unfamiliar with the piece, be prepared to explain and rehearse this.

Go back to the faster tempo at **reh. E** and stay in one. The brass should only play single *forte*, even when the trombones and tuba are added. Depending on what speed you choose, it is possible, and maybe necessary, to make a slight ritard going into the double bar after **reh. F**. The tempo should not be as slow as it was when the same material appeared in the third movement, but some relaxation feels right. If you can get the bassoons and tambourine to continue to feel this as 6/16, it makes a nice contrast to the other instruments in 3/8. Bring out the accents on the third beats of the melody line every so often.

Starting **reh. H** is tricky because you must let the violas and bassoon finish their three-note figure and, at the same time, set up the tempo for the violins. I stay in one for this but slightly increase my speed to the Vivo tempo. The pizzicatos in the second violins often sound as though the second and third notes are afterthoughts. In fact, the note in the middle is very important and should be brought out.

Do not let the horns cover the strings starting four bars after **reh. I**. When the first violins return to arco, the last note of the phrase can either be short or long. I prefer the latter, assuming the clarinet can still come through clearly.

At **reh. K**, the violas and cellos play double stops on the open strings; the musicians will automatically do this without being asked. I would suggest that you mark in the score—until the time comes that you know this passage from memory—the phrase structure as it pertains to the brass and percussion entrances, which can be confusing.

Look at the cymbal part nine and eight bars before **reh. L**. Rimsky-Korsakov appears to ask the player to switch immediately from two plates to one, hit with sticks. This cannot be accomplished, but remember, you have four percussionists, so the musician who is not playing helps out here. The music at **reh. L** pretty much repeats everything in a different key until **reh. M**.

All is straightforward here, but a problem lurks at **reh. N**. With a fast tempo, the violas might have difficulty playing the pizzicato sixteenth notes. They are marked *forte*, which only adds to the strain. Get as much sound as you can, but don't expect the volume you see on the page. A rough and aggressive sound is appropriate from the violins. As with the brass at **reh. K**, you need to memorize the phrase structure.

The horn must keep the tempo steady before and after **reh. O**. Balance can be an issue here. The flute and oboe should be prominent, but the first violins and clarinet must be about equal. Six measures before **reh. P**, the second violins have an octave to play, and I recommend bringing out the lower division.

At **reh. P**, pay attention to the difference between the *forte* and *fortissimo* measures. The dynamic drops down to *mezzo-forte* in the ninth bar. Four measures before **reh. Q**, encourage everyone to give maximum force, especially the woodwinds. The horns and trumpets use double-tonguing at **reh. Q** to play all the notes. Nevertheless, be aware of the tempo—even that technique has speed limits. Since these phrases are four bars in length, counting does not present a problem.

Do not slow down at **reh. R** because the fast tempo is still in effect four bars later. As before, stay in one for the *pesante*, getting back up to speed when the dotted line ends. Keeping a steady tempo at **reh. S** will allow you to continue beating in one. Adding a slight ritard three and four bars after **reh. T** will make this similar to the transition back at **reh. F**.

At **reh. U**, the violins should play on the string, somewhat near the tip. Because of what is coming up for the piccolo and flute, conductors often hold back the tempo at **reh. V**, even going into two. Considering the number of notes the violins have to play, I think it makes sense to do that for clarity.

The fermata at *Più stretto* does not have to last very long, only for the length of an eighth note, according to Rimsky-Korsakov. If some of your string players are approaching this work for the first time, one or more of them may jump the gun and overlook the fermata. It is not the worst idea to warn them that this pause is coming. I do it by putting my left arm out, index finger up, to get everyone's attention.

*Più stretto*, as used here, means gradually faster. I think of it as a stringendo, so when it starts, the tempo is the same as before the fermata. A crescendo begins in the ninth bar, but it takes a while to reach *fortissimo*. You might consider putting in various dynamic marks along the way.

We reach the final fast tempo at **reh. W**. Be sure to save enough energy to make a crescendo going into the 6/4. A few commentators have argued that this is the climax of the movement, but I beg to differ; we will reach that point in a minute. The metronome indication is $\d. = 60$, making it slightly faster than the first movement's Allegro. If ever there was a place to add the word *maestoso*, this is it.

Rich and sonorous, this is another moment when having two harps is useful. I also suggest the use of a hard mallet for the bass drum to distinguish the eighth-note figures. Notice that Rimsky-Korsakov has the percussionist play on the first note of each eighth-note sextuplet, as opposed to the trumpets' tied first note. I suppose it is possible to eliminate the bass drum's first eighth note, but I have not encountered this alteration.

Two bars after **reh. X**, the woodwinds playing the chromatic scale need to start as loudly as possible because the lower notes of the scale can be obscured by the other instruments. To achieve maximum sound, the violins and violas should play the two bars before **reh. Y** on the string.

Two possible retouches can take place after **reh. X** for the purpose of elevating the moving lines above the dense texture. Eight and twelve bars after **reh. X**, the first two horns and first trombone can double the clarinet an octave lower. At **reh. Y**, all the violins can play the first two bars plus the downbeat. Meanwhile, the violas can continue down the chromatic scale in the second bar, doubling the cello.

Stay in tempo five bars after **reh. Y**, although some conductors slow down; my guess is that they go into six. For that to work, the clarinets and trumpets have to do a bit of math to figure out how their rhythm fits in, but it is not that hard. An easier solution, however, is staying in two and only subdividing the second half of the sixth bar of **reh. Y**.

I believe the actual climax of the work appears here. Everyone should make a crescendo into the only *fortississimo* in the entire piece, which appears in the trombones, along with an accent. Many conductors ask for the sole stroke of the tam-tam to be quite loud, reinforcing the idea of this place as the high point.

Stay in tempo until two bars before *Poco più tranquillo*. Then, relax and get back to the same speed as the Allegro of the opening movement. Make sure you allow enough time for the violas to cut off before starting their pizzicato.

Rimsky-Korsakov certainly understood formal structure, as the final metronome mark at the *Tempo come I* indication is the same as the very opening bar of the suite. Notice that he specifies two violins at this *Alla breve*. I believe he was anticipating possible intonation difficulties, but since they both play a harmonic, the likelihood of this sounding good is diminished. Most concertmasters play the whole thing alone. You can conduct this in two, but I have seen and heard some performances conducted in six.

The four *Midsummer Night's Dream*-like chords appear, just as they did when you started forty-five minutes ago. Their diminuendo six bars before the end can commence right away, and they can be cut off during the violin soloist's F♯. Conduct the final two bars as you did the end of the first movement, except now the violin and timpani, rather than the fourth horn, hold the note.

Ormandy made an interesting change to the arpeggio. After the first E, he had the concertmaster go down to the low G♯ and then continue with the ascending arpeggio until reaching the last note. In a way, it coincides with the end of the first solo, which also covers a three-octave span.

The conductors of my generation and those before it did this piece at least once a year. Although still popular, it does not seem to hold that much interest for the younger generation. Regardless, *Scheherazade* is a work that everyone needs to learn, as it contains a wealth of value for all musicians. It is such great music.

## Conductor's Etiquette

This is one of the more complicated set of post-performance bows in the entire repertoire, but perhaps not for the reason you might think. In almost every other piece, the conductor signals for the whole orchestra to rise, goes offstage, and then returns for the solo acknowledgments. But here, as with Strauss's *Ein Heldenleben*, we usually acknowledge the concertmaster before leaving the platform.

You must, however, clearly indicate that the bow is for the concertmaster in a way that does not prompt the whole orchestra to stand. As conductors, we typically finish a piece and gesture for the entire ensemble to rise before we turn to the audience. In this case, you have to slightly shift to the left and gesture to our storyteller to stand. After you shake hands, signal to everyone else to get up.

With that out of the way, when you return to the stage, it is a question of not only who is singled out but also in what order. In the situation of multiple bows, I usually work from the back of the stage to the front. The challenge here is to indicate exactly who is supposed to stand. Make eye contact with that musician, and if they are looking away, catch the attention of the person sitting next to them.

My preferred order is trumpet, trombone, bassoon, clarinet, oboe, flute, cello, and harp, followed by another bow for the concertmaster. Once a musician gets up, proceed to the next one on the list, as this process can otherwise feel as if it might last forever. Upon your next entrance, recognize the orchestra, without soloists. If by some chance the audience demands another bow, the concertmaster can rise again.

***

"Orchestration is part of the very soul of the work. A work is thought out in terms of the orchestra, certain tone-colors being inseparable from it in the mind of its creator and native to it from the hour of its birth."

—Nikolai Rimsky-Korsakov

## Notes

1. Nikolay Andreyevich Rimsky-Korsakoff, *My Musical Life*, trans. Judah A. Joffe, ed. Carl Van Vechten (New York: Alfred A. Knopf, 1924), 248.
2. Nikolay Rimsky-Korsakov, *Scheherazade* (New York: Dover, 1984).

# Pyotr Ilyich Tchaikovsky: Symphony No. 6, "Pathétique"

"To regret the past, to hope in the future, and never to be satisfied with the present: that is what I spend my whole life doing."

— Pyotr Ilyich Tchaikovsky

Portrait of Pyotr Ilyich Tchaikovsky, Public domain, via Wikimedia Commons

# Pyotr Ilyich Tchaikovsky: Symphony No. 6, "Pathétique"

Just as some famous people are remembered by the significance of their last words, some composers leave us with profound and prescient last works. The final completed symphony by the Russian master Tchaikovsky is indeed a fitting epitaph to an incredibly fruitful life. This work seemingly coalesces all the elements of his turbulent life into a definitive musical statement with a surprising Finale few could have foreseen.

The precise reason for Tchaikovsky's death, just a week after the symphony's premiere, will never be known. The composer certainly considered the "Pathétique" his masterpiece and worked at a feverish pace to complete it, despite the absence of a commission or even a scheduled performance. Tchaikovsky was the most revered of Russian composers in 1893, at home in virtually all forms of music: symphony, opera, song, chamber music, and ballet. His successes far outnumbered his failures, so to view the Sixth Symphony autobiographically, we have to search inward to his personal life to understand its bleak nature.

Although composers had utilized slow movements to conclude sonatas and chamber works, this practice had never extended to a symphony. With the "Pathétique," Tchaikovsky alters the standard four-movement form. The first three movements follow down a mostly traditional path with some unusual twists. However, instead of placing a slow movement (Andante or Adagio, perhaps) second or third, he saves this gravitas for the fourth movement, a choice that does not become commonplace until Mahler again breaks with convention and redefines the symphonic mold. This final movement establishes the autobiographical nature of the entire work as a summation of the composer's conflicted personal life.

Originally, Tchaikovsky planned to call the piece "Program Symphony," but his brother Modest persuaded him to change this unusually bland and odd title. Our typical understanding of the word "Pathétique" is sad or tragic. However, in this case we should look to its Russian origins, in which the meaning is closer to "impassioned suffering" and thus quite different in tone and atmosphere. Even though the work starts bleakly, the transformations over the course of the first three movements suggest that Tchaikovsky is looking back upon happier times. Those reflections are shattered in the fourth movement, which begins with a vague harmonic sequence and ends in darkness.

Tchaikovsky's manuscript shows a composer very much in conflict, with passages scratched out and notes added here and there. Overall, the various publishers of this work have made very few changes to his score. We will use the Breitkopf edition, which includes rehearsal letters.[1] I strongly recommend adding measure numbers to your score as well.

The instrumentation is similar to that of the second and fourth symphonies, with additional percussion. Symphony No. 6 is scored for an orchestra comprising three flutes (third doubling piccolo), two oboes, two clarinets (in A), two bassoons, four horns (in F), two trumpets (in A and B♭), three trombones, tuba, three timpani, cymbals, bass drum, tam-tam (*ad lib.*), and strings. Note that for one passage in the first movement, conductors sometimes substitute a bass clarinet for the bassoon. My preferred string section is 14-12-10-10-8 players, but you might need to adjust based on the size of the orchestra or hall.

Performance time is usually around forty-five minutes, but some conductors have stretched this out to almost an hour.

## First Movement: Adagio; *Allegro non troppo*

Bleak is just one possible word we could use to describe this opening. Tchaikovsky marked the speed at ♩ = 54. Since original metronome markings are provided throughout, we can get a great sense of the desired pacing of not only this introduction but also the entire symphony.

The first bar warrants much consideration. More than likely, this is the first symphony to open with just the double basses, here divided into two parts. What about the disposition of the divisi itself (by stand or by front/back)? What kind of sound should be invoked? Is it in the distance, barely audible? Should it be played without vibrato? How loud will it get by the fifth bar? There are no straightforward answers to these questions because these decisions will depend on how you perceive the overall mood. Some choices will also be influenced by the level of quiet dynamics that the solo bassoon can achieve.

Since this introduction is so crucial to the complete view of the symphony, I encourage you to carefully consider the above questions and answer them before the first rehearsal. Given the multitude of variables, I will share with you what I do, and then you can make your own judgments. Remember that every decision you make as a conductor must be justified by a musical or practical reason and not by just saying, "I feel it that way."

For the sake of this discussion, assume that the orchestra comprises eight double basses. The higher note will always be easier to hear, so you might ask the group assigned the lower note to play a bit louder or vice versa. I also suggest that musicians sharing a stand play the same note for purposes of matching intonation. The divisi choice also depends on whether the bass section is arranged in a single line or in rows, as well as the acoustics of the hall. Be ready to tell the musicians how you want to handle this division.

Intonation can be a problem if the section plays without vibrato, so I always ask for just a little at the beginning. As the lower line moves downward, the consequences of your choices become more apparent. Correspondingly, I prefer to divide by stand rather than assign the first four players the upper part. The further away from the audience the basses are, the more difficult it is to hear this important line and the harmonic function it serves.

To some degree, the piece is devoid of tempo until the bassoon begins to play. You can wait a bit before inviting the soloist to enter. More so than in his previous symphonies, Tchaikovsky calls for exaggerated dynamics, but I can assure you that even the most distinguished musicians struggle to play the low E very softly. The bassoon color should emerge out of the bass sound but still be expressive and soloistic. The kind of instrument the bassoonist is playing automatically affects the sound: if it is a German model, it will sound darker and if French, a little reedier. You cannot change this, since the choice of maker is up to the individual.

This leaves us with the question, "How do we get what we want in this opening, setting the tone for our interpretation of the entire piece?" You can control the tempo, shaping the subtleties of how the phrase is played and the time between each entrance. However, you cannot alter the basic sonority that the soloist has been honing for years. Collaboration is key, and you must be willing to find the best solution given what is available. Who knows? Maybe the bassoonist's ideas might be even better than yours.

Great! We figured out the first bar. Obviously, the bassoon must be in the foreground but should not be obtrusive. While the solo line includes many expressive hairpins, the basses only have a single long crescendo. They should not follow the dynamic contours of the bassoon. We can get a good idea of how to gauge the crescendo by observing the dynamic markings in the strings. Should the viola entrance in **m. 4**. represent a sudden color shift or dynamic change? From my point of view, it should sound like a continuation of the growing intensity, and therefore I ask the violas to start a bit softer and under the level of the basses. Rather than being present immediately, they simply emerge organically from what has been taking place.

The same idea applies to the dynamics in the upper line of the violas. Contrary to the double basses dividing by alternating stands, I feel that splitting the violas inside/outside on the stand makes the most sense because it helps spread the sound evenly to the back of the section. To achieve a longer phrase and unified color, I ask the upper divisi to enter on the downbeat in unison with the lower part, playing *pianissimo* and not making a crescendo until the third beat of the bar. They should do this on a down bow and avoid any trace of accent on their first note.

The opening phrase culminates in the *sforzando* at **m. 5**. It ought to sound like a sting, but as Tchaikovsky has written a full-bar diminuendo and not a *forte/piano*, the sting should disappear gradually. Since the upper viola is the only voice that resolves to F♯ in the middle of the bar, perhaps they should not come down quite as much as the others until after the third beat. Give the cutoff for all instruments very gently and allow for a brief silence during which you should not move.

Although the next five measures basically repeat the opening, for reasons that I will never understand, the third bar of the phrase always feels like something different is happening. The music gives the impression of a glimmer of light coming through the darkness, yet the printed notes are exactly the same. Perhaps the effect changes because we know that in the fourth bar, Tchaikovsky has the violas enter on a different note than they played the first time, and we are subconsciously preparing this harmonic shift. In any event, the same questions of balance and phrasing apply until five bars before the ritenuto marking. As with the opening bassoon note, sometimes the horn will have a little difficulty making a *pianissimo* entrance without some sort of miscue. The player knows this entrance is coming, so avoid staring and potentially inciting nervousness.

At **m. 13**, dividing the violas inside/outside on the stand no longer works because the sound is thin. I suggest that the first few stands play the upper line. Some conductors ask the whole section to play to here, but I find that the appropriate volume and color can be achieved with as few as four musicians. Make sure to give a clear cutoff for the woodwinds and horns, together with the violas.

Four bars before the Allegro non troppo, the viola melody can either be performed as one continuous line or with a little separation following the quarter notes. During the ritenuto, subdivide the eighth notes and remember that these two bars are part of one long diminuendo. I ask everyone to be at a dynamic of single *piano* at the start of the bar with the fermata.

How much time should pass between the end of the introduction and the Allegro non troppo? This is not easy to surmise. Tchaikovsky puts a fermata on the last beat of **m. 18**, and yet he also writes three beats of rest at the beginning of the next bar, which represents a lot of silence. For the sake of the audience, you should not move a muscle prior to the faster music, so wait a few seconds before giving a very discreet three beats to prepare the next entrance. Clearly establishing this tempo makes the following passage much easier for the musicians and helps to settle you down.

The question of divisi arises again at the outset of this section. With music that contains groups of consecutive fast notes or syncopations, keeping the musicians physically close helps them hear each other and play together, and saves rehearsal time as well. This passage is tricky, and thus dividing the violas and cellos front/back helps with both ensemble and intonation issues. The sixteenth notes in the lower part of the cellos are often overlooked but can sound wonderful when in proper balance with the violas.

It appears that Tchaikovsky himself put in many of the bowings found in the manuscript. He was not a string player and only an adequate pianist, so he likely relied on others to give him advice. For the most part, the suggested bowings in the score work quite well. Still, music notation is notoriously imprecise. You are going to find questions of length, inconsistencies, and individual discrepancies in music by almost every composer. At the opening of the *Allegro non troppo*, the bowings are good, but the length of the eighth notes is unclear. They are slurred and have dots. In this case, I think we can consider the slurs to be a bowing indication, and the notes should be slightly separated but not off the string.

A common phrasing miscalculation that occurs because of a bowing choice has to do with the last note of a phrase that follows a slur. In the second bar of this section, for example, we have an eighth note that is clearly shorter than the preceding quarter. Often, however, it is clipped so short that we do not even hear it as a resolution to the appoggiatura. It is wise to pay attention to these situations in virtually any score you conduct. The same phrasing and articulations apply to the woodwinds' answer. Note that because the last note of the strings in **m. 23** does not have a dot, the flute entrance needs to begin louder to be audible at all.

You must maintain a very steady and clear beat throughout the opening of the Allegro, especially when the cellos pick up the sixteenth-note figure in **m. 28**, as those playing the upper line can be tempted to come in too soon. In the bar before **reh. A**, the first violins have the curious indication "1. Hälfte," which appears to be a choice made by the engraver and not Tchaikovsky. In any event, the front half of the section should play this, for the same reasons as above: ensemble and intonation. Keep paying attention to maintaining a steady sixteenth-note pulse with the cellos so that the tempo does not vary.

Following a very strong half note in **m. 38**, the composer switches to French and writes, *restez*, which usually translates to "stay in position." It is best to ignore this indication. Are the violins supposed to sustain through the first note of the next bar or, what comes naturally, insert a space before beginning the downward scale? I usually ask for a little separation after the ties and do the sixteenth notes off the string. Importantly, there is no diminuendo on the long notes. The descending lines have what amounts to a four-bar diminuendo.

*Saltando* (**mm. 42–43**) means that the bow is bounced off the string, but here it cannot be allowed to bounce too high, as the sixteenths must be in the precise rhythm and not rushed. Play these first four bars as softly as possible and ensure that the *subito piano* that follows is slightly louder. Note the first entrance of the piccolo two bars before **reh. B** and check that it isn't too loud. At **reh. B**, the dynamic goes up only one degree to *mezzo piano*. The horns are *espressivo*, which some conductors interpret as marcato, but that seems contrary to what the composer wants; this little downward phrase is lyrical and should be played legato.

Beginning in **m. 54**, Tchaikovsky includes a series of hairpins that should be exaggerated. Pay particular attention to which notes have dots and which appear with lines over them. These articulation contrasts are important and prevent the passage from all sounding the same. Often orchestras play crescendos with gusto and then ignore the reciprocal full return to a softer dynamic. Do not forget that everything is relative to the basic dynamic that begins any given passage.

The next tempo modification appears five bars after **reh. C** but in reality starts two beats earlier. *Un poco animando* may be more about the feeling of anxiety than an increase in speed. Since he does not assign a metronome mark, Tchaikovsky may be telling us that the moving forward is quite minimal. The dynamic is only single *forte*, so the full force must be saved for the *fortissimo* that follows.

The trumpets and trombones make their first appearance in the symphony with a martial fanfare. Note that Tchaikovsky gives a triplet to the second trumpet but only duple sixteenths to the second trombone. Did he really intend for a two-against-three feeling? These days, it is certainly not a technical problem for trombone players to tongue quickly enough, and thus I ask them to add the extra note to match the trumpet. One nuance that you rarely hear is the following eighth notes played at full value. The composer certainly is diligent when it comes to these annotations, and it might be interesting to hear these eighths, and the quarters after them, played in a more sustained manner. In **m. 70**, *détaché* for the sixteenths indicates that these are to be played on the string and slightly longer, with each note treated equally.

The notation for the series of falling eighth notes in the bassoons, trumpets, and trombones in the next two bars, **mm. 70–71**, looks unusual. This really is just a six-note figure distributed among several players, and the idea works very well if you make sure that all the accents are observed, followed by a quick decay. A moment of eye contact with the timpanist is advised for this musician's initial entrance.

The next tempo indication is Un poco più animato, ♩ = 132 (**m. 73**). Keep in mind that the Allegro tempo is ♩ = 116, so even if you don't achieve the metronome marks exactly, the increase in speed needs to be noticeable. I am not so certain that Tchaikovsky wanted this adjustment to be sudden, so it is certainly possible to gradually accelerate until this point. For the first time in this movement, all the instruments are playing at the same time.

Four bars after **reh. D**, the sixteenth-note figure in the cellos should stay off the string, for the sake of rhythm and pitch, as the *pianissimo* dynamic can make both murky. By the time the slurs appear, we already have these notes embedded in our ears. The trombones and tuba tend to be just a hair late with the final two entries, so give them a good cue. They will be relying on you in this moment, as it is difficult for those in the back of the orchestra to hear the cellos.

The *ritardando molto* at **m. 84** is also built into the music: the rhythmic figure goes from sixteenths to triplets and then eighth notes. Nevertheless, you must do more to slow down all the way to Adagio. Try to think of your desired arrival tempo and gauge the ritardando to feel organic and gradual instead of sudden. Slightly enhance the size of your beat to show the increase in time to fill.

Although the score makes clear that the melody in the violas (**m. 86**) is a continuation of the previous line in the cellos, the connection between the two instrumental groups is difficult, as their sonorities are radically different. Notice that the cellos play their entire line at the dynamic of *pianissimo* with no further diminuendo indicated, and the violas are expected to pick up not only their dynamic but the whole melodic line as well. One possibility to create a more seamless takeover is to add a soft A after the final F♯ in the cello line. This is also risky, however, especially if one of the cellists holds on to that added note too long or plays it too loudly. The violas usually expect a subdivision in **m. 87** so that they know where to place the final eighth note in the measure.

Remember the long pause between the opening Adagio and the Allegro? Here is another pause, but this time the second subject, a passionate Andante, follows. All the strings are asked to play *con sordini*. Whenever possible, try to encourage mutes on/off ahead of time to avoid disrupting the music during a quiet passage. The violins and basses have plenty of time to put their mutes on prior to their entrance. The violas can put theirs on once the tune begins, but the cellos should do so during the three measures prior to the double bar, ideally during the violas' *mezzo piano* and as discreetly as possible.

The metronome indication is ♩ = 69. This is not a lugubrious Largo. As with the earlier passage, maintain a silence by not moving during the fermata. You can start the tune directly, but I prefer to give two quiet beats to establish the basic tempo.

There are many ways to interpret these twelve measures. Tchaikovsky gives us tempo indications almost every two bars, and for the melody, he writes, *teneramente, molto cantabile, con espansione*. That, plus the multitude of hairpins and dynamic markings, should suffice to tell us how to perform this passage. But these instructions are not enough, and the exact gradations of dynamics and rubato are up to you and the musicians, based on the information in the score. Keep in mind that this passage will return two more times, and each of those iterations should probably be more exaggerated than the last. From my point of view, the first time around ought to be on the simpler side, as if Tchaikovsky were saying, "Here is the tune, but wait until you see what comes next!"

You must decide whether the first three notes of the tune are in tempo or held back. In line with keeping this music uncomplicated on first hearing, I do nothing fancy. Ask yourself, if you were to sing the phrase, would you breathe after the half note in the third bar? Then, look ahead to the seventh bar of the phrase where Tchaikovsky adds a rest instead of a tied note in the parallel spot and see if that changes your opinion. Based on this specific detail, I go against the idea of vocalizing and play the first phrase with no separations until six bars before the Moderato. In addition, pay particular attention to the accents, which do not come on the first note of the phrase but rather in the middle. Treat them more like high points than attacks.

Getting into the *Moderato mosso* (♩ = 100) can be tricky. You can subdivide the fourth beat of the previous bar (**m. 100**) so that the eighth note, which is already part of a ritenuto, becomes the new quarter. Alternatively, you can let the ritard flow naturally and start the Moderato directly at a new tempo, showing the musicians how fast or slow you want it to go.

In the fifth bar, **m. 105**, you will see *poco più forte* and then, in the next bar, *poco crescendo*. Is there a difference? Probably not, but in any event, this suggests a two-bar increase in dynamic. One measure before **reh. E**, as well as eight bars later, the first violins' ascending line imitates the clarinets, including the crescendo. However, if you listen to many recordings, quite often this line is performed with a diminuendo, which is what all the other instruments have. I admit that I also do this, as every time I have tried to conduct what is on the page, it just sounds wrong. In particular, the scale passage leading into **reh. F**—with even more notes—feels awkward and out of place. Maybe Tchaikovsky really wanted us to feel uncomfortable.

Note that the piccolo switches to third flute at **reh. F**. If you have the luxury of doubled woodwinds, this is a good place to utilize them, especially the bassoons. Their line, as well as the clarinets' line five bars later, tends to get obscured. As the upper strings make a crescendo, pay attention to their switch from *saltando* to legato notes, an important detail. In **m. 124**, it will seem as if the dynamics have dropped down when the first violins stop playing. Keep the intensity up in the seconds and violas to account for this until the firsts return two bars later.

When you arrive at the fourth beat of **m. 126**, just prior to the ritenuto, allow the music to end abruptly and do not bring your arms down. Instruct the strings to hold their position, as any motion during the silence will disturb the effect. This physical pause also forces you to wait a bit longer before commencing the *fortissimo* woodwind phrase, still doubled if you have the players. The strings are instructed to remove their mutes, but I suggest they wait until the winds have begun to play to preserve the silence.

You have a few decisions to make in this phrase. Should you insert a breath before the fourth beat of **m. 128**? Should the players make a crescendo into the ensuing *sforzando*? What is the ending dynamic of the hairpin? We have no instructions from the composer about these choices, so they are up to you. Amid the flurry of decisions, do not forget about the ritenuto: make sure the tempo is noticeably held back.

When you cut off the winds, ensure that your gesture ends low; keep your right arm still during the fermata and in position to give a normal upbeat to the next section. Essentially, you are giving the third beat twice: first as the cutoff and second to set up the new tempo. As you prepare your upbeat, think about the triplet rhythm, focusing on this rather than the tune. All the instruments must play each note in the same manner and articulation, with Tchaikovsky's instruction, *pesante, non-staccato* being exactly correct (and for some reason only marked in the wind parts). I usually linger on the third beat just a little longer than indicated before beginning the melody. Imagine a video in which the action suddenly freezes and then resumes. This pause allows a little space for the music to settle as well as the opportunity for you to show the expression needed in advance of the melody.

Although we have heard this music before, the feeling this time is much expanded, both in dynamics and orchestration, with important differences to highlight. In **m. 134**, the trumpet and trombone play the music originally given to the violas, but here the first three notes are *mezzo forte*, and then the downbeat is a *subito piano*. Gone are the accents and some of the hairpins in the sweeping theme, making the whole phrase broader.

The next section—marked Moderato assai, ♩ = 88—cannot drag because it is a transitional episode meant to take us down from the very emotional second theme. Keep in mind that the melodic line always starts from the third beat. Some phrases might require rehearsal and emphasis to bring clarity to the structure. At **reh. G**, for example, you do not need a lift before the third beat, but an indication that the four-bar phrase is in segments helps. Tchaikovsky gradually reduces these to just one bar and then simply two notes.

The clarinet solo should be delayed just a little, allowing the preceding material to fade away. You would think that this dynamic, triple *piano*, would be the softest level, but with three more degrees of *piano* to go, a bit of weight should be infused into the initial entrance. The last four notes of this section are marked as a sextuple *piano* and are assigned to the bassoon, but a bassoon cannot play softer than a clarinet. I do not know when the practice began, but a common solution is to have the bass clarinet cover these notes. Tchaikovsky used bass clarinet in other works such as *Manfred* and *Nutcracker* but did not include it in any of his numbered symphonies. Because it is impractical to hire a musician just for a few notes, often the second clarinet doubles on bass for just this measure. This means they will miss a few of the following bars while they switch back to clarinet, but since the next section begins quite loudly, and the second clarinet music doubles the fourth horn and violas, the omission will not be noticeable.

For the clarinet solo, it is not necessary to conduct in a clear four-beat pattern. The accompanying instruments all have the same rhythms and dynamics, so just let everyone follow the clarinet's lead. For the timpani, treat the eighth note at the end of each group as a release rather than a clearly articulated note. The interesting tempo marking *Adagio mosso* must allow for a slower tempo, and thus the *ritardando molto* ought to be as slow as possible. You can think of the final bar as if it were in eight, giving just a single pickup to coordinate the pizzicato. This must be barely audible, as if the musicians were just blowing air across the strings.

The downbeat of **m. 161** ranks as one of the biggest "shock moments" in classical music, along with the start of the "Infernal Dance" in the suite from Stravinsky's *Firebird* (1947 version). The *Allegro vivo* may be marked only as *fortissimo*, but conductors try to make the first note as loud as possible. I would like to think that the audience comprises at least one person who has never heard this symphony, and this chord should jolt the listeners out of their seats—if not their slumber.

One more element, a bit theatrical, can add to the surprise. Going against expectations, you can very quietly give a small preparatory beat or two, concealing the torrent of sound that will be released with this entry. Any visual indication of the subito *fortissimo* will come too early to make the same kind of impact. Once the notes have exploded, I go back to a more vigorous conducting style. If you choose to do this, be sure to inform the orchestra, lest more than a few of them forget to play forcefully.

Talk about the storm after the calm! We now encounter the most unrelenting development in any symphony written up to this time. Tchaikovsky marks this section *Allegro vivo*, ♩ = 144. Every ounce of energy is packed into nearly four-and-a-half minutes of music that race by at a furious clip. Earlier, you will recall a passage in which the trumpet and trombone had two different rhythms at the same time. A similar conflict occurs in **m. 161**, **m. 165**, and **m. 169** between the strings, who have triplet sixteenths, and the winds and brass, who have duple sixteenths. The tempo is so fast that you do not need to alter anything. The C♮ pedal tones, both long and short, keep the tension almost unbearable, particularly in the bassoons. Note that Tchaikovsky has the timpani and tuba make a quick diminuendo to silence to ensure enough clarity on the faster notes.

To heighten the closing figure two bars before **reh. H**, and to set up the ensuing fugato, consider asking the musicians playing eighth notes to insert a crescendo in the bar before **reh. H**. Some conductors also add a ritard on these five accented notes, but this feels forced and unnecessary to me.

The word *feroce* suits this section perfectly. The main subject should be played near the frog, and the scalelike passages are on the string. Surprisingly, Tchaikovsky marks the brass at only *mezzo forte* in the fourth bar of the phrase and similar spots. As long as you can make the brass entrances sound like one continuous line, this dynamic works.

Starting at the third measure of **reh. I**, the woodwinds clearly have slurs on each beat, but the strings do not. Should they sound radically different? Considering that the strings do not have a dot on the eighth notes, I think the notes in this passage should be played at full value. This lends even more weight to the music while still maintaining a contrast.

I find that **m. 189**, nine bars before **reh. K**, requires a dynamic adjustment. If the brass and timpani enter triple *forte* as marked and sustain that level, then they can easily overwhelm the rest of the orchestra. I place an accent on this upbeat and then immediately drop the horns, trombones, tuba, and timpani down to single *forte*. I make the same alteration the next two times this appears. Five bars before **reh. K**, I apply an accent to the quarter note on the last beat and then drop the dynamic to single *forte* again after the downbeat of the next bar. I add a crescendo for the brass in the bar before **reh. K**, with very strong accents on the two eighth notes.

At **reh. K**, strive to keep up the intensity when the brass drop out, all the way until the diminuendo. You may find that by the third bar, when the cellos and basses are the only instruments playing, the sixteenth notes lack clarity. Be careful not to change the tempo, however. Tchaikovsky purposefully sets up a diminuendo and then a rhythm change to triplets. He does not intend for us to relax the tempo, though that is easy to do here. The trumpet and trombones are marked *cantabile* and should play quite legato. Again, do not allow the sustained phrasing to drag down the tempo.

Eight bars after **reh. K** marks a wonderful one-off moment. The upper strings start a scale that the woodwinds then continue. I disagree with Tchaikovsky's up bow, as it encourages the strings to crescendo, a direction reserved for the winds on the subsequent beat. The two-beat scale should sound like one instrumental group. Although the composer does not specify a final dynamic for the woodwinds, I suggest finishing *forte* for maximum effect and to contrast with the upcoming brass entrance marked *piano*.

Remain in the same tempo for the eight-bar crescendo, which should be properly managed to save some intensity for later, and at **reh. L**. Three elements to be aware of here include the motor-like sixteenth notes in the lower strings, on-the-beat quarter notes in the brass and most of the woodwinds, and syncopations in the flutes and upper strings that sort-of respond to the quarters.

Tchaikovsky writes *diminuendo un poco* in the third bar after **reh. L** and then *forte* at the end of the subsequent bar. From my perspective, this indicates that the diminuendo arrives at *forte*, but conductors are divided about how to interpret this, and many perform the *forte* as a *subito* change.

The music six bars before **reh. M** appears to lack melodic material. However, if you bring out the trombones a little and separate the first note from the dotted half, it feels like a tune. Of course, the horns are anticipating what is coming, so make sure they are clearly heard as well.

It feels natural to hold back the tempo two bars before **reh. M** but not by so much that you diminish the anxiety created by the pulsating horns. Try to find a balance between the tempo of the first Allegro of the movement and the one at the onset of the development. Provide a clear beat to help the horns play together and to prevent the violins from dragging during their melodic fragments. Although you can begin to return to the faster tempo almost anywhere, my preference is to start moving forward four measures before **reh. N**, in conjunction with the crescendo.

The nature of Tchaikovsky's scoring suggests a slower, more *pesante* tempo at the pickup to **m. 249**. A good place to return to the faster tempo is at the *pianissimo* right after **reh. O**.

In the sixth bar after **reh. O**, I ask the players to bring out the repeated sixteenth notes that have been added to the triplets. At **reh. P**, Tchaikovsky includes the instruction *pesante* for the brass, but the meaning of this directive is different from that which I applied to the music a few measures earlier. Since this passage features sixteenths moving at a speedy pace, the tempo should not be altered. In this context, the marking indicates that the brass should play long notes. The dynamic drops to double *forte* six bars before **reh. Q**, but this is usually played with the same intensity as the previous passage.

One bar before **reh. Q**, we encounter a paradox. All the music in the symphony thus far has been leading to this point, as if it were the climax of the movement. Yet, instead of having the timpani make a crescendo, Tchaikovsky very clearly calls for the reverse. The cellos and basses have no decrescendo, although the cellos briefly drop out before returning *sempre fortissimo*. What are we to do? Let's assume that we all consider **reh. Q** to be one of the sonic high points of this work. The timpani cannot be so overwhelming as to cover the whole orchestra, so perhaps Tchaikovsky writes a diminuendo for practical purposes. One option is to ask the timpanist to remain *fortissimo* until just after the attack at **reh. Q** and then drop to a single *forte*. Whether to make the diminuendo is really a matter of how to deliver the appropriate impact in this moment.

The passage at **reh. Q** is simply magnificent. The buildup of tension is almost unbearable, and you can intensify it even more by asking the strings to use "free" bowing, meaning that on the long notes, the musicians can change bow direction several times, independently of their colleagues. Furthermore, full bow strokes are mandatory, and the violins should play the first few bars on the G string to get the richest sound. Common practice is to perform this section just a bit slower and heavier, although Tchaikovsky has already built in that feeling by writing longer and more sustained notes. The basses can play a tremolo instead of the printed sixteenths.

The upbeat to the third bar after **reh. Q** in the second and fourth horns must be heard clearly, as this figure becomes increasingly prominent over the next several bars. I strongly advise against adding the first and third horns or having them play an octave higher. If an assistant horn player is helping to relieve some of the principal horn's burden in this piece, you can ask that musician to join in here.

Finally, in **m. 284**, the timpani has a crescendo, although please note that the arrival point is still one volume level less than that of the strings and winds. The sweeping triple-*forte* upbeat is usually stretched out, delaying the downbeat just a bit. As an answer to the downward motion in the woodwinds and strings, the low brass have an almost fanfare-like set of interjections. They are marked marcato, but as far as I am aware, no one separates the upbeat. Moreover, the sixteenth note of the group is typically played *pesante* rather than quickly.

The printed bowings at **reh. R** may be misleading for the strings. At this point, at least two strokes are needed in each bar to sustain the volume. Even with free bowing, a down bow will come naturally to produce a strong *sforzando* on the downbeats.

On the page, it looks like the timpani should reattack the F♯ in the fifth bar of **reh. R**. While a rearticulation may be desired in other similar passages for the timpani, logic tells us that this is more like what the cellos have, which is just a release of the note. You, as well as the timpanists, will need to make this choice throughout the repertoire, using your judgment to determine whether a separate stroke is appropriate.

The four bars before the key change very clearly specify the dynamic levels at each bar of the diminuendo. Cutting off the winds together with the last pizzicato in the strings—as opposed to holding a bit longer—works well.

After a moment of silence, at your discretion, begin the next section, which requires you to be both clear and vague at the same time. As the thirty-second notes in the cellos occur simultaneously with triplet sixteenth notes in the bass, the intended effect is a murky sound. The cellos and basses should play near the tip of the bow. Coming out of the silent fermata, just a little flick of the wrist in tempo should be enough to get the correct *pianissimo* sound after the eighth-note rest. All the inflections and choices from the first two statements of this material are in play again, with the addition of many more variables. I think that these nuances should be brought out and exaggerated. For example, you can urge the orchestra to play the *incalzando* measures with even more speed and intensity than earlier in the movement.

The ritenuto in **m. 315** is very effective if you can really stretch it out before returning to *Tempo I*. Note that the transition material is only marked at *mezzo forte*, and observing this properly will work well. The cellos can sing out in their melodic material, without too much diminuendo.

At **reh. T**, allow some space to let the chord die away completely before cueing the solo clarinet to enter. Once again, the last note in the timpani looks like a reattack when it is really a release. It is not necessary to conduct the clarinet; focus your attention solely on the accompanying chords and timpani. Regarding the latter, some timpanists will play the first four notes with just a single mallet, depending on the tempo. In any event, these notes must be articulate enough so that you can hear them to know when to start the next phrase. Under some circumstances, I have even seen the whole passage played with a single stick. This can impart an evenness to each stroke that is sometimes missing when two are used.

Follow the clarinet's lead for the *animando* unless the musician is really not in line with your concept. I cannot explain why the timpani has a slur when the rallentando starts, but I can say that this time, the final note is reattacked. The two bars of rallentando going into the *quasi adagio* can be done in eight, but only start beating in eight at the third beat of **m. 332**. The tempo should slow down enough so that the eighth note becomes the quarter at the *Andante mosso*.

The metronome mark of ♩ = 80 suggests a nice, moderate tempo for the Coda. Ask the strings to play the pizzicato notes with a bit of vibrato to give them some life. When the woodwinds answer the brass at **m. 340**, you have to decide whether they should add a breath at the end of their fourth bar. In my opinion, since the next entrances are not part of the previous rhythmic pattern, this two-bar phrase needs to be separate from the preceding one. Avoid making a ritard when the trombones enter; it is already difficult enough for them to play these long notes softly, in tune, and in one breath. You must decide if the low brass should cut off with the timpani's last note (similar to the choice at **m. 304**) or hold on a little longer.

Tchaikovsky puts a fermata on the rest in the last bar for a reason. He wanted the silence after the music to be maintained. We should honor that request and remain still for a few seconds after the final reverberations of the chord have faded away. This is a big movement, with incredibly emotional highs and lows, so allow plenty of time before continuing to the more lighthearted music that follows.

## Second Movement: Allegro con grazia

The operative word to describe this movement is elegance, just as if it were written by Johann Strauss (either of them). But Strauss never wrote a waltz with five beats! How is this possible? How does Tchaikovsky distribute the beats to convey some semblance of a waltz?

With the indication ♩ = 144, Tchaikovsky implies that we should hear this music "in five," but that is not how it is conducted today. At this speed, conductors show the macro beat, meaning two unequal beats per bar, 2 + 3. Why not 3 + 2? The slurs in the first few measures of the cello part reveal the composer's preferred phrasing. However, if you only consider the clarinets and bassoons, you could interpret the beats as 3 + 2. With less-experienced orchestras, you will have to specify which beat pattern you will use. Be aware that you may choose to alter the beat for a few bars in the movement.

When you study, it is always wise to consider not only the entirety of the score but also what the musicians see in their individual parts. For example, at the beginning of this movement, we must think about musicians who don't enter until later. Their music will contain whole-bar rests that do not communicate five beats per bar or in which subdivision.

Having established that we will be in 2 + 3, we have to decide how to give a clear upbeat that shows both the tempo and a clear entrance for those playing pizzicato. When considering how to give an upbeat, think of what the first part of the upcoming bar contains. Since in this case we have determined that it has two beats, that is what you should show.

Once you start, there are important matters of balance to consider. The horns should sound equal to the woodwinds, as if they were playing a single line of music. It is good to rehearse this separately so that they can hear each other. Even though the sixth bar is written as a 2 + 3 grouping, you can lend a touch of gracefulness to this measure by conducting a 3 + 2 pattern.

Every so often, you can help the orchestra by adding subtle subdivisions to the second half of the bar. This preparation is especially beneficial to musicians who have not yet played. A good example is **m. 8**, when the woodwinds pick up the tune after the cellos. While looking at this bar, make sure the cellos observe the glissando, which should be audible but still charming.

The repeat is structurally essential and should never be omitted. Furthermore, I can think of no musical reason to play the repeat of this opening phrase group any differently than the initial statement.

At the second ending, I usually ask the violins to make a slight diminuendo on the eighth notes, meaning that the next passage will start a bit softer than *mezzo forte*. This creates more contrast for the upcoming crescendo. I also prefer that the strings insert a slight space after the second quarter in **m. 17** but not at the *più forte* two bars later. The same will apply to the winds at **reh. A**. Repeat this when it makes sense.

The strings' lengthy pizzicato passage at **m. 32** will reveal whether the tempo you established is too fast or not. Keep these pizzicatos in mind when you set your speed; the players should not have to scramble for notes. Five measures after **reh. B**, bring out the cellos and basses. At this point, we have already heard the tune several times, so the other interjections are welcome.

In many performances, the horns sound like the primary voice at **reh. C**, but in fact, the woodwinds have the tune, so make sure they can be heard. When the trumpets and trombones take over the line in the fifth bar of **reh. C**, a dynamic of single *forte* is loud enough. Use a small, subdivided beat to help the musicians place their eighth note accurately at the end of the second and fourth bars of this phrase.

The Trio, commencing at **reh. D**, has no metronome indication and should stay in the same tempo. Some conductors choose to hold it back a little, perhaps to give more pathos to this B-minor section. Tchaikovsky uses the term *con dolcezza e flebile*, which literally translates as "with sweetness and feebleness." Perhaps this is to tell us not to overdo the expression. For instance, the many hairpins in the upcoming passages can evoke a seasick-like feeling if exaggerated.

The music is quite repetitive, so I find that bringing out inner voices on the repeats provides a lovely change in color without violating Tchaikovsky's instruction. For example, on the first repeat, I have the first violins and cellos play softer while increasing the volume of the seconds and violas. This lends an even greater sense of yearning to the phrase. You must also find the right balance between the bassoons, timpani, and double basses. Interestingly, Tchaikovsky notates eighth notes for the timpani but gives the other instruments quarter notes with tenuto marks. We can consider these tenuto indications to represent slight pulses on each note. When the recap of the opening of this Trio occurs at **reh. F**, the phrases are shorter, so I bring out the dynamics of the inner voices every four bars instead of eight.

The transition back to the opening material occurs at **reh. G**, but the way it appears in the score can be confusing. This is a two-bar diminuendo, not a reattack with a new dynamic in the second measure.

One bar before **reh. H** is another place about which conductors are divided. It appears that the composer is creating a crescendo to get back to the initial subject. Some conductors, however, interject a diminuendo and rallentando, beginning the recapitulation closer to *piano* than *mezzo forte*. I usually count myself among those who slow down and decrease the dynamic, but I may reconsider this position. Upon examining the phrase further, I think the addition of the first violins to the melody is different enough from the opening of the movement to warrant a stronger sound. We shall see what happens the next time I conduct the piece.

Once we arrive at **reh. I**, the music tracks the initial section without further alterations to the orchestration. The Coda begins at the pickup to **reh. N** and consists of an upward scale accompanied by descending chords. Observe the accent on the second note in the winds—and later in the brass—which is a gentle push rather than an exaggerated expression.

Four bars before **reh. O**, the quarter notes are marked just like the strokes that began the Trio (minus the timpani) and thus should be played similarly. It is possible to consider the woodwinds' A as the final note of the cello melody. Be careful that the winds are not covered by the strings at **reh. O**. While I have heard conductors slow down a little here, I advise against it, as I think it feels out of place in the middle of this phrase.

Consider performing the last seven bars as a continuous diminuendo. I recommend following Tchaikovsky's bowing in the first bar of **reh. P**, but two bars later, just play the whole phrase triple *piano* in one long down bow. I also ask the orchestra to treat the third bar before the end as an echo.

I am not sure why many conductors take the final two measures out of tempo. The 5/4 meter is still in play, and Tchaikovsky's carefully laid out rhythm is thrown out of kilter if you slow down or delay these bars. They contain an element of humor, and I believe we must observe that. Go into five for these two measures and conduct a very abrupt, yet soft, cutoff just after the final beat. As with the end of the first movement, maintain a moment of stillness and silence before lowering your arms.

## Third Movement: Allegro molto vivace

As with the preceding movement, this section can stand alone as an almost balletic statement or even an encore. Who can resist the rhythmic thrust and boisterous elements contained within?

Is this a march? If so, the ♩ = 152 metronome marking tells us it is a fast one. Furthermore, the time signature shows four beats in the bar instead of two, and to make it even more interesting, Tchaikovsky gives both a common-time and 12/8 meter simultaneously. We will have to get deeper into the movement to discover what is going on.

To start, I quietly give a full bar in four. Safety and security come first here, as the tempo can be difficult for the musicians to predict. While it is possible to start in two if the orchestra really has the hang of it, it is nonetheless dangerous. I like to bring out the duples that seem to disrupt the quicker notes. I recommend rehearsing the first few pages slowly at first to help everyone hear and understand how they fit in with each other.

Note the string divisi at the beginning. I suggest dividing by stand instead of by person to allow the audience to hear both lines equally. The violas have the trickiest passage, ensemble-wise, no matter how you divide it. With fast music like this being passed back and forth from one voice to another, the split sections tend to rush. An effective solution, although time-consuming to rehearse, is to ask the violas to add the first note of the other group's triplet to their own lines. A four-note pattern, with everyone meeting together on each beat, stabilizes the speed. Still, you should certainly try the passage as written before suggesting changes.

Two bars after **reh. A**, Tchaikovsky presents the first hint of the main theme in the oboe line. Playing in octaves, both musicians have a crescendo that ends at an unspecified dynamic around *mezzo forte*. Trombones, trumpet, and horn follow, but they make a diminuendo instead. By **reh. B**, the tempo should be stable enough to go into two. The pizzicato high C can often sound coarse, but it does have to be strong enough for the pitch to register clearly. One way to help is to ask the lower division to play louder.

The violins are *leggiero* when they return to arco, but the horns, who have a similar phrase two bars later, are marked *un poco marcato*. The difference in timbre is probably the reason for this distinction. Perhaps the horns should not simply answer the violins but do so in a slightly more aggressive manner.

You can conduct in either two or four at **reh. D**. Regardless of the beat pattern, the triplet groups should sound equal in volume to feel like a single, continuous line. Certainly, going back into two is appropriate six bars before **reh. E**. This is the first appearance of the piccolo since the first movement, and because its first note is so high, it runs the risk of sticking out too much. I suggest asking the violins to play their pizzicato notes stronger here to achieve better balance.

Note that the horns' and trumpets' dramatic upbeats to the marcato descending line (at the pickups to **m. 45** and **m. 46**, for example) are always marked a dynamic level lower than the strings/winds so as not to overshadow the melody.

In the third bar of **reh. F**, pay attention to the length of the first note. Whereas this was previously a staccato eighth, it is now an accented quarter to be played at full value. Rehearse this pattern with the various instruments involved to achieve the proper dynamic levels.

At **reh. G**, bring out the accents in the winds. In the second measure (and subsequently every two bars), you may choose to add an E to the timpani part to match the other instruments carrying the melody. A substantial crescendo must precede the first entry of the bass drum at **m. 69**, followed by an extreme diminuendo all the way back to *pianissimo*.

Finally, at **reh. H**, Tchaikovsky shows us that we are indeed in a march. You can interpret this tune as a series of two-bar phrases, a four-bar grouping followed by two more measures, or a single six-bar phrase. I prefer to perform this with the single phrase in mind, adding a slur after the long notes to connect the ideas. The clarinets and horns are playing quietly and *leggieramente*, and thus the strings need to play as softly as possible. Ask the woodwinds to make a truly big crescendo in the bar before **reh. I**, followed by a quick diminuendo.

At **reh. I**, apply the same phrasing to the violins, and make sure that their dynamic is *pianissimo*. Ensure that the horns' rhythmic figure four bars before **reh. K** can be heard clearly, as sometimes the sixteenth notes are muddy, and watch that the brass does not overwhelm the strings with their *fortissimo* at **reh. K**. Notice that the brass and upper winds have a rest written after their long notes, but the strings and bassoons do not. It makes sense for both groups to play with similar articulation, so I suggest putting a space between their notes as well.

Speaking of space, composers do not always need to put in a rest to accomplish it. Look at the violin figure in the fifth bar of **reh. K**, where Tchaikovsky clearly desires space between notes by writing two down bows that require a retake.

In the ensuing music, place importance on the hairpins in the second bassoon and double basses, as this will come up again in a much stronger way later in the movement. At **reh. M**, the violins should reduce their dynamic to allow for the melody in the low strings to be heard. However, when their roles are reversed a few bars later, the balance is fine, and nothing needs to be altered.

We have been conducting in two for quite a while, but I advise that you go into four two bars before **reh. O** to help with the entrances. After **reh. O**, you are welcome to return to two because this music is a more elaborate reiteration of the opening section of the movement, and you have the advantage of a well-established tempo to help maintain control.

At **reh. T**, Tchaikovsky redevelops the two-bar motif with which he began the march. Take a look at the timpani roll in the second and third bars (**m. 194** and **m. 195**). While the crescendo goes to *fortissimo* on the third beat of **m. 194**, musical logic tells us that the high point is at the start of **m. 195**, where you might consider adding an accent on the downbeat to denote the start of a new section.

In the ensuing buildup, make sure that the two-note motif sounds equal as it passes through various instruments and builds to a crescendo. Likewise, the moving lines in the strings should convey one continuous voice. Be aware that these are not tremolos but measured sixteenths. I put a very discreet accent on the first beat of each note change to prevent this passage from sounding murky.

Follow the composer's dynamics carefully during this lengthy crescendo. The texture shifts at **reh. V** when the double basses change from sixteenth notes to triplets, although I do not believe I have ever heard the triplets with clarity here. Watch out for the trombones' entrance in the third bar of **reh. V**; they should sneak in so that their whole note does not sound intrusive.

If you are not a string player, it is worth noting that the slurs that start two bars before **reh. W** in the upper strings are not tied notes but rather bowing indications. The dots over the notes tell us that the articulation should match that of the upper winds and brass. The bass drum will dominate to some extent at **reh. X**, as it should. The flurry of scales played triple *forte* is amazing, but to counteract the natural tendency to play softer as the scale descends, you may have to remind the players to continue at maximum volume toward the end of each group.

Reflecting a curious choice of orchestration, the pickup to **reh. Y** often feels like a letdown after all the scales have been played simultaneously by many instruments. You must insist that the violas and cellos ferociously attack these notes as if they were the culmination of the section. Even though you might be tempted to hold back the tempo, keep it steady because you will have an opportunity to slow down later.

The first cymbal crash occurs at **reh. Z**, and the score reveals that the instruments must ring and not be stopped. Even though the dynamic is very loud, Tchaikovsky's phrasing for the six-bar motif remains the same, so you must perform it consistently. Much of the music is a repeat of previous material, so observe the changes in dynamics, key, and orchestration carefully.

At **reh. CC**, the first violins have trouble competing with the triple *forte* of the brass or being audible at all, depending on the reverberation in the hall. Since the chords in the second violins reinforce the brass harmonies, I often ask the seconds to double the firsts here. It is possible to ask the brass to reduce their dynamic, but you do not want to diminish the energy and intensity. The seconds should return to their own part one bar before **reh. DD**.

When the march tune comes back one measure after **reh. DD**, the notation changes significantly. Instead of short eighth notes, beats one, three, and four now contain quarter notes. This change permits us the possibility of lengthening the quarters and holding back the tempo slightly. I suggest returning to beating four to the bar and making the next eight measures *pesante*. The ritardando must be slight enough that you can get back to tempo at the pickup to the second bar of **reh. EE** unobtrusively. I realize that some interpreters don't slow down at **reh. DD** and instead hold back at this spot, but since the music after **reh. EE** is a reprise of earlier material, I think it is more appropriate to play it at the same main tempo.

Jump ahead to three bars before **reh. HH** (m. 304). Unless you have at least one hundred string players, their material is going to be inaudible. Even though everyone is marked *sempre fortississimo*, sometimes a dynamic is not about the volume but rather the nature of the sound. This is one of those cases, so after the first outburst, I bring all the brass down at least one level and sometimes more, depending on the orchestra and hall. Five bars before **reh. II**, I ask them to add a crescendo to full volume. Tchaikovsky adds yet another *forte* to the orchestra, as well as a tremendous bass-drum thwack in the next measure, completely transforming the seemingly easygoing march.

The eight-bar crescendo is very clear, with each starting and ending dynamic as indicated until **reh. KK**. The dialogue between upper winds and strings that begins in the third bar after **reh. KK** doesn't quite work as printed because the four or five woodwinds playing the upward scales cannot sound equal to forty or more strings alternating the same passage. To balance this section, the strings should drop down in dynamic when the winds play, just enough to allow these eight notes to cut through the texture.

At **reh. LL**, some conductors reduce the brass and timpani dynamic and make a three- or four-bar crescendo. This is a matter of personal preference. Five measures after **reh. LL**, pay attention to the bass drum, making sure that the triple *forte* does not obliterate the other instruments playing the same figure.

For maximum intensity and effect, ask the timpanist to add a crescendo two bars before the end of the movement. To hear the triplet figure clearly, I ask everyone playing—including the timpani—to cut off just before the final four notes.

Prior to discussing the Finale, I should address the audience's response after the third movement. Numerous pieces of music contain spots where audiences tend to clap before the movement has concluded, or movements whose endings seem to invite applause, even though they are not finales. Tchaikovsky's two last symphonies both have moments that tend to elicit premature outbursts. The early applause in the Fifth Symphony is especially regrettable because it occurs before the last movement has concluded.

If the audience is so stirred that they want to applaud after the third movement of the Sixth Symphony, I think there is no stopping them, and we should not even try. Tchaikovsky certainly must have anticipated this when he wrote this triumphant music. Some audiences know the piece well and are familiar with the contemporary symphony-hall etiquette to refrain from clapping until the end of a piece. However, the majority of the public is likely unfamiliar with the work, and Tchaikovsky certainly wrote it in a way that sounds like the symphony has concluded. Yet, some conductors feel offended by this applause, and some have gone so far as to reprimand the public for interrupting the musical flow.

This, of course, undermines the continuity even further, and may discourage some concertgoers from ever returning. The supposed reason for asking for respectful silence in between movements—that a symphony must be heard in its entirety without acknowledgment to avoid losing the musical thread—is nonsense. We do not condemn anyone for applauding after arias in opera, even though this clearly stops the performance and interferes with not only the musical line but the continuation of the story as well. When audience members show their appreciation, why stop them?

On one occasion, at the conclusion of the five-minute cadenza that connects the third and fourth movements of Shostakovich's First Violin Concerto, the audience was so thrilled that they applauded and cheered for several bars while we were playing the last movement. It was like being in a jazz club after a big drum solo.

Rather than verbally castigating or glaring at the audience, some conductors choose to go straight into the Finale without a pause of any kind. This is predicated solely on the idea that it might prevent applause, as I can think of no musical defense for this choice, considering the lack of relationship between the keys and the extremely different moods.

I advise a total reset before launching the Finale. I take close to two minutes before giving the downbeat, not only to catch my breath but also to put myself in the proper frame of mind and heart for what is to come.

In summary, when the last note of the third movement has sounded, let the audience clap if they are so moved, but do not turn around or bow to them. Simply remain focused and use the time to gather your wits until the applause has subsided.

## Fourth Movement: Finale. Adagio lamentoso; Andante

This movement must have come as a shock to those attending the premiere. Knowing that Tchaikovsky's first five symphonies featured optimistic and even bombastic endings, they likely did not anticipate a slow movement. Certainly no one could have foreseen a movement so dark and lacking in the joy of Tchaikovsky's earlier finales.

This movement is one of the most complex pieces to conduct, and not just for technical reasons. This is a work more about meaning and emotion than abject clarity. I choose to conduct it without a baton, as I find the angularity of the stick incongruous to the music. Conductors who perform the piece from memory must find a place to put the baton, assuming they used it for the first three movements, usually between the stand and music folder of the musicians sitting to the right.

You must have the whole somber world of this movement in your mind and body before giving the downbeat. How you start will determine the path for the next twelve minutes. Conduct the first four bars in six, without much emphasis on the eighth notes, to impart the feeling of three. Notice the line over the last note in the first bar, which could be interpreted either as a slight lift or just as a brief tenuto. Assigning the three flutes and bassoons a unison F♯ in the second measure and subsequent bars is a wonderful stroke of orchestration. In almost any other composer's hands, this probably would have been allocated to the clarinets.

The opening melody is distributed between the first and second violins to create a composite line. The idea behind this choice has to do with the split seating of the violins to the left and right of the conductor. Dividing this melody across the stage clearly had some appeal as both an aural concept and a visual one. Does this mean that we must split up the violins when performing the symphony? No, but we do have to remind the seconds that the higher notes of the phrase are part of the melody. In **m. 5** and **m. 7**, note that the strings' slurs connect the first two repeated notes, but the eighths have tenuto marks above them. As we have seen previously, this is a bowing indication and not a traditional tie. The repeated note is rearticulated.

By the fifth bar, you can safely go into three. For the first time in this symphony, Tchaikovsky gives the direction *affrettando*. This word implies a combination of getting faster and more agitated, like an accelerando that accumulates tension over a period of time. Gauge the rallentando after **reh. A** to arrive at the Andante naturally. This tempo, at ♩ = 69, should clearly be faster than the opening Adagio. To put it more succinctly, we start at Adagio, move forward with the *affrettando*, slow back down to the Andante, and then recommence the Adagio.

Go back into six for the sixteenth notes at **m. 19**, as we are setting up the same material with which we began the movement. Tchaikovsky writes that the next Adagio is *poco meno che prima* which means a little "less adagio" than earlier and thus slightly faster than the opening of the movement, but only by six metronome clicks. Six bars before **reh. B** is marked single *piano* but should be played somewhat expressively so that the echo two bars later has more contrast. Throughout this entire passage, the dark timbre of the bassoons becomes increasingly evident as the line descends. Do not let the accompaniment's crescendos to *forte* cover this incredible sonority.

It feels natural to allow the tempo to slow down from **reh. B** onward. In **m. 34**, when the bassoons get to the sixteenth notes, the more relaxed speed gives them freedom to play these in their most expressive manner. The second horn's change in pitch plays an important role here. Because you are setting up the next tempo, I advise that you cue these notes.

Customarily, I put a bit more space than the score suggests before commencing the Andante section. This hesitation preserves the tension right before the only optimistic moments in the whole movement. The horns should play their rhythmic pattern legato but articulated enough to convey the triplet pattern. Ensure that this new tempo is different than the previous Adagio, taking care not to get swept up in the preceding emotions and proceed too slowly.

The four eight-bar phrases starting at **reh. C** are similar to each other but contain important differences in instrumentation, dynamics, and speed. It seems that for every *animando*, Tchaikovsky provides a corresponding ritenuto to get back to the original tempo. From my perspective, each phrase increases the dramatic content of the music, and therefore the peaks should become more intense as well. However, each of you must decide how you want this extended buildup to unfold.

Finally, four bars before **reh. F**, the composer writes an *animando* without a rallentando, bringing us to the *Più mosso* (♩ = 96) tempo. Be careful not to get too fast, too soon, as stringendo and Vivace indications lie ahead. Asking the strings to play with full bows, maybe even as many as three strokes per dotted half note, will produce maximum power. The strings must also play with long strokes for the eighth notes to yield enough sound.

In **m. 81**, I have heard some conductors add a second C for the timpani to match the other instruments. I do not think this is necessary because in my experience, the instruments playing on the second beat provide plenty of sound.

Do not move a muscle during the fermata! The tension lies not in the notes but rather in the silence. Begin the Andante with two somewhat small beats so that the audience can respond to the sound they hear rather than the gesture they see. I can tell you from experience that several musicians will erroneously enter on the upbeat with the first violins and cellos, no matter how hard you try to prevent it. This mistake is simply part of the learning curve, and they will not do it again after you rehearse this a couple of times.

The Andante continues the drama of the movement, so apply an abundance of intensity here. In the third bar, the woodwinds move to an adjoining eighth note that settles the harmonic discord of the suspension, but this important pitch is often hard to hear. Ask everyone to hold their quarter notes for the full value until you cut them off. In addition, the oboes and clarinets need to make a crescendo to the last note and then sustain it. The same holds for the subsequent three phrases. Even though the dynamic markings change, you could make the case that the strings should follow the diminuendo pattern of the woodwinds, certainly in the last statement of the passage.

I suggest returning to six in the bar before **reh. G**. Interestingly, Tchaikovsky writes *Andante non tanto* here, even though the metronome mark is the same as the earlier *Adagio poco meno*. Moreover, the opening tune is no longer divided between the violin sections but rather presented as a single melodic line played by the full instrumental group, presumably to impart a level of intensity that the split forces cannot match.

Return to conducting in three in the fifth bar, watching that the horns are not late on beat two. However, you must return to beating in six at **reh. H**. After that, you can decide when returning to three is appropriate. Two measures after **reh. H**, I push the tempo ahead a little and do not draw attention to the last note of the bar. Tchaikovsky provides the instruction *stringendo molto*, but the next metronome mark is curiously only ♩ = 88, which is not very fast. Between *animando* and *incalzando* markings, we know that the music ought to press forward. Whatever you do regarding these indications, the ritenuto must get you back to Andante at **reh. K**.

A lot will now depend on the ability of the two horn players to project their low notes marked *gestopft*. Placing the hand in the bell of the instrument tends to produce a growl-like sound in this register. Furthermore, the stopped-note technique often distorts the pitch and prevents the possibility of a *fortissimo*. These notes are even harder to produce when Tchaikovsky writes them down an octave four bars later. If an assistant is sitting in the section, I recommend that this musician also play with the low horns here. You might also consider asking the assistant to play without hand-stopping to improve the clarity of the note, being sure to do so very discreetly. Some players might opt to use a stopped mute, which is more secure but produces a slightly different color.

As the music winds down, it is as if we are giving up hope. Two bars before **reh. L**, I slow down so that the eighth notes sound like sighs. In the instrumentation list for the work, the tam-tam is listed as *ad lib*. However, in the score at this point, such an option is not indicated. I have not been able to determine the reason to suggest the potential omission of this important instrument. Perhaps it involves superstition about the ominous nature of the trombone chorale. In any event, I have not heard it left out in any performance or recording.

The music at **reh. L** is sublime, to say the least. Frequently, the trombones and tuba players like to rehearse this on their own, and I welcome them to do so. On some occasions, I have let them play without conducting, but more often I find that they prefer to have guidance to better gauge the tempo and the amount of space between rests.

The shattering Coda is marked *Andante giusto*, ♩ = 76, around the same tempo as the second theme. You may be tempted to take it a bit slower, but do not allow it to approach the Adagio pace of the opening. What a brilliant stroke of genius to have this most passionate of endings played with muted strings, including the double basses! The basses should play this on the string, but it must sound marcato enough to convey a timpani-like sense of pulse. This articulation also helps to keep the tempo steady.

Maintain the intensity by asking for full bows, with as much expression as possible on the crescendos. At **reh. N**, the melodic line in the violins should land on an F♯, but since the violins do not have that note available, the clarinets and bassoons finish the phrase. This must be performed delicately so that the wind color does not sound like it comes out of the blue. Ask the violins to hold on to the G a bit longer and invite the woodwinds to approximate the strings' sonority so that it sounds like one continuous line.

At this point, the bass line divides. The continuing triplets are more important than the long melodic notes, and therefore I usually ask the front of the section to keep the rhythmic figure going while the back takes the top line.

A similar divisi unfolds in the cellos. Whereas those playing the top line have no problem projecting, those playing the bottom line have trouble, simply because it is written an octave lower. If the cellos are seated on the outside of the stage, they should divide this passage by stand. If they are on the inside of the orchestra, they should follow standard divisi—in other words, outside players on the top line, inside on the bottom.

Finally, it can make a huge difference in the sonic quality of your orchestra to specify on which string certain passages should be played. I can point to one such instance here. I ask the upper division of cellos to play on the D string until the end of the fifth bar of **reh. N (m. 159)**. Then, starting on the downbeat of the next measure, they switch to the G string, adding a bit of portamento to highlight the new color on the very same pitch. If you try this, I advise you to have the principal cellist demonstrate what it sounds like before asking the others to join. Done properly, it can be a tear-inducing moment.

What should we make of the *sforzando* markings eight and six bars before the end? Should this sudden emphasis be loud or within the context of the surrounding *piano* dynamic? I compromise and ask the first one to be played a bit aggressively and the second one less so.

Even though Tchaikovsky changes the divisi assignments of the double basses eight measures before the end, rely on your ear to determine which musicians should play which line because stage placement may impact the decision. You need to hear both the written-out rhythmic ritardando of the arco passage as well as the final heartbeat pizzicato notes. Rehearse this until you are satisfied that you have found the optimal balance.

I find it useful to have the arco instruments play with vibrato until the last bar, when I ask them to stop vibrating gradually. Even though the fermata is on the rest, you can hold on to the note until it has faded away. Indicate the cutoff with the simplest of gestures, perhaps just closing your fingers. Imagine that the silence is part of the musical fabric, and do not move at all. When you feel that sufficient time has passed, relax your shoulders to signal to the audience that they can applaud. If you are very fortunate, they will continue to maintain the stillness. Everyone should feel exhausted at the conclusion of this masterpiece.

## Conductor's Etiquette

Once the applause commences, ask the entire orchestra to rise. When you come back for the next bow, it is customary to acknowledge the principal bassoon first, followed by the solo clarinet. Then, I usually ask the trombones and tuba to stand. Recognizing the contributions of the other sections is appreciated but not imperative.

\*\*\*

"Music is an incomparably more powerful means and is a subtler language for expressing the thousand different moments of the soul's moods."

— Pyotr Ilyich Tchaikovsky

## Notes

1. Pjotr Iljitsch Tschaikowsky, *Symphony No. 6 in B Minor, Pathétique, Op. 74*, ed. Martin Schmeling (Wiesbaden, Germany: Breitkopf & Härtel, Partitur-Bibliothek Nr. 4959, 2005).

# Bibliography

Beethoven, Ludwig van. *Symphonies 1–9.* Edited by Jonathan Del Mar. Kassel: Bärenreiter Urtext, 1996-2000.
Beethoven, Ludwig van. *Symphony No. 3 in E Flat Major, "Eroica," Op. 55.* Edited by Peter Hauschild. Wiesbaden, Germany: Breitkopf & Härtel Urtext, 1999.
Berlioz, Hector. *Symphonie fantastique.* Edited by Nicholas Temperley. Kassel, Germany: Bärenreiter Urtext of the New Berlioz Edition 16, 1971.
Berlioz, Hector. *Symphonie fantastique.* Edited by Nicholas Temperley. Wiesbaden, Germany: Breitkopf & Härtel Urtext PB 4929, n.d.
Brahms, Johannes. *Complete Symphonies in Full Orchestral Score.* Edited by Hans Gal. New York: Dover Publications, 1974.
Brahms, Johannes. *Symphony No. 1, Op. 68.* Edited by Hans Gál. Leipzig: Breitkopf & Härtel, 1926–1927, Plate J.B. 1. https://imslp.org/wiki/Symphony_No.1,_Op.68 _(Brahms,_Johannes).
Cherniavsky, David. "Sibelius's Tempo Corrections." *Music & Letters* 31, no. 1 (1950): 54. http://www.jstor.org/stable/729017.
Del Mar, Norman. *Conducting Beethoven.* Oxford: Clarendon Press, 1992.
Del Mar, Norman. *Conducting Berlioz.* New York: Oxford University Press, 1997.
Dvořák, Antonín. *Symphony No. 9, "From the New World."* Edited by Jonathan Del Mar. Kassel, Germany: Bärenreiter-Verlag Urtext, 2019.
Dvořák, Antonín. "Symphony No. 9 in E Minor, Op. 95: Critical Edition Based on the Composer's Manuscript." In *Souborné vydání díla,* series 3, vol. 9. Edited by Otakar Šourek. Prague: SNKLHU, 1955.
"Dvořák, Antonín / Symphony No. 9, E Minor, Op. 95 (From the New World) (ID 4211–101–114." The New York Philharmonic Shelby White & Leon Levy Digital Archives. https://archives.nyphil.org.

Dyment, Christopher. *Conducting the Brahms Symphonies: From Brahms to Boult.* Woodbridge, Suffolk, UK: The Boydell Press, 2016.
Kipeläinen, Kari. "Afterword." In *Sibelius Symphony No. 2 in D Major, Op. 43.* Edited by Kari Kipeläinen. Wiesbaden: Breitkopf & Härtel, 2004. https://www.breitkopf.com/assets/pdf/6293_PDF_PB5376_NW.pdf.
Moussorgsky, Modest. *Pictures at an Exhibition.* Orchestrated by Maurice Ravel. London: Boosey & Hawkes Music Publishers Ltd., 1922.
Mussorgsky, Modest. *Pictures at an Exhibition.* In *Complete Collected Works, Volume VIII, Series 2.* Edited by Paul Lamm. Moscow: Muzgiz, 1931; reprinted New York: E. F. Kalmus, n.d. https://s9.imslp.org/files/imglnks/usimg/8/83/IMSLP107727-PMLP03722-Mussorgsky_Werke_Kalmus_Band_VIII_Folge_2_Tableaux_d_une_Exposition_filter.pdf.
Mussorgsky, Modest. *Pictures at an Exhibition.* Orchestrated by Maurice Ravel. Paris: Editions Russes de Musique, 1929. https://imslp.hk/files/imglnks/euimg/1/1a/IMSLP741261-PMLP3722-115525.pdf.
Mussorgsky, Modest. *Pictures at an Exhibition.* Orchestrated by Sergei Gorchakov. Berlin: Sikorski, 1954.
"Real Value of Negro Melodies." *New York Herald.* May 21, 1893. http://static.qobuz.com/info/IMG/pdf/NYHerald-1893-Mai-21-Recadre.pdf.
Rimsky-Korsakoff, Nikolay Andreyevich. *My Musical Life.* Translated by Judah A. Joffe. Edited by Carl Van Vechten. New York: Alfred A. Knopf, 1924.
Rimsky-Korsakov, Nikolay. *Scheherazade.* New York: Dover, 1984.
Sibelius, Jean. *Symphony No. 2.* New York: Associated Music Publishers, Inc., 1933.
Sibelius, Jean. *Symphony No. 2 in D Major, Op. 43.* Edited by Kari Kipeläinen. Urtext based on the Complete Edition "Jean Sibelius Works." Wiesbaden: Breitkopf & Härtel, 2004.
Simco, Andrew P. "Performing the Timpani Parts to *Symphonie fantastique.*" *Percussive Notes* 36, no. 2 (April 1998): 62–65. http://www.kettledrummer.com/wp-content/uploads/2014/11/Berlioz.pdf.
"*Symphonie fantastique,* H 48 (Berlioz, Hector)." International Music Score Library Project (IMSLP)/Petrucci Music Library. https://imslp.org/wiki/Symphonie_fantastique,_H_48_(Berlioz,_Hector).
"Symphony No. 2, Op. 43 (Sibelius, Jean)." International Music Score Library Project (IMSLP)/Petrucci Music Library. https://imslp.org/wiki/Symphony_No.2%2C_Op.43_(Sibelius%2C_Jean).
Tschaikowsky, Pjotr Iljitsch. *Symphony No. 6 in B Minor, Pathétique, Op. 74.* Edited by Martin Schmeling. Wiesbaden, Germany: Breitkopf & Härtel, Partitur-Bibliothek Nr. 4959, 2005.
Weingartner, Felix, and Jessie Crosland. *On the Performance of Beethoven's Symphonies.* London: Breitkopf & Härtel, 1907.

# About the Author

Internationally acclaimed conductor **Leonard Slatkin** is music director laureate of the Detroit Symphony Orchestra, directeur musical honoraire of the Orchestre National de Lyon, conductor laureate of the St. Louis Symphony Orchestra, principal guest conductor of the Orquesta Filarmónica de Gran Canaria, and artistic consultant to the Las Vegas Philharmonic. He maintains a rigorous schedule of guest conducting throughout the world and is active as a composer, author, and educator.

A recipient of the prestigious National Medal of Arts, Slatkin also holds the rank of chevalier in the French Legion of Honor. He has received the Prix Charbonnier from the Federation of Alliances Françaises, Austria's Decoration of Honor in Silver, the League of American Orchestras' Gold Baton Award, and the 2013 ASCAP Deems Taylor Special Recognition Award for his debut book, *Conducting Business*. His second book, *Leading Tones: Reflections on Music, Musicians, and the Music Industry*, was published in 2017, followed by *Classical Crossroads: The Path Forward for Music in the 21st Century* (2021) and *Eight Symphonic Masterworks of the Twentieth Century: A Study Guide for Conductors* (2024).

Slatkin has also held posts as music director of the New Orleans Philharmonic-Symphony Orchestra and National Symphony Orchestra, and he was chief conductor of the BBC Symphony Orchestra. He has served as principal guest conductor of London's Philharmonia and Royal Philharmonic, the Pittsburgh Symphony Orchestra, the Los Angeles Philharmonic at the Hollywood Bowl, and the Minnesota Orchestra. He makes his home in St. Louis with his wife, composer Cindy McTee.